NEW
Holiday
cookbook

Favorite Recipes® of
Home Economics Teachers

© Favorite Recipes Press MCMLXXIV
Box 77   Nashville, TN 37202
Library of Congress Catalog Card No. 74-80085
ISBN 0-87197-062-7

4 5 6 7 8 9 0

dEAR HOMEMAKER,

Favorite Recipes of Home Economic Teachers Cookbooks is proud to add this collection of Favorite Holiday Recipes to this invaluable series.

Home economic teachers from every section of the United States have contributed their excellent recipes for holiday and special occasion entertaining in order to make this edition possible. We want to thank these teachers who have generously shared their personally tested outstanding recipes. Each of these women is an expert in planning and preparing superior meals for every conceivable social event or family affair.

You will be thrilled with the variety of menus—elegant dinners, elaborate buffets, hearty get-togethers, delicious picnics and a before-the-game brunch. And, you will enjoy cooking beautiful desserts, attractive casseroles, colorful hors d'oeuvres and magnificent main dishes.

We hope that this cookbook will not only assist you in serving exceptionally delicious holiday foods, but also in creating imaginative menus of your very own. Also, your purchase of this cookbook will help home economic departments in many schools in supporting important school and community projects.

Sincerely yours,

Mary Anne Richards

Mary Anne Richards

board of advisors

Ruth Stovall
Branch Director, Program Services Branch
Division of Vocational—
Technical and Higher Education
Alabama Department of Education

Barbara Gaylor
Supervisor, Consumer Education Special Projects
Work Study and Co-op G Unit
Home Economics Education
Michigan Department of Education

Catherine A. Carter
Consultant, Consumer Homemaking Education
Illinois Division of Vocational
and Technical Education

Anne G. Eifler (Retired)
Senior Program Specialist
Home Economics Education
Pennsylvania Department of Education

Janet Latham
Supervisor, Home Economics Education
Idaho State Board for
Vocational Education

Christine E. Nickel
Consultant, Home Economics Education
Wisconsin Board of Vocational,
Technical and Adult Education

Frances Rudd
Supervisor, Home Economics Education
Arkansas Department of Education

Odessa N. Smith
State Supervisor, Home Economics Education
Louisiana Department of Education

PREFACE

Holidays and special occasions are among the most important times of the year in most American households.

Families going to grandmother's for a traditional Christmas dinner . . . Company employees picnicing at the local lake on Labor Day . . . Children celebrating that special birthday . . . Friends getting together to bring in the New Year . . . Neighbors cooking out in the backyard on July 4th . . . Or, the class of 1954 gathering for their 20-year Reunion.

These are times when the gracious hostess shares her culinary skills with family and friends. Whether in the traditions of the past or with a distinctive modern touch, today's hostess is ready for festive entertaining or informal hospitality.

Menus in this book are designed to assist you in selecting recipes that will complement your own personal type of holiday celebration. There are traditional holiday recipes. And, there are new ideas and suggestions to make this year's holiday affair different from last.

With this book of marvelous menus and recipes, you're ready for any type of entertaining . . . be it a very formal dinner or an outdoor picnic.

COVER RECIPE

FESTIVE STUFFING BALLS

  1/2 c. chopped onion
  1/2 c. chopped celery
  2 tbsp. butter
  1   12-oz. can vacuum-packed golden
       whole kernel corn, drained
  1   8-oz. package seasoned stuffing mix
  1/2 tsp. salt
  1/4 tsp. pepper
  1/2 tsp. crushed marjoram
  2 eggs
  1 c. milk
  1/2 c. melted butter

Saute onion and celery in butter in saucepan until tender, stirring frequently. Add corn, stuffing mix, seasonings, eggs and milk; mix well. Shape into 1 1/4 to 1 1/2-inch balls. Place in shallow 9 x 13-inch or 10-inch round pan; pour melted butter over stuffing balls. Bake, uncovered, in preheated 375-degree oven for 15 minutes. Delicious served with leftover turkey or chicken gravy. Yield: 25-28 stuffing balls.

Photograph for this recipe on cover.

CONTENTS

NEW YEAR'S

Horns blowing . . . balloons popping
Time for laughter and good cheer
Music playing, hardly stopping
Making plans for a happy New Year

The perfect time to entertain . . .
whether it be an elegant dinner or a
fireside gathering. Ringing in the New Year
is a great time for the hostess to delight friends
and relatives with her very special dishes. Try
something NEW this YEAR—a delicious company
buffet. Many recipes can be prepared in advance, leaving
less work so you too can enjoy the party. Use Old Man
Time for a centerpiece. Set the hands for one minute
'til midnight. Place mats are made from colorful poster
paper with the words to Auld Lang Syne printed on them.
For place cards, use small brass bells with the guests' names
painted on one side. Add party favors such as confetti, horn
blowers and firecrackers.

◊ Recipes on pages 19 and 21.

MENU

New Year's Celebration Buffet

Sausage Balls
Marinated Shrimp
Liver Paté
Party Cheese Ball
Haa's Holiday Salad
Old English Prime Rib
Pork Sausage Dressing
Good Luck Peas
New Year's Stuffed Tangerines
Easy Refrigerator Rolls
Eggnog Cake
Kahlua

MARINATED SHRIMP

5 lb. shrimp
1 8-oz. bottle remoulade sauce
1/4 c. lemon juice
1 1/2 c. mayonnaise
3/4 c. olive oil
2 cloves of garlic, minced
1/2 c. chopped chives
1/2 c. chopped parsley
1/2 c. finely chopped celery

Peel and devein shrimp; place in bowl. Add remoulade sauce, lemon juice, mayonnaise, olive oil, garlic, chives, parsley and celery; mix well. Cover. Place in refrigerator; marinate for 24 hours or longer, stirring occasionally. Drain shrimp; serve.

Mrs A. David Buealer
Mainland Sr HS, Daytona Beach, Florida

LIVER PATE

1 med. onion
1/2 lb. liver, cut in strips
1/4 c. butter
1 tsp. salt
1/2 tsp. pepper
1 tbsp. red wine
2 hard-cooked eggs, separated

Cut onion into eighths. Saute onion and liver in butter until liver is just done, stirring frequently; place in blender container. Add salt, pepper, wine and egg whites; cover. Process at high speed until smooth, scraping side of blender container with rubber spatula frequently. Place in serving bowl. Blend egg yolks until chopped fine; sprinkle over pate.

Mrs Kathleen Burns
Mahtomedi HS, Mahtomedi, Minnesota

PARTY CHEESE BALL

4 c. shredded Cheddar cheese
2 3-oz. packages cream cheese,
   softened
1/3 c. mayonnaise
2 tsp. sherry flavoring
1 tsp. Worcestershire sauce
1/8 tsp. onion salt
1/8 tsp. garlic salt
1/8 tsp. celery salt
1/2 c. chopped ripe olives
1/3 c. minced dried beef
1/3 c. minced fresh parsley

Combine cheeses, mayonnaise, sherry flavoring, Worcestershire sauce and onion, garlic and celery salts in large bowl; mix until smooth. Stir in olives; cover. Chill until nearly firm. Shape into ball. Combine dried beef and parsley; roll cheese ball in beef mixture. Place in bowl; cover and chill.

Alice Hansberger
Canton Sr HS, Canton, Illinois

OLD ENGLISH PRIME RIB

2 tbsp. Worcestershire sauce
1 tsp. paprika
1 tsp. monosodium glutamate
Salt and pepper to taste
Choice prime or standing rib roast,
   1/2 lb. per serving
Ice cream salt

Combine Worcestershire sauce, paprika, monosodium glutamate, salt and pepper; rub into meat. Line heavy roasting pan with foil; cover bottom of roaster with layer of ice cream salt. Dampen salt lightly with water until just moist. Place roast on salt in standing rib position. Cover roast completely with ice cream salt; repeat dampening procedure. Do not cover. Bake in preheated 500-degree oven for 12 to 20 minutes per pound, depending on degree of doneness desired. Remove from oven. Crack salt with mallet; pull salt sections away from meat. Brush all salt particles from roast. Place roast on serving platter; cut into serving portions.

Mrs Estella Hottel
Dimmitt HS, Dimmitt, Texas

9

SAUSAGE BALLS

1 10-oz. package Cheddar cheese
1 lb. hot bulk sausage
2 1/2 c. Bisquick

Cut cheese into cubes; place in top of double boiler. Cook over hot water, stirring frequently, until melted. Place sausage, Bisquick and cheese in large mixing bowl; mix well. Shape into small balls; place on cookie sheet. Bake in preheated 350-degree oven for 15 minutes. May be frozen before baking. Place on cookie sheet; freeze until firm. Place in plastic bags; freeze.

Mrs. Ruth Irwin
Shawnee HS, Wolf Lake, Illinois

HAA'S HOLIDAY SALAD

1 4-oz. can water chestnuts
1 10-oz. package frozen green peas
1 lg. head lettuce
1/4 c. chopped onion
1/4 c. chopped green pepper
1 1/2 c. mayonnaise
Grated Romano cheese to taste
Grated Parmesan cheese to taste
2 hard-boiled eggs, sliced
3 slices bacon, fried and crumbled

Drain and slice water chestnuts. Cook peas according to package directions; drain. Tear lettuce into small pieces; place in large salad bowl. Place onion, green pepper, water chestnuts and peas in layers on lettuce; spread with mayonnaise. Sprinkle with Romano and Parmesan cheeses; refrigerate overnight. Place eggs and bacon on top; garnish with parsley.

Mrs Dotti Andersen
Washington Park HS, Racine, Wisconsin

PORK SAUSAGE DRESSING

1 1/2 lb. bulk pork sausage
2 c. chopped celery
1/3 c. chopped onion
1/4 c. butter
1 recipe baked corn bread, coarsely crumbled
9 c. day-old bread cubes
2 tsp. salt
1/2 tsp. pepper
2 eggs, beaten
3 c. broth or water

Cook sausage in a skillet, breaking up and stirring frequently, until lightly browned; drain. Saute celery and onion in butter in saucepan until tender, stirring frequently. Combine corn bread, bread cubes, sausage, salt and pepper in large bowl. Add celery mixture, mixing lightly. Add eggs and enough broth to moisten; mix well. Place in large casserole or baking pan. Bake in preheated 325-degree oven for 45 minutes to 1 hour. May stuff about 2/3 of the dressing into cavity of turkey and remaining dressing into neck portion before baking, if desired.

Mrs Dorothy B. Vacek
Corsicana HS, Corsicana, Texas

NEW YEAR'S STUFFED TANGERINES

6 tangerines
1 tbsp. sugar
1 tbsp. margarine
1/2 c. orange juice
1/4 c. orange-cranberry relish

Make 8 cuts from blossom end to about 1 inch from bottom of each tangerine peel. Pull peel down; turn pointed ends in. Remove any white membrane. Loosen sections at center slightly; place tangerines in baking pan. May be prepared in advance, covered and refrigerated. Pull tangerine sections apart again slightly just before baking; add 1/2 teaspoon sugar and 1/2 teaspoon margarine to center of each tangerine. Pour orange juice over tangerines. Bake in preheated 325-degree oven for 30 minutes. Fill center of each tangerine with 2 teaspoons relish; place on serving platter. Small oranges may be substituted for tangerines.

Helen B. Boots
Lakeland Village Sch, Medical Lake, Washington

EASY REFRIGERATOR ROLLS

3/4 c. sugar
1 c. vegetable shortening
2 tsp. salt
1 c. boiling water
2 eggs, beaten
1 env. yeast
1 c. lukewarm water
6 c. flour
Melted butter, cooled

Place sugar, shortening and salt in large bowl; pour boiling water over sugar mixture. Stir well; cool to lukewarm. Stir in eggs. Sprinkle yeast over lukewarm water; let stand for 5 minutes. Stir well; add to sugar mixture. Add flour; mix well with wooden spoon. Cover with foil; place in refrigerator for 2 hours or longer. Roll out on floured surface into rectangle; brush with melted butter. Roll up as for jelly roll; cut into 1-inch slices. Place in greased muffin cups. Let rise for 2 hours or until doubled in bulk. Bake in preheated 400-degree oven for about 15 minutes or until brown.

Mrs Sue Stilley
Forestburg HS, Forestburg, Texas

EGGNOG CAKE

1 doz. macaroons
1 lg. angel food cake
1/2 lb. butter
Powdered sugar
5 egg yolks, beaten
1 c. chopped toasted almonds
Bourbon
Rum
1/2 tsp. almond extract
1 c. heavy cream, whipped

Toast and grind macaroons. Slice cake horizontally into 4 layers. Cream butter and 1 3/4 cups powdered sugar thoroughly. Add egg yolks; mix well. Stir in 3/4 cup almonds, 1/3 to 1/2 cup bourbon, 2 to 3 tablespoons rum, almond extract and macaroons. Spread between layers of cake; place layers together. Cover; refrigerate overnight. Add 2 tablespoons powdered sugar to whipped cream slowly; stir in 2 teaspoons rum or bourbon. Frost cake with cream mixture; garnish with remaining 1/4 cup almonds. Refrigerate until served. Yield: 15-20 servings.

Nancy McLain
East Texas State U, Commerce, Texas

GOOD LUCK PEAS

1   10-oz. package frozen green peas
1/4 c. chopped onion
1 clove of garlic, minced
1/2 c. sliced stuffed olives
1/4 c. vegetable oil
2 c. hot cooked rice
1/4 c. snipped parsley
1   2-oz. jar pimento strips,
*   drained*
1/2 tsp. salt
1/4 tsp. pepper

Cook peas according to package directions; drain and keep hot. Saute onion, garlic and olives in oil until onion is transparent, stirring frequently. Place peas and rice in serving bowl; toss gently. Add onion mixture, parsley, pimento, salt and pepper; toss gently. Serve hot.

Mrs Carl Sundbeck
Manor Independent Sch, Manor, Texas

KAHLUA

4 c. sugar
1 vanilla bean, split in half
*   lengthwise*
1   2-oz. jar instant Yuban coffee
1 fifth 80-proof vodka

Mix 3 cups water and sugar in saucepan. Bring to a boil; reduce heat. Simmer for 20 minutes; remove from heat. Add vanilla bean halves; let stand until cold. Mix 1 cup boiling water with coffee; let stand until cold. Mix sugar mixture, coffee and vodka. Place in 1/2-gallon container; cover well. Let stand for 2 weeks. Remove vanilla bean halves. Pour into decanters to serve.

Linda Armstrong
Union City Comm Schools
Union City, Michigan

MIDNIGHT WATCH PARTY

Hot Onion Appetizers

Pepper Steak Hors d'oeuvres

Philly Fondue

Pizza-Style Fondue

Toffee Fondue

Seven-Up Midnight Punch

HOT ONION APPETIZERS

1/2 c. butter
1/2 pkg. onion soup mix
1 10-count pkg. refrigerator biscuits

Melt butter in electric skillet at 150 degrees. Add soup; stir well. Cut biscuits into quarters; place in skillet. Cover skillet. Cook at 275 degrees for about 20 minutes, or until brown, turning once. Reduce heat to lowest setting; keep warm. Serve hot with toothpicks. Shake package of soup mix before measuring.

Betty Hagberg
Chisago Lakes Jr HS, Chisago City, Minnesota

PEPPER STEAK HORS D'OEUVRES

2 lb. boneless round steak
Prepared mustard
1/4 c. vegetable oil
1 1 3/4-oz. envelope mushroom
*   gravy mix*
Salt and pepper to taste
1 green pepper, cut in thin strips

Cut steak into thin strips. Spread each strip with mustard; roll as for jelly roll. Secure each roll with wooden pick. Cook in hot oil in skillet until brown. Blend gravy mix with pan drippings; add salt and pepper. Stir in 1 1/4 cups water gradually, blending until smooth. Cover; simmer for 13 minutes. Add green pepper strips; simmer for 2 minutes longer. Remove picks from steak rolls before serving. Keep warm in chafing dish, if desired. May be served with sweet-sour sauce, chili sauce or jalapeno sauce.

Mrs Jacquelyn Sanders
Taft HS, Taft, Texas

PHILLY FONDUE

1 3/4 c. milk
2 8-oz. packages cream cheese,
*   cut into cubes*
2 tsp. dry mustard
1/4 c. chopped green onions
1 2 1/2-oz. jar sliced dried beef

Pour milk into fondue pot; heat until scalded. Add cream cheese; cook at low heat, stirring until cream cheese is melted. Add mustard, onions and dried beef; cook, stirring, for 5 minutes longer. Serve with French bread cubes.

Sandra Parish
Kennedale HS, Kennedale, Texas

PIZZA-STYLE FONDUE

1/2 c. chopped onion
1/2 c. ground chuck
2 10 1/2-oz. cans pizza sauce
1 tbsp. cornstarch
1 1/2 tsp. fennel seed (opt.)
1 1/3 tsp. oregano
1/4 tsp. garlic powder
2 1/2 c. grated Cheddar cheese
1 c. grated mozzarella cheese

Place onion and ground chuck in electric fondue pot. Turn heat control to high; cook, stirring, until chuck is brown. Reduce heat to medium; add pizza sauce, cornstarch, fennel seed, oregano and garlic powder. Stir for about 5 minutes or until mixture comes to a boil and thickens. Reduce heat to low. Combine Cheddar and mozzarella cheeses. Add,

1/3 at a time, to fondue pot, stirring after each addition until melted. Spear toasted rye or French bread cubes with fondue fork; dip into fondue. Yield: 6-8 servings.

Frances W. Banner
Castlewood HS, Castlewood, Virginia

TOFFEE FONDUE

1 lg. package Kraft caramels
1/4 c. milk
1/4 c. strong black coffee
1/2 c. milk chocolate chips (opt.)
Apple wedges
Banana chunks
Marshmallows
Angel food cake, cut in 1-in. cubes

Place caramels, milk, coffee and chocolate chips in top of double boiler; cook over boiling water, stirring, until melted and blended. Place in fondue pot. Spear fruits, marshmallows and cake on fondue forks; dip into fondue.

Mrs Brett W. Slusser
Agra HS, Agra, Oklahoma

SEVEN-UP MIDNIGHT PUNCH

1 1-lb. can crushed pineapple
1 12-oz. package frozen
strawberries, thawed
1 46-oz. can pineapple juice
1 c. grenadine
6 7-oz. bottles Seven-Up
Orange rind curls

Chill fruits, pineapple juice, grenadine and Seven-Up. Combine pineapple and strawberries in punch bowl; stir in pineapple juice and grenadine. Pour in Seven-Up slowly; mix gently. Add 2 trays ice cubes; garnish punch bowl with orange rind curls. Yield: About 30 servings.

Mrs Betty Rassette
Central HS, Salina, Kansas

ZESTY CHEESE DIP

1 10-oz. package sharp Cheddar
cheese, grated
1 tbsp. grated onion
Dash of salt
1 tbsp. Worcestershire sauce
Mayonnaise

Place cheese, onion, salt and Worcestershire sauce in bowl. Add 2 tablespoons mayonnaise or just enough for dipping consistency; serve with crackers or Fritos. May be used to stuff celery or as spread for sandwiches; keeps indefinitely in refrigerator if stored in airtight container.

Mrs Dorthy G. Wood
Robert E. Lee HS, Staunton, Virginia

LIVER SAUSAGE-NUT BALL

1 lb. liver sausage
1/4 c. mayonnaise
2 tbsp. dill pickle juice
1 tsp. Worcestershire sauce
3 drops of Tabasco sauce
1/4 tsp. garlic salt
1 8-oz. package cream cheese,
softened
1/3 c. finely chopped dill pickle
1/4 c. finely chopped onion
1/2 c. chopped salted cocktail
peanuts

Place liver sausage in bowl; mash with fork until smooth. Add mayonnaise, pickle juice, Worcestershire sauce, Tabasco sauce, garlic salt and 1/3 of the cream cheese. Beat until smooth; stir in pickle and onion. Pack firmly into 2-cup mixing bowl lined with plastic wrap; chill for several hours or overnight. Turn out of bowl; remove plastic wrap. Frost sausage mixture with remaining cream cheese; chill. Cover with peanuts just before serving. Place on platter; surround with desired crackers. Yield: 16-20 servings.

Mrs Ann J. Hilliard
Plant City Sr HS, Plant City, Florida

CHEESE PUFF SQUARES

1 3-oz. package cream cheese
1/4 lb. sharp Cheddar cheese, cut
  into cubes
1/2 c. margarine
2 egg whites, stiffly beaten
1 1 1/2-lb. loaf thickly sliced
  bread

Place cream cheese, Cheddar cheese and margarine in top of double boiler; cook over hot
water until melted, stirring frequently. Remove from water; fold in egg whites. Cut
bread slices into squares; dip into cheese
mixture. Place on foil-lined cookie sheets.
Bake in preheated 400-degree oven for 10
minutes. Squares may be prepared ahead of
time, covered and frozen or refrigerated
until ready to bake.

Gerry Smith
Waco HS, Waco, Texas

DELICIOUS EGGPLANT APPETIZERS

6 tbsp. margarine
1 peeled eggplant, finely chopped
1 onion, minced
1/4 c. tomato paste
1/4 c. sour cream
2 tbsp. vinegar
1 1/2 tsp. salt
Dash of pepper

Melt margarine in saucepan. Add eggplant
and onion; cook until tender, stirring frequently. Add tomato paste, sour cream, vinegar, salt and pepper; mix well. Place in
bowl; refrigerate until chilled. Serve on
crackers or thinly sliced rye bread.

Mrs Clara Levins
Eastern Jr HS, Lynn, Massachusetts

FILLED CREAM CHEESE PASTRIES

1/2 lb. ground beef
1/2 3/4-oz. package spaghetti
  sauce mix

2 tbsp. chopped onion
1 peeled tomato, chopped
2 tbsp. grated Parmesan cheese
1/4 c. grated sharp Cheddar cheese
1 c. butter, softened
1 8-oz. package cream cheese,
  softened
1/2 tsp. salt
2 c. unsifted flour
1 egg yolk
2 tsp. milk or cream

Cook ground beef in skillet until brown, stirring frequently. Stir in sauce mix, onion,
tomato and 1/4 cup water; simmer for 20
minutes. Remove from heat. Add Parmesan
and Cheddar cheeses; mix well. Cool. Place
butter, cream cheese and salt in mixing
bowl; beat until smooth. Add flour, small
amount at a time, mixing well after each
addition. May have to work by hand toward
end of mixing. Place on large piece of foil;
flatten to form 6 x 8-inch rectangle. Fold
foil over pastry; seal. Refrigerate overnight
or for several days, if desired. Remove pastry
from refrigerator about 10 minutes before
rolling; divide in half. Roll out 1/8 to 1/16
inch thick on floured pastry cloth with
floured rolling pin; cut with 3-inch cookie
cutter. Place 1 rounded teaspoon beef filling
in center of each pastry circle. Moisten edge
of pastry; fold over filling. Seal edge with
fork. Beat egg yolk with milk; brush over
pastries. Place pastries on baking sheet. Bake
in preheated 350-degree oven for 20 minutes. Yield: About 4 dozen.

Dean V. Twait
Brookside Jr HS, Albert Lea, Minnesota

SAUERKRAUT-HAM BALLS

1/4 c. margarine
1 med. onion, chopped
1/2 clove of garlic, chopped
1/4 c. flour
1/2 c. beef broth
1 1/2 c. ground cooked ham
3 c. chopped sauerkraut, drained

1 tbsp. chopped parsley
2 eggs, beaten
1/4 c. milk
Dry bread crumbs

Melt margarine in skillet. Add onion and garlic; cook, stirring, until onion is transparent. Mix flour and broth until smooth. Add to skillet; cook, stirring, for 1 minute. Stir in ham, sauerkraut and parsley; cook until thick. Place in bowl; chill. Form into 1-inch balls. Mix eggs and milk. Dip balls into egg mixture; roll in bread crumbs. Fry in deep fat at 340 degrees until brown. Drain; serve warm. May be stored in refrigerator and reheated in oven. Yield: 6 dozen.

Jenny L. Curtis
Orrville HS, Orrville, Ohio

MUSHROOMS AVERY

1/2 lb. medium mushrooms
4 tbsp. oil
2 tbsp. minced onion
1/2 c. bread crumbs
1/4 tsp. Tabasco sauce
1/4 tsp. dried leaf thyme
1/4 c. sherry or water

Remove stems from mushrooms; chop only enough stems to make 2 tablespoons chopped stems. Heat 2 tablespoons oil in skillet. Add onion and mushroom stems; saute until tender. Add bread crumbs, Tabasco sauce and thyme; mix well. Fill mushroom caps with stuffing. Clean the skillet. Add remaining oil to skillet; heat. Add stuffed mushrooms; saute for about 3 minutes. Add sherry; cover. Simmer for about 10 minutes or until mushrooms are tender; serve immediately. Yield: About 12 stuffed mushrooms.

Photograph for this recipe on this page.

TABASCO AVOCADO DUNK

2 ripe avocados
1/2 c. mayonnaise
3 tbsp. lemon juice
1 tsp. chili powder
1 sm. garlic clove, pressed (opt.)
1/4 tsp. Tabasco sauce
1/4 tsp. salt

Mash avocados with fork or place in blender and blend until smooth. Stir in remaining ingredients; refrigerate for about 1 hour before serving to let flavors blend. Serve with fresh cauliflower buds, green pepper slices, carrot sticks and cucumber sticks. Yield: 1 1/2 cups.

Photograph for this recipe on this page.

TOMATO TEASERS

1 pt. cherry tomatoes
1/2 lb. sauteed bacon, crumbled
1/4 tsp. Tabasco sauce

Cut out small hole in top of each tomato. Combine crumbled bacon with Tabasco sauce; sprinkle bacon mixture into tomatoes. Serve with food picks. Yield: About 24 tomatoes.

Photograph for this recipe on this page.

SNAPPY CHEESE WEDGES

12 slices bread
1/2 c. processed Cheddar cheese
spread
1/4 tsp. Tabasco sauce
1/4 tsp. prepared mustard
Rolled anchovies (opt.)

Remove crusts from bread; slice bread diagonally to make 4 wedges from each slice. Combine cheese spread, Tabasco sauce and mustard until well blended; spread on bread wedges. Place on baking sheet. Bake in preheated 400-degree oven for 5 minutes or until cheese is bubbly. Place anchovies on wedges; serve immediately. Yield: 48 wedges.

Photograph for this recipe on page 15.

CONGEALED CRANBERRY SALAD

1 1/2 c. cranberries
1 sm. orange
1 c. sugar
1 3-oz. package lemon gelatin
1/2 c. chopped nutmeats (opt.)
1/2 c. chopped celery (opt.)
Lettuce leaves
Salad dressing or mayonnaise (opt.)

Wash and drain cranberries. Wash orange; cut into eighths. Remove seeds. Grind cranberries and orange; place in small bowl. Add sugar; let stand for at least 1 hour. Prepare gelatin according to package directions, decreasing water by 1/4 cup; chill until partially set. Stir cranberry mixture; add to gelatin. Add nutmeats and celery; mix well. Place in individual molds which have been rinsed with cold water; chill for about 3 hours or until set. Unmold; place each mold on lettuce leaf. Serve with salad dressing. Salad may be prepared day ahead of serving; will keep for 3 to 4 days in refrigerator. Yield: 6 to 8 servings.

C. Janet Latham
Idaho State Bd for Vocational Ed
Boise, Idaho

NEW YEAR'S EVE HOT CHICKEN SALAD

2 to 3 c. diced chicken
1 10 1/2-oz. can cream of chicken
soup
3 tbsp. minced onion
1/2 tsp. salt
3/4 c. mayonnaise
1/2 c. toasted almonds
1 tbsp. lemon juice
3 hard-cooked eggs, chopped
1 c. diced celery
1 1-oz. jar pimento strips,
drained
Crushed potato chips or Ritz
crackers

Combine chicken, soup, onion, salt, mayonnaise, almonds, lémon juice, eggs, celery and pimento in large bowl. Place in greased baking dish; cover with potato chips. Bake in preheated 350-degree oven for 30 to 40 minutes or until bubbly. Sliced water chestnuts may be used instead of almonds.

Mrs Marguerite Woods
Modesto HS, Modesto, California

RUSSIAN COLESLAW

8 c. shredded cabbage
3 green sweet peppers, chopped fine
3 red sweet peppers, chopped fine
1 med. onion, chopped fine
1 pt. vinegar
2 1/2 c. sugar
1 1/2 tsp. mustard seed
1 1/2 tsp. salt
1/2 tsp. turmeric
1 tsp. celery seed

Mix cabbage, green and red peppers and onion in stainless steel or glass bowl. Mix vinegar, sugar, mustard seed, salt, turmeric and celery seed in saucepan; bring to a boil. Pour over cabbage mixture; mix well. Cover; marinate in refrigerator for 24 hours before serving. Will keep indefinitely in refrigerator. Two small jars pimento strips, drained, may be substituted for red peppers.

Sara Coleman, Retired
South Range Mahoning Co Sch, Greenford, Ohio

FESTIVE CRAB-POTATO SALAD

8 med. Idaho Russet potatoes
Salt to taste
1/4 c. minced Idaho Spanish onion
Coarsely ground pepper to taste
2/3 c. white wine vinegar
2   7-oz. cans crab or lobster
1 c. coarsely chopped celery
1/2 c. coarsely chopped dill pickles
2 hard-cooked eggs, chopped
1 c. mayonnaise
1 c. sour cream
Salad greens

Place potatoes in Dutch oven; add 1 1/2 inches cold, salted water. Cover tightly. Bring to a boil; reduce heat. Simmer for about 30 minutes or until potatoes are just tender. Remove from heat; drain. Remove cover. Shake potatoes in Dutch oven over low heat until dry; peel potatoes while hot, holding on long fork or with paper towels. Halve lengthwise; place on cutting board, flat side down. Cut each potato half into 3/4-inch strips; cut crosswise to make bite-sized cubes. Place in warm bowl; sprinkle with salt. Add onion and pepper; stir in vinegar. Let stand at room temperature for 1 hour; refrigerate overnight. Drain crab; reserve larger pieces for garnish. Add remaining crab to potato mixture. Add celery, pickles and eggs; stir lightly. Mix mayonnaise and sour cream; add to potato mixture, stirring in just enough to coat ingredients liberally. Place salad in serving bowl; may be refrigerated. Tuck greens around edge of bowl just before serving; decorate with reserved crab. Serve remaining mayonnaise mixture with salad. Yield: 8 servings.

Photograph for this recipe on this page.

CHINESE NEW YEAR'S CHICKEN

1 fryer, cut into sm. pieces
Garlic salt to taste
Cornstarch
2 eggs, beaten
Oil
1 tsp. monosodium glutamate
3/4 c. sugar
1/4 c. chicken stock
1/2 c. wine vinegar
1 tsp. salt
1 tbsp. soy sauce
1/4 c. catsup

Sprinkle chicken with garlic salt; roll in cornstarch. Dip in eggs. Cook in small amount of oil in frying pan until brown; place in shallow casserole. Mix monosodium glutamate, sugar, stock, vinegar, salt, soy sauce and catsup; pour over chicken. Bake in preheated 350-degree oven for 1 hour and 15 minutes or until chicken is tender.

Kay Caskey
Manogue HS, Reno, Nevada

CURRIED OYSTER CASSEROLE

2 c. Uncle Ben's long grain and
   wild rice
1/2 c. melted butter
4 doz. oysters
Salt and pepper to taste
1 can cream of chicken soup
1 c. light cream
1 1/2 tbsp. onion powder
3/4 tsp. thyme
1 tbsp. curry powder
1/4 c. hot water

Cook rice according to package directions; combine with butter. Place half the rice in casserole; add half the oysters. Season with salt and pepper; repeat layers. Combine soup, cream, onion powder, thyme, curry powder and hot water in saucepan; heat through. Pour over oysters. Bake in preheated 300-degree oven for 45 minutes.

Mrs Virginia O. Savedge
Northampton Sr HS, Eastville, Virginia

TAGLIARINI

2 1/2 lb. ground beef
1 onion, chopped
1 can mushroom soup
1 can tomato soup
1 can whole kernel corn
Salt and pepper to taste
1 lg. package egg noodles
4 c. grated Cheddar cheese

Cook beef and onion in skillet over medium heat until brown. Add soups, corn, salt and pepper; simmer while cooking noodles. Prepare noodles according to package directions, cooking until nearly done; drain. Add to beef mixture; simmer for about 20 minutes. Add cheese; simmer, stirring, until cheese is melted.

Mrs Jesse Clausel
Kossuth HS, Kossuth, Mississippi

OKINAWAN-STYLE SHOYU PORK

1 3 to 4-lb. pork Boston butt
1 c. shoyu or soy sauce
1 c. (packed) brown sugar
1 c. water
4 1/2-in. pieces of gingerroot

Cut pork into 3-inch cubes. Place shoyu sauce, brown sugar, water and gingerroot in 5-quart saucepan; bring to a boil over high heat. Add pork; bring to a boil again. Reduce heat to low; simmer, uncovered, for 1 hour to 1 hour and 30 minutes or until pork is tender, turning pork occasionally. Serve with rice.

Mrs Patricia Takahashi
Makawao Sch, Makawao, Maui, Hawaii

SURPRISE CASSEROLE

1 lb. hamburger
Salt and pepper to taste
3/4 c. cubed cheese
1 pkg. egg noodles
1 can cream of mushroom soup
1 can cream of celery soup
2 tbsp. grated Parmesan cheese
1/2 c. bread crumbs

Season hamburger with salt and pepper; shape into bite-sized meatballs around cubes of cheese. Cook meatballs in skillet until brown on all sides; drain. Cook noodles according to package directions; place in lightly greased casserole. Stir in soups, Parmesan cheese and meatballs; top with bread crumbs. Bake in preheated 375-degree oven for 45 minutes. Yield: 4-6 servings.

Cathy DiOrio
Reavis HS, Burbank, Illinois

EGGNOG POUND CAKE

1/2 c. sliced almonds
1 pkg. yellow cake mix

1/8 tsp. nutmeg
2 eggs
1 1/2 c. commercial eggnog
1/4 c. melted butter or margarine
2 tbsp. rum

Grease 10-inch tube or bundt pan generously with soft butter; press almonds against buttered side and bottom. Combine cake mix, nutmeg, eggs, eggnog, melted butter and rum in large mixing bowl with electric mixer until blended. Beat at medium speed for about 4 minutes or until smooth and creamy. Pour into prepared pan. Bake in preheated 350-degree oven for 45 to 55 minutes or until long wooden skewer inserted in thickest portion comes out clean. Cool in pan for 10 minutes. Invert cake onto rack; cool thoroughly. One-fourth teaspoon rum flavoring may be used instead of rum. Yield: 10-12 servings.

Mrs Marjorie Harris
Greeley Public Sch, Greeley, Nebraska

TWELFTH NIGHT CAKE

1 c. butter or margarine
3 tbsp. Florida frozen concentrated
    orange juice, thawed
2 tsp. grated Florida orange rind
1/2 tsp. vanilla extract
1/4 tsp. salt
4 eggs, at room temperature
4 egg yolks, at room temperature
1 c. sugar
1 1/2 c. sifted all-purpose flour
1/4 c. sifted cornstarch
Confectioners' sugar

Combine butter, undiluted orange concentrate, rind, vanilla and salt in small saucepan; cook over low heat, stirring, until butter is melted. Remove from heat; cool to lukewarm. Place eggs, egg yolks and sugar in large, warm bowl; beat until tripled in bulk. Sprinkle flour and cornstarch over eggs gently. Add orange mixture; fold in very gently until there is no trace of butter. Pour into greased 9-inch tube pan. Bake in preheated 350-degree oven for about 50 minutes or until cake starts to come away from side of pan. Cool; remove from pan. Sprinkle top of cake with confectioners' sugar; garnish side with orange slices, if desired. Yield: About 12 servings.

Photograph for this recipe on page 6.

SNOWFLAKE PUDDING

1 c. sugar
1 env. unflavored gelatin
1/2 tsp. salt
1 1/4 c. milk
1 tsp. vanilla
1 3 1/2-oz. can flaked coconut
2 c. heavy cream, whipped
Crimson Raspberry Sauce

Mix sugar, gelatin and salt thoroughly in saucepan; add milk. Cook, stirring, over medium heat until gelatin and sugar are dissolved; chill until partially set. Add vanilla; fold in coconut, then whipped cream. Spoon into 1 1/2-quart mold or 8 to 10 individual molds; chill for at least 4 hours or until firm. Unmold; serve with Crimson Raspberry Sauce. Yield: 8-10 servings.

Crimson Raspberry Sauce

1 10-oz. package frozen red
    raspberries
2 tsp. cornstarch
1/2 c. red currant jelly

Thaw raspberries; crush. Place in saucepan. Add cornstarch; mix thoroughly. Add jelly; bring to boiling point. Cook, stirring, until mixture is clear and slightly thickened. Strain; chill. Yield: 1 1/3 cups.

Mrs Mary Ada Parks
Anna-Jonesboro HS, Anna, Illinois

ALMOND-COFFEE REFRIGERATOR CAKE

1 c. butter or margarine
1 1/2 c. confectioners' sugar
2 egg yolks, well beaten
1/2 c. cold strong coffee
1/8 tsp. salt
1 tsp. vanilla
1/2 c. chopped toasted almonds
18 to 20 ladyfingers, split
Whipped cream

Cream butter in mixing bowl; add sugar gradually. Add egg yolks; beat until smooth and fluffy. Add coffee, small amount at a time, mixing well after each addition. Add salt, vanilla and almonds; mix well. Line loaf pan with waxed paper. Cover bottom of pan with ladyfinger halves, flat side down. Spread half the coffee mixture over ladyfingers; cover with layer of ladyfingers. Add remaining coffee mixture, then layer of ladyfingers. Chill for at least 4 hours. Turn out on small platter; garnish with whipped cream.

Magdalene Beehler
Mt St Benedict HS, Crookston, Minnesota

NEW YEAR'S EGGNOG PIE

1 3-oz. package lemon gelatin
1 c. hot water
1 pt. French vanilla ice cream
1/4 tsp. nutmeg
2 eggs, separated
1 tbsp. dark rum
Golden Coconut Shell
Chocolate curls

Dissolve gelatin in hot water. Add scoops of ice cream; stir until melted. Add nutmeg; chill until partially set. Stir in well-beaten egg yolks and rum; fold in stiffly beaten egg whites. Pour into coconut shell; chill until set. Sprinkle with additional nutmeg; top with chocolate curls. Molded numerals may be used instead of chocolate curls to decorate pie as face of clock.

Golden Coconut Shell

4 tbsp. soft butter
2 1/2 c. flaked coconut

Combine butter and coconut; mix well. Press into 9-inch pie pan. Bake in preheated 300-degree oven for 20 minutes; cool.

Mrs Shirley S. Allen
Redford HS, Detroit, Michigan

EASY RUM CAKES

1 15 1/2-oz. can French vanilla pudding
1 tbsp. light rum
1/2 c. heavy cream, whipped
1 box yellow cake mix
Powdered sugar

Mix pudding and rum; fold in whipped cream. Prepare cake mix according to package directions; place in paper-lined muffin tins. Bake according to package directions; cool thoroughly. Cut circle from center of each cupcake with center section of doughnut cutter; scoop out some of the cake. Spoon filling into center of each cupcake; replace cake circle. Sprinkle with powdered sugar. Yield: 24 cupcakes.

Mrs Mary Tranquillo
Plant City HS, Plant City, Florida

EGGNOG DELIGHT

6 eggs, separated
1 c. confectioners' sugar
2 c. milk
2 c. heavy cream, stiffly beaten
1 pt. bourbon
1/4 c. rum
Nutmeg to taste

Beat egg yolks until thick. Add 1/2 of the sugar gradually; beat well. Beat egg whites until soft peaks form. Beat until stiff peaks form, adding remaining sugar gradually; fold in egg yolk mixture. Stir in milk; fold in whipped cream. Pour into punch bowl; stir in bourbon and rum. Sprinkle with nutmeg; serve. Brandy or sherry may be substituted for rum.

Katharine Rigby
Starr Washington Jr HS, Lancaster, Ohio

ICEBERG EGGNOG PUNCH

6 eggs
1/2 c. sugar
1 1/2 tsp. nutmeg
3 c. half and half
3 c. heavy cream
3 1/2 tsp. vanilla
7 sm. bottles Seven-Up
1/2 gal. vanilla ice cream
1/2 c. chopped maraschino cherries

Combine eggs, sugar and nutmeg in large bowl; beat until light. Stir in half and half, cream and vanilla; pour into punch bowl. Add Seven-Up slowly; mix gently. Spoon ice cream into punch; sprinkle cherries over top. Serve immediately. Yield: 32 servings.

Sharon Lea Bundy
Green River Sr HS, Green River, Wyoming

FESTIVE CHICKEN HORS D'OEUVRES

1 3-oz. package cream cheese, softened
1 5-oz. can chicken spread
1/3 c. chopped apple
1/4 c. chopped walnuts
2 tbsp. chopped parsley
1/2 tsp. Worcestershire sauce
Dash of cayenne pepper
Toasted wheat germ

Stir cream cheese in bowl until smooth; blend in remaining ingredients except wheat germ. Chill. Shape into 38 balls; roll in wheat germ. Place on serving platter.

Photograph for this recipe on this page.

GALA COCKTAIL

1 6-oz. can V-8 cocktail vegetable juice
1 oz. white port
Dash of aromatic bitters
2 diagonal slices celery
Stuffed olive

Fill 10-ounce glass 1/2 full with crushed ice. Add juice, port and bitters; stir. Spear celery slices and olive alternately on toothpick; garnish glass with the kabob. Yield: 1 serving.

Photograph for this recipe on this page.

RING-IN-THE-NEW-YEAR PUNCH

5 c. Florida orange juice
2 1/2 c. maraschino cherry syrup
5 c. lemon soda or sparkling water

Combine orange juice and cherry syrup in large punch bowl; add lemon soda slowly. Add block of ice or ice cubes just before serving; garnish with orange slices and cherries. Yield: 24-26 servings.

Photograph for this recipe on page 6.

lincoln and washington's birthday

Inspired by the traditions of two of our
country's greatest leaders, home economic
teachers from a cross section of the United
States have put together great menus and recipes
for hearty foods such as those prepared during the
days of Abraham Lincoln and George Washington.

Frontier Kentucky in the time of Abe Lincoln was surely
a land of much hard work and good simple food. Those were
the days when women served meals that really stuck to a
man's ribs. And, George Washington, "father of our country,"
certainly must have enjoyed this basic hearty fare as the com-
mander of the Revolutionary Army.

Why not celebrate the birthdays of these two famous presidents with
a hearty family supper such as the ones suggested on the next pages.
For Lincoln's, use a bright red and white checked gingham tablecloth
with the Lincoln Ham-Cheese Log for the centerpiece. Maybe some
member of your family can recite the Gettysburg Address with a little
help. And, for Washington's birthday, pick up the cherry tree legend
by making place mats from white construction paper then drawing
tiny red cherries and little brown hatchets along the borders. For a
centerpiece, use any house plants with branches so
that you can tie fresh cherries to the limbs.

Recipes on page 29.

Hearty Family Suppers

Lincoln's Birthday

Lincoln's Ham-Cheese Logs
Marie's Special Day Casserole
Fireside Macaroni Casserole
Boiled Custard
Abe's Apple Cake

Washington's Birthday

Special Cherry Salad
George's Cherry Chicken
Minuteman Broccoli Casserole
Potato Pancakes
Washington Cream Pie Cake

FIRESIDE MACARONI CASSEROLE

1 8-oz. package macaroni
1/2 c. mayonnaise
1/4 c. diced green pepper
1/4 c. chopped pimento
1 sm. onion, chopped
1/2 tsp. salt
1 can mushroom soup
1/2 c. cream
1 c. grated sharp cheese

Prepare macaroni according to package directions. Mix mayonnaise, green pepper, pimento, onion, salt, soup, cream, cheese and macaroni; place in casserole. Bake in preheated 325-degree oven for 30 minutes or until bubbly.

Venita Gill
Brewer Middle Sch, Ft Worth, Texas

ABE'S APPLE CAKE

2 c. sugar
1 1/2 tsp. soda
3 c. flour
1/2 tsp. nutmeg
1/2 tsp. cloves
1 tsp. cinnamon
1 tsp. salt
3 eggs, slightly beaten
1 c. salad oil
1 tsp. vanilla
3 c. diced apples
1 c. chopped nuts

Sift sugar, soda, flour, spices and salt together into bowl. Add eggs, oil and vanilla; mix well. Add apples and nuts; stir until mixed. Pour into greased and floured tube pan. Bake in preheated 350-degree oven for 1 hour. Remove cake from oven; place in heavy brown paper bag immediately. Close tightly; let stand until cool.

Sandy Shape
Jackson Sch, Garland, Texas

BOILED CUSTARD

4 eggs
1 c. sugar
2 qt. milk
1 tbsp. butter
1 tsp. vanilla
1 orange peel, quartered

Place eggs in top of double boiler; beat well. Add sugar gradually; stir in milk. Cook over boiling water, stirring frequently, until mixture coats spoon. Add butter; cool. Stir in vanilla; add orange peel. Chill overnight. Remove peel before serving. Yield: 10-12 servings.

Mrs Marian G. Craddock
Colorado HS, Colorado City, Texas

MARIA'S SPECIAL DAY CASSEROLE

1 1/2 lb. ground beef
1/2 c. chopped onion
1 tsp. salt
1/2 tsp. thyme
1/8 tsp. pepper
1/2 c. sour cream
1/3 c. milk
3/4 c. rolled oats
1 16-oz. can tomato sauce
1 6-oz. can tomato paste
1 c. water
1 med. head cabbage, coarsely
   shredded

Combine ground beef, onion, seasonings, sour cream, milk and oats; set aside. Combine tomato sauce, tomato paste and water. Pour 1/3 of the sauce into Dutch oven; place 1/2 of the cabbage over sauce. Spread beef mixture over cabbage. Cover with remaining cabbage; pour remaining sauce over cabbage. Cover tightly. Simmer for 1 hour or until cabbage is tender and beef mixture is done.

Maria Campo
Glenrock Jr-Sr HS, Glenrock, Wyoming

LINCOLN'S HAM-CHEESE LOGS

1 c. shredded sharp cheese
1 8-oz. package cream cheese
1 4 1/2-oz. can deviled ham
1/2 c. chopped ripe olives
1/2 c. finely chopped pecans

Have cheeses at room temperature. Place cheeses in small mixing bowl; beat until blended. Beat in deviled ham; stir in olives. Chill until almost firm. Shape into two 8-inch logs; roll in pecans. Serve with crackers.

Sandra Gilliland
Gustine HS, Gustine, Texas

SPECIAL CHERRY SALAD

1 No. 2 can fruit cocktail
1 No. 2 can crushed pineapple
1 12-oz. carton cottage cheese
1 pt. Cool Whip
1 3-oz. package black cherry
gelatin

Drain fruit cocktail and pineapple in colander. Place cottage cheese on fruits; drain well. Place in bowl; fold in Cool Whip and gelatin. Chill. Any flavor gelatin may be used in place of black cherry.

Mrs Edith May Bryan
Harrisonburg HS, Harrisonburg, Virginia

GEORGE'S CHERRY CHICKEN

1 fryer
1 tbsp. oil
1/2 c. water
1 1-lb. 4-oz. can frozen pitted sour cherries, thawed
1 3/4-oz. envelope au jus gravy mix
1 tsp. grated orange peel
1/4 c. honey

Cut fryer into serving pieces; brown in oil in large skillet. Add water; cover. Cook over low heat for 30 minutes or until tender. Drain cherries, reserving liquid; add enough water to reserved liquid to make 1 cup liquid. Add gravy mix, orange peel, cherry liquid and honey to chicken; bring to a boil. Cover; cook for 10 minutes longer. Stir in cherries; cook just until cherries are heated through. Canned cherries may be substituted for frozen cherries. Yield: 4 servings.

Deanna Juehd
Needles HS, Needles, California

MINUTEMAN BROCCOLI CASSEROLE

2 10-oz. packages frozen broccoli spears
1 can cream of mushroom soup
2 eggs, well beaten
1 c. grated sharp cheese
1 med. onion, chopped fine
1 c. mayonnaise
1/2 pkg. Pepperidge Farm stuffing mix
Butter

Cook broccoli according to package directions; drain. Place in casserole. Combine soup, eggs, cheese, onion and mayonnaise; pour over broccoli. Sprinkle with stuffing mix; dot with butter. Bake in preheated 350-degree oven for 25 to 30 minutes or until bubbly. Yield: 5-6 servings.

Mrs Frances VanLandingham
Greene Central HS, Snow Hill, North Carolina

POTATO PANCAKES

2 eggs
2 tbsp. flour
1/2 med. onion, grated
1 1/2 tsp. salt
1/4 tsp. pepper
6 med. potatoes, grated
Parsley flakes to taste (opt.)
3 or 4 tbsp. margarine

Beat eggs in large bowl; beat in flour. Add onion, salt and pepper; stir in potatoes and parsley. Heat margarine in heavy skillet. Drop potato mixture by spoonfuls into skillet; flatten. Cook until brown. Turn; cook until brown. Serve hot with sour cream or applesauce.

Mable Whisnant
East Lincoln HS, Denver, North Carolina

WASHINGTON CREAM PIE CAKE

3 eggs
1 1/2 c. sugar
1 tbsp. lemon juice
1 c. sifted cake flour
1 tsp. baking powder
3/4 tsp. salt
3 tbsp. butter
1/2 c. hot milk
4 tbsp. cornstarch
1 1/2 c. milk
2 egg yolks, slightly beaten
1 tsp. vanilla
1   1-lb. 4-oz. can frozen tart red
*   cherries, thawed*
1 c. whipping cream
1 tbsp. confectioners' sugar

Grease bottom of 8-inch baking pan; line with waxed paper. Set aside. Beat eggs until thick. Add 1 cup sugar gradually; beat until light and fluffy. Stir in lemon juice. Sift flour, baking powder and 1/4 teaspoon salt; fold into egg mixture just until blended. Melt 1 tablespoon butter in hot milk; stir into batter quickly. Pour into prepared pan. Bake in preheated 350-degree oven for 30 minutes. Let stand for 10 minutes. Invert onto wire rack to cool; remove waxed paper. Combine remaining sugar, 3 tablespoons cornstarch and remaining salt in saucepan; add milk gradually. Cook over medium heat, stirring constantly, until thick; cook for 2 minutes longer. Blend small amount of hot mixture into egg yolks; stir back into saucepan. Cook for 1 minute. Stir in remaining butter and vanilla. Press circle of waxed paper over surface of filling; chill. Cut cake crosswise into 2 layers; fill with cream filling. Drain cherries, reserving 3/4 cup syrup. Combine remaining cornstarch and reserved syrup in 1-quart saucepan. Cook over medium heat, stirring constantly, until thick; cook for 2 minutes longer. Add cherries; spoon over top of cake. Chill. Whip cream in chilled bowl until stiff; fold in confectioners' sugar. Frost sides of cake with whipped cream; flute whipped cream around edge of cake.

Jolinda Willis
Northern Burlington Co Reg HS
Columbus, New Jersey

SOUR CREAM MEAT PIES

1 1/2 c. lean hamburger
1 c. finely chopped mushrooms
1 lg. onion, finely chopped
3 tbsp. butter
1 1/2 c. sour cream
1 1/2 tsp. salt
1/4 tsp. pepper
2 c. flour
1 tbsp. sugar
1/2 c. shortening
1 egg, separated

Saute hamburger, mushrooms and onion in butter until hamburger is lightly browned. Remove from heat; stir in 1/2 cup sour cream, 1/2 teaspoon salt and pepper. Mix flour, remaining salt and sugar in bowl; cut in shortening. Mix egg yolk and remaining sour cream. Add to flour mixture; mix well. Roll out on floured surface; cut into circles with sour cream carton. Place 1 heaping teaspoon filling in middle of each circle of pastry. Fold over; seal edges. Mix egg white with 1 tablespoon water; brush over pies. Place on baking sheet. Bake in preheated 400-degree oven for 15 to 20 minutes. Chopped cooked roast may be substituted for hamburger. Yield: 1 1/2 dozen.

Mrs Judy Stetson
W. R. Myers HS, Taber, Alberta, Canada

FAMILY-STYLE MEAT LOAF

2 lb. ground beef chuck
1 c. Gerber oatmeal cereal
1/2 c. chopped onion
1/2 c. chopped green pepper
2 eggs, slightly beaten
1 1/2 tsp. salt
1/4 tsp. rosemary
1/4 tsp. oregano
1/4 tsp. basil
1 8-oz. can tomato sauce

Combine all ingredients thoroughly in large bowl; place in 9 x 5 x 3-inch loaf pan. Bake in preheated 400-degree oven for about 50 minutes or until brown; drain off fat. Let stand in pan for 5 minutes; transfer to serving platter. Garnish with parsley or watercress, if desired. Yield: 6-8 servings.

Photograph for this recipe on this page.

BAKED VERMICELLI CASSEROLE

3/4 lb. ground beef
3/4 lb. ground pork
2 onions, chopped
1/3 c. diced green pepper
3 stalks celery, diced
Salt and pepper to taste
1 4-oz. package vermicelli
1 or 2 cans stewed tomatoes
1 can cream of celery soup
1 tbsp. Worcestershire sauce
2 c. grated Cheddar cheese
1 2 1/2-oz. jar mushroom stems and
   pieces, drained

Cook beef and pork in skillet until lightly browned, stirring frequently. Add onions, green pepper, celery, salt and pepper; cook, stirring frequently, until vegetables are tender. Prepare vermicelli according to package directions. Mix beef mixture, vermicelli, tomatoes, soup and Worcestershire sauce; place in 9 x 13-inch baking dish. Bake in preheated 350-degree oven for 30 minutes. Sprinkle cheese and mushrooms on top. Return to oven; bake until cheese is melted. Almonds may be added with cheese and mushrooms, if desired.

Mrs Mildred Anderson
Moorhead Sr HS, Moorhead, Minnesota

MOLASSES ROLLED COOKIES

3/4 c. shortening
1/2 c. sugar
1/2 c. Grandma's unsulphured molasses
1 egg yolk
2 c. sifted all-purpose flour
1/2 tsp. salt
1/2 tsp. soda
1 tsp. baking powder
1 tsp. cinnamon
1/2 tsp. ginger
1/2 tsp. cloves
Ornamental Frosting

Cream shortening, sugar, molasses and egg yolk in large bowl. Sift in flour, salt, soda, baking powder and spices; mix well. Chill for 1 hour or until ready to bake. Roll out 1/8 inch thick on lightly floured board or pastry cloth; cut into desired shapes. Place on ungreased baking sheets. Bake in preheated 375-degree oven for 10 minutes; cool. Decorate with Ornamental Frosting forced through cake decorator. Yield: About 4 dozen.

Ornamental Frosting

1 1/4 c. sifted confectioners' sugar
1/8 tsp. cream of tartar
1 egg white
1/2 tsp. vanilla

Combine all ingredients in mixing bowl; beat with rotary beater or electric mixer until frosting holds shape. Cover with damp cloth until ready to use.

Photograph for this recipe on page 22.

GINGERBREAD VALENTINES

2 1/2 c. sifted all-purpose flour
1 tsp. salt
2 tsp. baking powder
1/2 tsp. soda
1 tsp. ginger
2 tsp. cinnamon
1/2 tsp. cloves
1/2 c. shortening
1/2 c. sugar
1 c. Grandma's unsulphured
   molasses
2 eggs
1 c. hot water

Sift flour, salt, baking powder, soda, ginger, cinnamon and cloves together. Cream shortening and sugar in bowl; blend in molasses. Stir in 1/2 cup flour mixture; beat in eggs. Add hot water alternately with remaining flour mixture, mixing well after each addition; turn into greased and floured 9-inch square pan. Bake in preheated 350-degree oven for 40 minutes; cool. Cut out with heart-shaped cutter; top each heart with whipped cream or whipped topping and candy heart. Yield: 10 hearts.

Photograph for this recipe on page 22.

MOLASSES LINCOLN LOG

2/3 c. Grandma's unsulphured molasses
2/3 c. peanut butter
1 c. instant nonfat dry milk
3/4 c. coarsely chopped peanuts

Mix molasses and peanut butter in bowl; stir in dry milk. Knead on board lightly sprinkled with additional dry milk to keep from sticking. Roll into log shape 2 inches thick; chill for 30 minutes. Roll log in peanuts. Mixture may be rolled into rope 3/4 inch in diameter for individual pieces. Cut into 1 1/2-inch lengths; wrap pieces in waxed paper or transparent plastic wrap. Yield: About 1 pound.

Photograph for this recipe on page 22.

DATE-NUT LOG

2 eggs, beaten
1 c. sugar
1 tsp. vanilla
1/4 tsp. almond flavoring
1 c. chopped dates
1 c. shredded coconut
1 c. chopped nuts

Mix eggs and sugar; stir in vanilla, almond flavoring, dates, coconut and nuts. Spoon into ungreased casserole. Bake in preheated 350-degree oven for 30 minutes. Remove from oven; beat well while hot. Cool; form into balls, using about 1 tablespoon for each. Roll in additional sugar, coating well. May be shaped into logs and sliced for more servings. Yield: 20 servings.

Ruth Nolte
Waco HS, Waco, Texas

DUTCH APPLE PIE

6 tbsp. flour
Sugar
6 med. Winesap or Rome Beauty
   apples, quartered
1 unbaked 9-in. pie shell
3/4 c. sour cream
Cinnamon to taste

Mix flour, 2 tablespoons sugar and apples in mixing bowl; place in pie shell. Spoon sour cream over apple mixture; sprinkle 1/2 cup sugar, then cinnamon over top. Bake in preheated 400-degree oven until crust browns. Reduce temperature to 325 degrees; bake for 30 minutes longer or until apples are tender.

Marge Schudel
Lincoln East HS, Lincoln, Nebraska

CHERRY BERRIES ON A CLOUD

3 egg whites
1/4 tsp. cream of tartar
1 1/4 c. sugar
1 3-oz. package cream cheese,
   softened

1/2 tsp. vanilla
1 c. whipping cream
1 c. miniature marshmallows
1 can cherry pie filling
1 tsp. lemon juice

Cover baking sheet with heavy brown paper. Beat egg whites and cream of tartar until foamy. Beat in 3/4 cup sugar, 1 tablespoon at a time, beating until stiff and glossy; do not underbeat. Shape meringue into 9-inch circle on brown paper, building up side. Bake in preheated 275-degree oven for 1 hour; cool. Remove from paper. Blend cream cheese, remaining sugar and vanilla. Pour cream into chilled bowl; beat until stiff. Fold gently into cream cheese mixture; fold in marshmallows. Pile into shell. Cover; chill for at least 12 hours. Mix pie filling and lemon juice; spread over cream cheese mixture. Cut into wedges.

Eva Jo Hoyle
Metz R-2 Sch, Metz, Missouri

DOUBLE CHERRY PIE

2 c. frozen pitted tart cherries
1 c. frozen pitted dark sweet
   cherries
1/4 c. sugar
2 1/3 tbsp. quick-cooking tapioca
1 1/2 tbsp. cornstarch
1 tsp. lemon juice
Pastry for 2-crust pie

Thaw cherries; drain, reserving juices. Mix sugar, tapioca and cornstarch in saucepan; add 2/3 cup reserved tart cherry juice and 1/3 cup reserved sweet cherry juice. Mix well. Cook over high heat until thickened; cool. Line 9-inch pie pan with half the pastry. Add cherries and lemon juice to tapioca mixture; pour into pastry-lined pie pan. Cover with remaining pastry; make slits in top with knife. Bake in preheated 425-degree oven for 30 to 35 minutes or until browned. Bake on lowest oven shelf for brown undercrust.

Jo Nita Schwarz
Miles Independent Sch, Miles, Texas

CHERRY DUMP CAKE

1/2 c. butter
1 1-lb. can crushed pineapple
1 1-lb. can cherry pie filling
1 box yellow cake mix

Spread half the butter over bottom of 9 x 11-inch pan; spread pineapple over butter. Spread pie filling over pineapple; spread cake mix over top. Dot with remaining butter. Bake in preheated 350-degree oven for 1 hour. Cool; remove from pan. Chill; top with whipped cream or Dream Whip.

Dorothy Thruston
Redwood Valley Jr HS
Redwood Valley, California

EASY CHERRY PUNCH

1 1-qt. bottle cherry punch mix
6 qt. cold water
1 pkg. cherry Kool-Aid
1 c. sugar
1 46-oz. can pineapple juice
1 1-pt. bottle lemon juice
Red food coloring (opt.)

Mix punch mix, cold water and Kool-Aid, stirring well. Add sugar; stir until dissolved. Add fruit juices; mix well. Stir in enough food coloring for desired shade. Serve from punch bowl with ice ring or ice cubes, if desired.

Elizabeth Muennink
Cedar Bayou Jr Sch, Baytown, Texas

POPCORN CRUSTED CHERRY PIE

1 5-oz. pan Jiffy Pop Popcorn
3/4 c. light corn syrup
1 tbsp. butter

Pop popcorn according to frypan directions. Cool slightly; crush by rolling with rolling pin. Place popcorn in bowl. Mix corn syrup and butter in saucepan; cook to soft-ball stage or 240 degrees on candy thermometer.

Pour over popcorn; toss with greased wooden spoon. Press firmly, with buttered hands, against bottom and side of buttered 9-inch pie plate; refrigerate for 30 minutes or until set.

Cherry Filling

1 env. unflavored gelatin
2 tbsp. lemon juice
2 tbsp. orange juice
2 1-lb. 5-oz. cans cherry pie filling
1 c. frozen whipped topping, thawed
1/2 tsp. brandy extract
Mace or nutmeg

Mix gelatin with lemon juice and orange juice in saucepan; let stand for 5 minutes. Place over low heat; stir until gelatin is dissolved. Mix with pie filling; pour into popcorn crust. Stir brandy extract into whipped topping. Drop by spoonfuls in center of cherry filling; sprinkle with mace. Refrigerate until ready to serve.

Photograph for this recipe on this page.

NEW YEAR'S EVE LAMB CURRY

3/4 c. butter
4 lb. boneless leg or shoulder of lamb,
    cut in 1-in. cubes
2 cloves of garlic, crushed
3 c. chopped celery
2 med. onions, sliced in thin rings
1 c. flour
4 tsp. curry powder
1 tsp. ground ginger
1/2 tsp. cayenne pepper
2 qt. lamb or chicken broth
1 c. yogurt
2 tbsp. lime juice
2 cored apples, sliced in thin wedges
Salt to taste
3/4 c. chutney
Lime slices
Parsley sprigs
Hot cooked rice

Melt 1/2 cup butter in large skillet. Add lamb and garlic; cook, stirring, until brown. Remove lamb and garlic; set aside. Add remaining butter to skillet. Add celery and onions; cook, stirring, until lightly browned. Blend in flour, curry powder, ginger and cayenne pepper. Combine broth, yogurt and lime juice, blending thoroughly; add to skillet gradually, stirring constantly. Cook over low heat, stirring constantly, until thickened and smooth. Return lamb and garlic to skillet; add salt. Cover. Simmer for 20 minutes. Add apples; simmer for 25 minutes longer or until lamb is tender, stirring occasionally to prevent sticking. May sprinkle several of the apple slices with lime juice and reserve for garnish, if desired. Blend chutney into lamb mixture just before serving; heat through. Garnish with lime slices and parsley sprigs. Serve with rice and condiments of sliced green onions, diced tomatoes, shredded lettuce, sliced radishes and cucumber cubes. Yield: 12-16 servings.

Photograph for this recipe on page 33.

CORNED BEEF AND CABBAGE SALAD

2 tbsp. sugar
1 tsp. salt
1/2 tsp. celery seed
1/2 tsp. dry mustard
1/4 tsp. pepper
1/2 c. white vinegar
1/4 c. Planters peanut oil
1 tsp. minced onion
4 c. finely shredded cabbage
2 c. cooked corned beef, cut in
   2-in. julienne strips
1 c. Planters cocktail peanuts
1/2 c. diced green pepper

Combine sugar, salt, celery seed, mustard, pepper, vinegar, oil and onion; blend thoroughly. Combine cabbage, corned beef, peanuts and green pepper in large bowl. Add vinegar mixture; toss. Cover; refrigerate for at least 3 hours. Toss before serving; drain off excess liquid. Yield: 6-8 servings.

Photograph for this recipe on page 34.

IRISH STEW WITH PEANUTS

1 1/2 lb. lean boneless lamb, cut
   into 1 1/2-in. cubes
1 1/2 c. water
1   8-oz. can stewed tomatoes
1 1/2 c. sliced onion
1/2 c. chopped celery and leaves
1/4 c. chopped parsley
1 lg. clove of garlic, crushed
1 beef bouillon cube
1 tsp. salt
1/4 tsp. ground thyme
1/8 tsp. pepper
6 carrots, peeled and quartered
6 sm. potatoes, peeled and quartered
1 tsp. cornstarch
1 c. Planters cocktail peanuts

Combine lamb cubes, water, stewed tomatoes, onion, celery, parsley, garlic, bouillon cube, salt, thyme and pepper in Dutch oven or large saucepot. Bring to a boil. Reduce heat to low; cover. Simmer for about 1 hour and 30 minutes or until lamb is tender. Add carrots and potatoes; bring to a boil. Reduce heat to low; cover. Simmer for about 30 minutes or until vegetables are tender. Blend 2 tablespoons hot broth mixture into cornstarch. Pour into remaining broth mixture; stir in peanuts. Cover; cook for 5 minutes longer or until stew is slightly thickened. Yield: 6 servings.

Photograph for this recipe on page 34.

VALENTINE'S

Cupids, Hearts, Flowers and Old Lace

Since the Victorian Era, women of all ages have anxiously awaited St. Valentine's Day . . . the day the man in her life tells her just how really special she is to him.

For this romantic holiday, let's have a delicious candlelight affair— a dinner for two. A gourmet meal, complete with savory appetizers and wine, that will say "I love you, too" in your own personal language. The following menu and recipes will serve as an excellent guideline in planning a distinctive repast that will suit your individual taste.

A lacey tablecloth and a pretty candelabra . . . Your very best silver and china . . . A vintage bottle of wine, and perhaps for this special occasion you will want to splurge a little—some carnations from the florist.

◁ Recipe on page 44.

MENU
Candlelight Dinner

Paté Pineapple
Savory Buttered Shrimp Appetizers
Strawberry Salad Supreme
Easy Veal Cordon Bleu
Baked Cheesy Green Beans
Rice-Mushroom Medley
Pink Meringue Hearts
Coffee

PATE PINEAPPLE

1 lb. chicken livers
1/2 c. minced onion
2 tbsp. oil
1/2 tsp. salt
1/4 tsp. pepper
2 tbsp. cream sherry
1/4 tsp. dried dill
Sliced olives
Greens

Heat livers and onion in oil. Add salt and pepper; cook until livers are no longer pink. Chop coarsely. Pour sherry into blender. Add dill and liver mixture; blend lightly. Do not liquefy. Turn out onto platter; shape lengthwise on platter to resemble half of a pineapple. Score into diamond shapes; place olive slice in each diamond. Place greens at top of pate on platter for crown.

Mrs B. Sachs
Westlake HS, Thornwood, New York

SAVORY BUTTERED SHRIMP APPETIZERS

1 clove of garlic, minced
2 tbsp. lemon juice
Basil and rosemary to taste
1/2 tsp. salt
1/4 tsp. pepper
Tabasco sauce to taste
1 c. melted butter or margarine
2 lb. peeled deveined shrimp

Mix seasonings with butter. Place shrimp in shallow pan; broil for 5 minutes. Spoon sauce over shrimp; broil for 5 to 8 minutes longer. Serve immediately. Yield: 8 servings.

Mrs Susan McAlexander
Abernathy HS, Abernathy, Texas

STRAWBERRY SALAD SUPREME

1 6-oz. box strawberry gelatin
2 c. boiling water

1 pt. frozen strawberries, partially thawed
2 bananas, finely chopped
1 lg. can crushed pineapple

Dissolve gelatin in boiling water. Add strawberries, bananas and pineapple; mix well. Spoon into individual heart molds; chill until firm. May be placed in 9 x 13-inch pan or dish and chilled.

Mrs Dorothy S. Ray
East Yancey HS, Burnsville, North Carolina

EASY VEAL CORDON BLEU

8 3-oz. tenderized veal steaks
4 thin slices ham
4 slices Swiss or Monterey Jack cheese
1/2 c. vegetable oil
1 egg
1 tbsp. water
Salt and pepper to taste
Garlic salt and onion salt to taste
1 c. cracker crumbs
Mushroom Sauce

Layer 1 veal steak, 1 slice ham, 1 slice cheese and top with another veal steak for each stack, trimming edges of ham and cheese smaller than steak. Press edges together securely. Heat oil in a heavy frypan. Beat egg with water. Dip steak stacks into egg mixture. Sprinkle with salt, pepper, garlic salt and onion salt; roll in crumbs. Fry on each side until golden brown; transfer to casserole. Bake in preheated 325-degree oven for 30 minutes. Serve with Mushroom Sauce.

Mushroom Sauce

1 c. medium white sauce
1 c. sliced mushrooms
1 tbsp. grated onion

Mix white sauce, mushrooms and onion in saucepan; cook, stirring, for about 3 minutes.

Mrs Dorothy Wuertz
John Marshall Sch, Los Angeles, California

BAKED CHEESY GREEN BEANS

1 10-oz. package frozen green beans
1 can cream of celery soup
1 5-oz. jar bacon and cheese
  spread
1 3 1/2-oz. can French-fried
  onions
3 slices crisply fried bacon,
  crumbled

Cook beans according to package directions; drain. Combine soup and cheese spread. Toss beans with soup mixture; place in 6-cup casserole. Top with onions and bacon. Bake in preheated 325-degree oven for 30 minutes. Yield: About 6 servings.

Phyllis T. Krumrine
Susquehannock HS, Glen Rock, Pennsylvania

RICE-MUSHROOM MEDLEY

1 6-oz. package long grain and
  wild rice
1 can beef broth
1 1/4 c. water
1 sm. onion, chopped
1/2 c. chopped celery
4 tbsp. butter or margarine
1 3-oz. can broiled in butter
  mushrooms, drained and sliced

Prepare rice according to package directions, substituting beef broth and 1 1/4 cups water for liquid called for on package. Cook onion and celery in butter until tender but not brown. Stir into rice 5 minutes before end of cooking time; stir in mushrooms. Cook until all liquid is absorbed. Yield: 6-8 servings.

Vivian B. Hicks
Corsicana HS, Corsicana, Texas

PINK MERINGUE HEARTS

3 egg whites
1 tsp. vanilla
1/4 tsp. cream of tartar
Dash of salt
1 c. sugar
Red food coloring
1 qt. vanilla ice cream
1 pt. fresh strawberries, sliced and
  sweetened

Beat egg whites with vanilla, cream of tartar and salt until frothy. Add sugar, small amount at a time, beating until stiff peaks form and sugar is dissolved; add enough food coloring for delicate pink tint. Cut heart pattern from 4 1/2-inch square of paper. Cover baking sheet with brown paper; draw 6 hearts on brown paper from pattern. Spread meringue over each heart shape, making 1/4-inch thick layer. Pipe rim about 3/4-inch high with pastry tube. Bake in preheated 275-degree oven for 1 hour. Turn off heat; let dry in oven for 1 hour for crisper meringues. Fill meringues with scoops of vanilla ice cream; top with strawberries. One 10-ounce package frozen strawberries, thawed, may be substituted for fresh strawberries.

Mrs Kay Nemetz
Southern Door Schools, Brussels, Wisconsin

ASPARAGUS-CHEESE CANAPES

1 egg
1 4-oz. package cream cheese
1 4-oz. package blue cheese
1 loaf sandwich bread
1 can asparagus stalks, drained
Melted butter or margarine

Blend egg with cream cheese and blue cheese. Trim crust from sandwich bread slices; roll each slice lightly with rolling pin. Spread with cheese mixture. Cut asparagus stalks in half; place on edge of bread. Roll as for jelly roll; brush generously with butter. Place in plastic container; cover. Freeze. Remove from freezer; cut each roll crosswise in 1 1/2-inch lengths. Place on greased cookie sheet. Bake in preheated 325-degree oven for 9 to 11 minutes or until golden brown. Serve hot.

Mrs Obera B. Pruitt
Belton-Honea Path HS, Belton, South Carolina

HEART CUTOUT SANDWICHES

1 c. ground cooked ham
1/2 c. grated carrot
1/2 c. salad dressing
1 1/2 tsp. prepared horseradish
1/4 tsp. salt
1/8 tsp. pepper
1 loaf sandwich bread
Soft butter

Mix ham, carrot, salad dressing, horseradish, salt and pepper thoroughly in mixing bowl. Cut small heart from center of half the bread slices with heart-shaped cookie cutter; spread hearts with butter. Remove crusts from whole bread slices; spread slices with ham salad. Place hearts on whole bread slices to serve.

Lillian B. Cockram
Floyd Co HS, Floyd, Virginia

TWO-IN-ONE VALENTINE SALAD

3 env. unflavored gelatin
1 c. cold water
4 c. tomato juice
1 tsp. salt
4 peppercorns
1 bay leaf
2 stalks celery, chopped
1/4 c. lemon juice
1 tsp. onion juice
Chicken Salad
Salad greens

Soften gelatin in cold water. Mix tomato juice, salt, peppercorns, bay leaf and celery in saucepan; bring to a boil. Reduce heat; simmer for 10 minutes. Strain. Add softened gelatin to hot liquid; stir until completely dissolved. Mix in lemon juice and onion juice; pour into twelve 1/2 cup heart-shaped molds. Chill until firm. Unmold onto serving platter. Spoon Chicken Salad on top of each serving; garnish with salad greens. May be poured into 9-inch square pan, chilled and cut with heart-shaped cutter.

Chicken Salad

1/2 lb. chopped cooked chicken
1 c. finely chopped celery
2 tbsp. finely chopped parsley
1/2 c. real mayonnaise

Mix chicken with remaining ingredients; chill.

Photograph for this recipe on this page.

Valentine's

ROLLED CHICKEN BREASTS

6 chicken breasts, boned and skinned
Salt to taste
1 6-oz. package sliced Swiss cheese
6 thin slices ham
Flour
2 tbsp. butter
1 tsp. instant chicken bouillon
1 3-oz. can sliced mushrooms
1/3 c. sauterne
Toasted almonds

Place chicken breasts, boned side up, on cutting board. Pound chicken lightly with wooden mallet to make 1/4-inch thick cutlets, working from center out; sprinkle with salt. Place cheese slice and ham slice on each piece of chicken; tuck in sides and roll up, pressing to seal well. Coat with 1/4 cup flour. Heat butter in skillet; brown chicken in butter. Remove to 11 x 7 x 1 1/2-inch baking pan. Combine 1/2 cup water, bouillon, mushrooms and sauterne in same skillet; heat, stirring to remove crusty bits from skillet. Pour over chicken; cover. Bake in preheated 350-degree oven for 1 hour to 1 hour and 15 minutes or until tender; transfer to warm serving platter. Blend 2 tablespoons flour with 1/2 cup water; stir into liquid in baking pan. Cook, stirring, until thickened. Pour small amount over chicken; garnish with almonds. Pour remaining gravy into sauceboat; serve with chicken. Yield: 6 servings.

Vicki Ann Sommers
Roosevelt Jr HS, Coffeyville, Kansas

CHICKEN VERMOUTH WITH RICE

3 lb. fryer pieces
3 tsp. salt
1/2 tsp. pepper
3 med. carrots, sliced
2 stalks celery, thinly sliced
1 med. onion, thinly sliced
4 cloves of garlic
2 tbsp. chopped parsley
1/3 c. dry vermouth
1 c. rice
2 c. chicken broth
1/4 c. sour cream

Place chicken in greased 2-quart casserole; sprinkle with 2 1/2 teaspoons salt and pepper. Add carrots, celery, onion, garlic, parsley and vermouth; cover. Bake in preheated 375-degree oven for 1 hour and 30 minutes. Combine rice, chicken broth and remaining salt in buttered casserole; cover with foil or lid. Bake for 30 minutes. Remove rice and chicken mixture from oven. Discard garlic from chicken mixture; add sour cream. Serve chicken mixture on rice. Yield: 6 servings.

Martha W. Good
DuPont Jr High, Belle, West Virginia

CRAB DELIGHT

1/2 c. diced celery
1/4 c. diced onion
1/4 c. diced green pepper
3 tbsp. margarine
1/2 c. flour
2 c. milk
1/2 tsp. dry mustard
1 tsp. Worcestershire sauce
Salt and pepper to taste
1 1-lb. can crab meat
1/2 c. bread crumbs

Saute celery, onion and green pepper in margarine until tender. Add flour; blend. Add milk slowly; cook, stirring, until mixture comes to a boil. Add seasonings and crab meat; pour into greased 1-quart casserole. Sprinkle with bread crumbs. Bake in preheated 350-degree oven for 30 minutes; serve hot.

Mrs Earl T. Charlesworth
North East HS, Pasadena, Maryland

DELICIOUS STUFFED MUSHROOMS

24 med. mushrooms
2 tbsp. butter

1 tbsp. minced onion
1/2 c. herb-seasoned stuffing mix
1/4 c. chopped almonds
4 strips fried bacon, drained and
    crumbled
1/4 tsp. salt
Chicken broth

Wash and dry mushrooms. Remove stems; chop. Heat butter. Add mushroom stems and onion to butter; saute until tender. Combine stuffing mix, almonds, bacon and salt; stir in enough broth to moisten. Fill mushroom caps; place in shallow baking dish. Bake in preheated 350-degree oven for 8 to 10 minutes or until heated through.

Margenia F. Keeton
Cumberland Co HS, Burkesville, Kentucky

LEMON LOVE SQUARES

1 bottle liquid fruit pectin
2 tbsp. water
1/2 tsp. soda
1 c. sugar
1 c. light corn syrup
2 tsp. lemon extract
10 drops of yellow food coloring
Sugar or colored sugar

Combine fruit pectin and water in 2-quart saucepan. Stir in soda; mixture will foam slightly. Mix sugar and corn syrup in large saucepan. Place both saucepans over high heat; cook both mixtures, stirring alternately, for 3 to 5 minutes or until foam has thinned from fruit pectin mixture and sugar mixture is boiling rapidly. Pour fruit pectin mixture in slow, steady stream into boiling sugar mixture, stirring constantly; boil, stirring, for 1 minute longer. Remove from heat; stir in lemon extract and food coloring. Pour immediately into buttered 9-inch square pan or 9 x 5-inch loaf pan; let stand at room temperature for about 3 hours or until mixture is cool and firm. Invert pan onto waxed paper which has been sprinkled with sugar; cut into 3/4-inch squares. Roll in

sugar. Let candy stand a while; roll in sugar again to prevent stickiness. Let stand overnight, uncovered, at room temperature before packaging or storing. Yield: 1 pound candy.

Carole Phillips
Sierra Joint Union HS, Tollhouse, California

ITALIAN CREAM CAKE

1/2 c. margarine
1/2 c. vegetable shortening
2 c. sugar
5 eggs, separated
2 c. all-purpose flour
1 tsp. soda
1 c. buttermilk
1 tsp. vanilla
1 4-oz. can flaked coconut
1 c. chopped pecans

Cream margarine and shortening. Add sugar gradually; beat until smooth. Add egg yolks; beat well. Combine flour and soda; add to creamed mixture alternately with buttermilk. Stir in vanilla. Stir in coconut and pecans; fold in stiffly beaten egg whites. Pour into 3 greased and waxed paper-lined 8-inch cake pans. Bake in preheated 350-degree oven for 25 minutes; cool.

Cream Cheese Frosting

1 8-oz. package cream cheese,
    softened
1/4 c. margarine, softened
1 1-lb. box confectioners' sugar
1 tsp. vanilla
Chopped nuts to taste

Mix cream cheese and margarine; stir in sugar, small amount at a time. Beat until smooth. Stir in vanilla and nuts. Spread between layers and on top and side of cake.

Kathleen Burchett
Southwest Area Home Economics Supvr
Bristol, Virginia

AVOCADO COEUR A LA CREME

1 c. pineapple juice
3 env. unflavored gelatin
1/3 c. sugar
2 or 3 California avocados
1 8-oz. package cream cheese,
    softened
1 8-oz. package cottage cheese
1 c. heavy cream
3 grapefruit, cut into sections
1/3 c. grenadine

Combine pineapple juice and gelatin in saucepan; let stand for 5 minutes. Stir over low heat until gelatin is dissolved. Stir in sugar; cool. Cut avocados into halves lengthwise. Whack sharp knife into seed; remove seed. Peel; mash with fork or press through sieve or food mill. Stir in pineapple mixture. Beat cream cheese until fluffy; beat in cottage cheese and heavy cream gradually. Fold in avocado mixture. Line 1 1/2-quart heart-shaped mold with damp cheesecloth; pour avocado mixture into mold. Chill until firm. Marinate grapefruit sections in grenadine. Invert mold onto platter; remove mold. Strip off cheesecloth carefully. Drain marinated grapefruit sections; garnish platter with sections. Decorate top with flower formed of additional avocado slices and grapefruit sections. Cut leaves and stem from avocado peel with scissors; place on mold with flower. May be molded in individual heart-shaped molds.

Photograph for this recipe on page 36.

PLEASE-BE-MINE VALENTINES

5 c. puffed rice cereal
4 c. miniature marshmallows
2 tbsp. butter or margarine
1/2 c. red cinnamon candies
6 wooden skewers

Place puffed rice cereal in shallow baking pan. Bake in preheated 350-degree oven for about 10 minutes. Pour into large greased bowl. Place marshmallows and butter in saucepan; heat, stirring occasionally, until smooth. Add candies; cook, stirring, for about 2 minutes or until mixture is deep pink, but all candies are not melted. Pour over puffed rice cereal; stir until evenly coated. Shape mixture with greased hands to form 6 hearts. Insert wooden skewer into each heart; decorate skewers with red ribbon bows.

Mrs Charles Caperton
Mississippi College, Clinton, Mississippi

CHERISHED SWEETHEART BARS

Flour
1/4 tsp. soda
Salt
1/2 c. (packed) brown sugar
1 c. rolled oats
1/3 c. melted butter
3/4 c. sugar
2 eggs, beaten
3/4 c. chopped maraschino cherries
1/2 c. flaked coconut
1/2 c. chopped nuts

Sift 1/2 cup flour, soda and 1/8 teaspoon salt together. Add brown sugar, oats and butter; mix well. Press firmly into greased 9-inch square pan. Combine 1/4 cup flour, sugar, 1/2 teaspoon salt and remaining ingredients thoroughly; spread over mixture in pan. Bake in preheated 350-degree oven for about 30 minutes; cool. Cut into bars.

Esther Engelhardt
Mt Pleasant Jr HS, Mt Pleasant, Iowa

PINK VALENTINE CAKE

2 1/2 c. sifted cake flour
1 1/2 c. sugar
3 1/2 tsp. baking powder
1 tsp. salt
1/2 c. shortening
3/4 c. milk
1/4 c. maraschino cherry juice

1 tsp. vanilla
2 tsp. almond extract
4 egg whites
18 well-drained maraschino cherries,
   finely chopped
1/2 c. chopped walnuts
Pink Valentine Frosting

Sift flour, sugar, baking powder and salt into mixing bowl; cut in shortening. Combine milk and cherry juice; add 3/4 cup milk mixture to flour mixture. Add flavorings; beat for 200 strokes, scraping bowl frequently with spoon. Add remaining milk mixture and egg whites; beat for 200 strokes. Add cherries and walnuts; mix well. Pour into 2 greased 9-inch cake pans. Bake in preheated 375-degree oven for 20 to 25 minutes; cool. Remove from pans; frost with Pink Valentine Frosting. May be mixed with electric mixer, if desired.

Pink Valentine Frosting

2 tbsp. shortening
2 tbsp. butter
1 tsp. vanilla
1/2 tsp. almond extract
1/2 tsp. salt
4 c. sifted confectioners' sugar
9 tbsp. scalded cream
Red food coloring

Combine shortening, butter, vanilla, almond extract and salt in bowl; blend. Beat in 1/2 cup sugar. Add cream alternately with remaining sugar, beating well after each addition; add only enough cream to make spreading consistency. Add enough food coloring to tint delicate pink.

Elizabeth Muennink
Cedar Bayou Jr Sch, Baytown, Texas

SWEETHEART CHERRY-WALNUT CAKE

1 box white cake mix
1/4 c. maraschino cherry juice
2 tsp. almond extract
2 egg whites

1 c. water
18 maraschino cherries, finely
   chopped
1/2 c. chopped walnuts

Place cake mix, cherry juice, almond extract, egg whites and water in mixing bowl; blend with electric mixer on low speed. Increase speed to medium; beat for about 4 minutes. Add cherries and walnuts; mix. Pour into 2 greased and floured heart-shaped cake pans. Bake in preheated 350-degree oven for 20 to 25 minutes; cool.

Icing

1 pt. heavy cream
6 tbsp. sugar
Red food coloring
6 maraschino cherries, cut in half

Whip cream until stiff, adding sugar gradually. Add enough red coloring to make icing delicate pink. Spread between cake layers and over top and sides of cake. Decorate with cherries.

Mrs Mable P. Nichols
Marjorie Stansfield Sch, Haledon, New Jersey

MARASCHINO CHERRY TARTS

2 c. flour
1/2 tsp. salt
1/3 c. finely chopped maraschino
   cherries
2/3 c. lard or shortening
5 to 6 tbsp. maraschino cherry juice
Vanilla or cherry ice cream
Whipped cream
Whole maraschino cherries

Sift flour and salt together into bowl; add chopped cherries. Cut in lard; add enough cherry juice to hold ingredients together. Roll out 1/16 inch thick on floured cloth; line individual heart-shaped molds with pastry. Bake in preheated 400-degree oven for 8 to 10 minutes or until lightly browned; cool. Fill pastries with ice cream; top each with whipped cream and cherry.

Dean V. Twait
Brookside Jr HS, Albert Lea, Minnesota

VALENTINE HONEY COOKIES

3/4 c. honey
1/4 c. butter
4 1/2 c. sifted flour
1 tsp. soda
1 tsp. cinnamon
1/2 tsp. nutmeg
2 eggs
3/4 c. sugar
1/2 c. ground almonds
1 tbsp. grated lemon rind
Tinted confectioners' frosting

Mix honey and butter in saucepan; bring to a boil. Cool until lukewarm. Sift flour, soda, cinnamon and nutmeg onto waxed paper. Beat eggs in large bowl until fluffy; beat in sugar gradually. Stir in honey mixture slowly; stir in almonds and lemon rind. Stir in flour mixture gradually to make very stiff dough. Cover; refrigerate overnight. Roll out on floured surface to 1/4-inch thickness; cut in desired shapes. Place on lightly greased baking sheets. Bake in preheated 350-degree oven for 10 minutes. Cool completely; spread with frosting.

Mrs Vickie Blubaugh
Orrville HS, Orrville, Ohio

VALENTINE SUGAR COOKIES ✗

1 1/2 c. margarine
4 c. sugar
4 eggs
2 tbsp. cream
4 c. all-purpose flour
1/8 tsp. salt
4 tsp. baking powder
2 tsp. vanilla
1/2 c. milk
Red food coloring

Cream 1 cup margarine and 2 cups sugar in bowl; add eggs, one at a time, beating well after each addition. Stir in cream. Sift flour with salt and baking powder; add to creamed mixture. Mix well; stir in 1 teaspoon vanilla. Chill for 20 minutes. Roll out very thin on floured surface; cut with heart-shaped cookie cutter. Place on greased cookie sheet. Bake in preheated 400-degree oven until brown; cool. Combine remaining sugar, milk and remaining margarine in saucepan; bring to a boil. Cook until mixture forms soft ball when dropped into cool water. Remove from heat; add desired amount of food coloring and remaining vanilla; cool. Glaze cookies quickly.

Judy Kelso
Fulton Co HS, Hickman, Kentucky

REMEMBRANCE STRAWBERRY PIE

1 c. sugar
3 tbsp. cornstarch
1 c. water
3 tbsp. strawberry gelatin
1 to 2 pt. stemmed strawberries
1 baked 8-in. pie shell
Cool Whip

Mix sugar and cornstarch in saucepan; stir in water. Cook until thickened, stirring constantly. Remove from heat; stir in gelatin. Pour over strawberries; mix well. Pour into pie shell; refrigerate until set. Spread Cool Whip over top. Other toppings may be used in place of Cool Whip.

Mrs Wilma Blide
Mayberry Jr HS, Wichita, Kansas

VALENTINE CHOCOLATE-CHERRY PIE

1 1/3 c. vanilla wafer crumbs
3/4 c. margarine, softened
3/4 c. sugar
1 sq. unsweetened chocolate, melted
   and cooled
1 tsp. vanilla
2 eggs
2 tbsp. chopped maraschino cherries
Whipped cream
Whole maraschino cherries

Combine crumbs and 1/4 cup margarine; press onto bottom and side of 8 or 9-inch pie plate or heart-shaped pan. Bake in pre-heated 375-degree oven for 8 minutes; cool. Cream remaining margarine and sugar; blend in chocolate and vanilla. Add eggs, one at a time, beating for 5 minutes after each addition; stir in chopped cherries. Spread in pie shell; chill for 4 hours. Top with whipped cream; garnish with whole cherries. Yield: 6-8 servings.

Janet Scheurich
Wilmington HS, Wilmington, Illinois

CHILLED STRAWBERRY-CAKE DESSERT

 2 1/2 c. boiling water
 2 3-oz. packages strawberry
    gelatin
 3 tbsp. sugar
 2 10-oz. packages frozen
    strawberries
 1 pt. whipping cream, whipped
 1 angel food cake

Mix water with gelatin and 1 tablespoon sugar in bowl; stir in most of the strawberries. Chill until thickened. Mix whipped cream and remaining sugar. Fold 3/4 of the whipped cream into gelatin mixture. Break cake into bite-sized pieces; place half the cake in large, shallow baking dish. Spoon half the gelatin mixture over cake. Add remaining cake; add remaining gelatin mixture. Refrigerate for several hours. Cut into squares; garnish each square with remaining whipped cream and 1 of the remaining strawberries.

Mrs Glenda Willoughby
Hamlin HS, Hamlin, Texas

PINK PEPPERMINT VALENTINE MOLD

 1 env. unflavored gelatin
 1/2 c. sugar
 1/8 tsp. salt
 2 eggs, separated
 1 1/4 c. milk
 1/4 tsp. peppermint flavoring
 Red food coloring
 1 c. heavy cream, whipped

Mix gelatin, 1/4 cup sugar and salt in sauce-pan. Beat egg yolks with milk; add to gelatin mixture. Cook over low heat, stirring constantly, for about 5 minutes or until gelatin dissolves and mixture thickens slightly. Remove from heat; add peppermint flavoring. Tint with several drops of food coloring; chill until slightly thicker than unbeaten egg whites. Beat egg whites until stiff, but not dry. Add remaining sugar gradually; beat until very stiff. Fold into gelatin mixture; fold in whipped cream. Turn into 5-cup heart-shaped mold; chill until firm. Unmold. Garnish with additional whipped cream. One-half cup crushed peppermint candy may be substituted for peppermint flavoring. Yield: 6 servings.

Neldalea Dotray
LaGrove HS, Farina, Illinois

SWEETHEART CHEESECAKE

 1 box vanilla Whip 'n' Chill
 1 3 3/4-oz. box instant vanilla
    pudding mix
 1 8-oz. package cream cheese,
    softened
 Juice of 1 lemon
 1/2 tsp. lemon extract
 1 angel food cake
 1 sm. carton Cool Whip
 1 c. canned cherry pie filling

Prepare Whip 'n' Chill and vanilla pudding mix according to package directions. Mix Whip 'n' Chill, pudding, cream cheese, lemon juice and lemon extract; place in oblong baking dish. Chill until firm. Cut cake crosswise into 3 layers. Spread cheese mixture between layers of cake; place layers together. Frost with Cool Whip; cover top with pie filling. Yield: 16 servings.

Margaret Raburn
Mustang HS, Mustang, Oklahoma

HEART'S DELIGHT VALENTINE CAKE

1 1/4 c. sifted cake flour
3/4 c. sugar
2 tsp. baking powder
3/4 tsp. salt
1/4 c. Mazola corn oil
1/2 c. water
2 eggs, separated
1 tsp. vanilla extract
1/8 tsp. cream of tartar
1 recipe Rich Chocolate Frosting
1 recipe Pink Decorator's Frosting

Sift flour, sugar, baking powder and salt together into mixing bowl. Make well in center; add corn oil, water, egg yolks and vanilla in order listed. Beat with spoon until smooth. Beat egg whites and cream of tartar until mixture forms very stiff peaks; fold in flour mixture gently, blending well. Do not stir. Pour into ungreased 9 x 1 1/2-inch layer pan. Bake in preheated 350-degree oven for 25 to 30 minutes or until cake springs back when touched lightly with finger; place on rack until cold. Loosen edge of cake with spatula; remove from pan. Fold 8 x 8 1/2-inch sheet of paper in half crosswise; cut out heart shape. Place heart pattern on top of cake layer; cut out heart shape carefully with serrated knife. Cut 2 small hearts from remaining cake pieces. Frost sides of cake with Rich Chocolate Frosting; swirl frosting on top, reserving about 1/3 cup for small hearts. Frost small hearts; position on top of cake. Decorate cake as desired with Pink Decorator's Frosting.

Rich Chocolate Frosting

1/4 c. Nucoa or Mazola margarine
3 tbsp. dark or light Karo syrup
1/8 tsp. salt
1/4 tsp. vanilla extract
1/2 c. cocoa
2 tbsp. (about) milk
2 c. sifted confectioners' sugar

Blend margarine, syrup, salt and vanilla in bowl; stir in cocoa. Add enough milk to make good spreading consistency alternately with confectioners' sugar, beating until smooth and creamy after each addition.

Pink Decorator's Frosting

1/4 c. Nucoa or Mazola margarine
1 c. sifted confectioners' sugar
Red food coloring

Combine margarine and confectioners' sugar in bowl, beating until smooth; tint pink with food coloring.

Photograph for this recipe on this page.

AVOCADO-CREAM MERINGUES

3 eggs, separated
1/2 tsp. vanilla extract
1/4 tsp. cream of tartar
1 1/3 c. sugar
1 c. light cream
3 tbsp. lemon juice
2 California avocados, peeled and
    mashed
2 to 3 drops of green food coloring
Raspberry or lingonberry preserves

Combine egg whites with vanilla and cream of tartar in bowl; beat until soft peaks form.

Add 1 cup sugar gradually, beating until very stiff peaks form. Cover large cookie pan with brown paper; draw 8 hearts about 3 inches in diameter on paper. Spread meringue on each heart, using back of spoon to shape sides higher than middle. Bake in preheated 275-degree oven for 1 hour; cool. Combine egg yolks, cream and remaining sugar in saucepan; bring to a boil over low heat, stirring constantly. Simmer for 3 minutes; cool to lukewarm. Stir in lemon juice, avocados and coloring; spoon into cooled shells. Drizzle raspberry preserves over top; garnish with sour cream. Yield: 8 servings.

Photograph for this recipe on this page.

VALENTINE FRUIT PUNCH

1 pkg. cherry Kool-Aid
1 pkg. strawberry Kool-Aid
2 c. sugar
3 qt. water
1 6-oz. can frozen orange juice
1 6-oz. can frozen lemonade
1 qt. ginger ale

Mix Kool-Aids, sugar and water. Add orange juice and lemonade; mix until thawed. Add ginger ale just before serving. Yield: Twenty-five 3/4-cup servings.

Mrs Dorothy Smith
Virginia HS, Virginia, Illinois

SWEETHEART RASPBERRY PUNCH

1 46-oz. can pink grapefruit juice
1 10-oz. package frozen
*   raspberries*
1 qt. ginger ale, chilled
1 pt. raspberry sherbet

Combine grapefruit juice and raspberries in punch bowl; stir until raspberries thaw. Add ginger ale and sherbet just before serving. Yield: Twenty 1/2-cup servings.

Patricia Shradel Mundy
Perry Jr HS, Perry, Iowa

ST. PATRICK'S DAY

Whether Emerald, Chartreuse, Lime or Sea . .
GREEN's the color you wearing must be;
Singing "Rosie O'Grady" or "Danny Boy"
Irish together good times we enjoy

Almost every American has a little Irish in him and he's proud of it.
And, no matter, everyone enjoys the lighthearted fun that accompanies
the celebration of Ireland's patron saint, St. Patrick. Traditional
parades . . . wearing of the green . . . and a lot of blarney.

This year, plan your festivities around a delicious Irish meal such as the
ones on the next pages. For your Dublin feast, use plenty of green. The
three-leaf clover, dubbed the Shamrock, is an excellent shape for
invitations and for place mats. And, for a unique centerpiece, try
making leprechauns using a potato for the body and pipe stems for the
arms and legs . . . a green felt hat to top him off. Let the little fellows
recline on a bed of clover.

◊ Recipe on page 55.

MENU

WEARING-OF-THE-GREEN GET-TOGETHER

Soup of The Balladeers
Cucumber-Lime Cream Mold
Baked Corned Beef
with Peppered Cabbage
Wine Potatoes
Crunchy Bread Twists
Emerald Isle Dessert Cups
Coffee

SOUP OF THE BALLADEERS

2 11 1/4-oz. cans green pea soup
2 4-oz. packages bacon and
    horseradish cheese spread,
    softened
2 soup cans water

Combine soup and cheese spread in saucepan; add water gradually. Heat, stirring occasionally. Garnish with shamrock-shaped croutons, if desired. Yield: 6 servings.

Mrs Martha Jo Mims
Mississippi State College for Women
Columbus, Mississippi

CRUNCHY BREAD TWISTS

1 egg
1/4 c. green goddess salad
    dressing
2 c. herb-seasoned stuffing mix,
    coarsely crushed
1/2 c. grated Parmesan cheese
1 c. refrigerator crescent rolls

Combine egg and salad dressing in a small bowl. Combine stuffing mix and cheese in a shallow dish or on waxed paper. Unroll crescent rolls; separate into 4 rectangles. Pinch diagonal perforations together; flatten slightly with rolling pin. Cut each rectangle lengthwise into 1-inch wide strips. Dip each strip into egg mixture; roll in cheese mixture, coating well. Twist each strip several times; place on ungreased cookie sheet about 1 inch apart. Bake in preheated 375-degree oven for 15 minutes or until golden brown. Serve warm. Yield: 16 twists.

Joann Gardner
Pembroke HS, Hampton, Virginia

BAKED CORNED BEEF WITH
PEPPERED CABBAGE

1 3 to 4-lb. corned beef brisket
3/4 c. sugar
1/2 tsp. ginger
1/2 tsp. cloves
1/2 tsp. dry mustard
1 tbsp. honey
1 med. head white cabbage, grated
1/4 c. butter
2 tbsp. sour cream
Dash of salt
1 tsp. freshly ground pepper

Boil beef in water to cover for 2 to 3 hours or until tender. Remove from water; trim off excess fat. Place in roasting pan. Make a paste of sugar, ginger, cloves, mustard and honey; spread over beef. Bake in preheated 325-degree oven for 25 to 30 minutes. Saute cabbage in butter for 2 to 3 minutes or until crisp-tender, stirring constantly. Stir in sour cream; season with salt and pepper. Serve with corned beef. Yield: 6 servings.

Margery Juk
Wolcott Jr HS, Warren, Michigan

EMERALD ISLE DESSERT CUPS

1 c. white cream mints
3/4 c. milk
Several drops of green food coloring
1 c. heavy cream, whipped
1 6-oz. package semisweet
    chocolate bits
2 tbsp. margarine

Combine mints and milk in saucepan; cook over low heat until mints are melted, stirring frequently. Let cool. Fold in food coloring and whipped cream; pour into refrigerator tray. Freeze until firm. Melt chocolate bits and margarine over hot water, stirring until smooth. Let cool. Place paper baking cups in muffin tins. Swirl chocolate mixture around inside cups with a teaspoon, covering entire surface with a thin layer of chocolate. Chill until firm. Tear off paper; fill cups with rounded scoops of mint ice cream. Top each dessert with a chocolate mint wafer, if desired. Yield: 8 servings.

Carolyn Reif
Western Dubuque HS, Epworth, Iowa

53

CUCUMBER-LIME CREAM MOLD

3 3-oz. packages lime gelatin
1 1/2 tsp. salt
2 2/3 c. boiling water
2 tbsp. vinegar
3 c. sour cream
2 c. cucumbers, finely chopped
2/3 c. chopped green onions

Dissolve gelatin and salt in boiling water in large bowl; stir in vinegar. Chill until partially congealed. Beat in sour cream; fold in cucumbers and onions. Pour into 8-cup mold; chill for about 4 hours or until firm.

Jane A. Bower
Del Norte HS, Crescent City, California

WINE POTATOES

5 or 6 lg. potatoes
Salt and pepper to taste
1/2 c. cubed Cheddar cheese
1/2 c. minced white onion
1 can golden mushroom soup
1/2 c. white cooking wine

Preheat oven to 400 degrees. Pare and slice potatoes; arrange half the slices in a greased casserole. Season with salt and pepper. Sprinkle 1/2 of the cheese and 1/2 of the onion over the potatoes. Spoon 1/2 of the soup over top, then pour 1/2 of the wine over the soup. Repeat layers; cover casserole. Bake for 1 hour. Remove cover; bake 15 minutes longer.

Mrs Nora Foster
Benton HS, St Joseph, Missouri

HOT BROCCOLI DIP

3 stalks celery, finely chopped
1/2 lg. onion, chopped
1 sm. can mushrooms, drained
Margarine
1 pkg. frozen chopped broccoli
1 can mushroom soup
1 6-oz. roll garlic cheese spread

Saute celery, onion and mushrooms in margarine. Cook broccoli until tender; drain well. Combine all vegetables and soup; mix well. Melt cheese in double boiler. Mix all ingredients together in fondue pot; serve with cubes of French bread, if desired.

Mrs Jane Silvey
Parker Middle Sch, Ft Worth, Texas

CREAMY BEEF AND CHEESE DIP

1 8-oz. package cream cheese,
softened
1/4 c. coarsely chopped walnuts
1 2 1/2 or 3 oz. jar dried beef,
finely chopped
1/4 c. sour cream or salad dressing
2 tbsp. chopped onion
2 tbsp. chopped green pepper
2 tbsp. milk
1 tsp. pepper

Place cream cheese in 1-quart casserole. Add remaining ingredients; stir until well blended. Cover; place in 225-degree oven. Bake for 10 to 15 minutes, stirring once. Serve with toast and crackers. May serve cold, if desired. Yield: 1 1/2 to 2 cups dip.

Jean Searcy
Silver Lake HS, Silver Lake, Kansas

GRAPEFRUIT SHAMROCK

1 10-oz. package frozen chopped
spinach
3 Florida grapefruit
1 6-oz. package lime gelatin
1 1/2 c. boiling water
1 6-oz. can sliced mushrooms,
drained
1 tbsp. instant minced onion

Thaw spinach; drain well. Cut slice from top of grapefruit; cut off strips of peel from top to bottom, cutting deep enough to remove white membrane. Cut slice from bottom. Peel may be cut off round and round in spi-

ral fashion. Go over grapefruit again, removing any remaining white membrane. Cut along side of each dividing membrane from outside to middle of core; remove section by section over bowl to retain juice from grapefruit. Remove seeds and discard. Drain grapefruit, reserving all juice; cut sections into small pieces. Place gelatin in bowl. Add boiling water; stir until dissolved. Add enough cold water to reserved grapefruit juice to make 2 cups liquid; stir into gelatin. Chill until slightly thickened. Fold in grapefruit pieces, spinach, mushrooms and onion. Turn into 6-cup shamrock mold; chill until firm. Garnish with additional grapefruit sections and watercress, if desired. Yield: 10 servings.

Photograph for this recipe on this page.

PADDIE'S AVOCADO MOLD

1   6-oz. package lime gelatin
1 tbsp. instant minced onion
1 tsp. curry powder
1 tsp. garlic salt
1 1/2 c. boiling water
1 c. cold water
2 tbsp. vinegar
2 California avocados
1/2 c. mayonnaise
1/2 c. chopped green pepper
1/3 c. sliced stuffed olives

Combine gelatin, onion and seasonings in bowl. Add boiling water; stir until gelatin is dissolved. Stir in cold water and vinegar; chill until mixture mounds when dropped from spoon. Cut avocados lengthwise into halves; remove seeds. Peel and sieve avocados; blend with mayonnaise, green pepper and olives. Stir into gelatin mixture; pour into 5-cup mold. Chill until set. Unmold; garnish with avocado slices, if desired. Yield: 6-8 servings.

Photograph for this recipe on page 50.

55

HEARTY CORNED BEEF SALAD

1 7-oz. package macaroni, cooked
   and drained
2 c. canned corned beef
1 c. diced celery
1/4 c. diced onion
1/2 c. tart pickle relish
1/2 c. mayonnaise
1 tsp. mustard
1 tsp. salt

Let macaroni cool. Break up corned beef in mixing bowl. Mix beef, macaroni, celery, onion and relish together. Combine remaining ingredients; stir into the beef mixture to blend well. Garnish with sliced stuffed olives, if desired.

Carolyn Rose
Marion L. Steele HS, Amherst, Ohio

ST. PATRICK'S SPECIAL SALAD

1/2 lb. fresh spinach
1 sm. head lettuce
1 tsp. grated onion
2 hard-cooked eggs, chopped
4 slices bacon, fried crisp and
   crumbled
4 tbsp. vinegar
2 tsp. sugar
1/2 tsp. salt

Tear spinach and lettuce in salad bowl; add onion, eggs and crumbled bacon. Combine remaining ingredients in small bowl; stir until well mixed. Pour over salad; toss gently. Yield: 6-8 servings.

Rita Nell Davis
Rankin HS, Rankin, Texas

ST. PATRICK'S FRUIT SALAD

1 1/2 c. boiling water
1 pkg. lime gelatin
1 sm. package cream cheese, softened
1 med. apple, chopped
1/2 c. finely chopped nuts

1 sm. can crushed pineapple with
   juice
12 pecan halves

Stir boiling water into gelatin until gelatin is dissolved. Pour into electric mixer bowl; add cream cheese. Beat at medium speed until cheese is dissolved. Add apples, nuts and pineapple; pour into mold. Cover; chill in refrigerator until partially congealed. Stir, then place pecan halves on top of salad for decoration. May serve as accompaniment to main dish, if desired. Yield: 8 servings.

Mrs Lillian J. Rhodes
Hickory Attendance Center
Hickory, Mississippi

LUCK-OF-THE-IRISH STEW

4 lb. neck of lamb, sliced
3 lg. onions
3 lb. potatoes
Salt and pepper to taste
Chopped parsley

Preheat oven to 325 degrees. Trim all fat from lamb slices. Peel onions; slice thin. Peel potatoes; slice 1/4 inch thick. Place a layer of onions in large heavy casserole. Cover with a layer of lamb; season with salt and pepper. Add a layer of potatoes. Repeat layers until all ingredients are used, ending with a layer of potatoes. Pour in enough water to fill the casserole 3/4 full. Place casserole over high heat; bring to a boil. Cover; transfer to oven. Bake for 1 hour. Let cool, then skim off any fat. Reheat for 30 minutes; sprinkle with parsley before serving. Yield: 6-8 servings.

Mary Johnson
Deshler Public Sch, Deshler, Nebraska

ST. PATRICK'S ROMAN FEAST CASSEROLE

4 c. flour
3 lg. eggs
1/2 lb. fresh spinach, cooked and
   pureed
1 tsp. salt

1 lb. ground beef
1 lb. chicken, diced
Chicken giblets, diced
1 carrot, chopped
1 onion, chopped
4 cloves of garlic, chopped
1 stalk celery, chopped
Chopped parsley
2 c. chopped tomatoes
Freshly grated nutmeg to taste
1 c. white wine

Pour flour in a mound on table top; make a well in the center. Break eggs in the middle; add spinach and salt. Mix together with fingers, adding small amounts of flour from the edge, and a drop of water at a time until the dough clings together. Pat into a ball. Flour board lightly; knead dough for 10 minutes or until very smooth and elastic. Roll out very thin; cut into thin strips. Cook in boiling salted water for 10 minutes. Plunge noodles into bowl of cold water; stretch out on towels to dry. Brown beef in a large heavy saucepan; stir in diced chicken, and giblets. Add vegetables, then stir in nutmeg and wine. Cook until the vegetables are tender and the Bolognese sauce thickened. Arrange noodles and sauce in alternate layers in buttered casserole. Bake in preheated 375-degree oven for 30 minutes or until heated through and bubbly.

Gwladys Jeanneret
Kettle Falls HS, Kettle Falls, Washington

CHICKEN-BROCCOLI CASSEROLE

1 4-lb. chicken, cooked
2 cans cream of chicken soup
1 can mushroom soup
1/4 c. melted butter
1/2 c. mayonnaise
2 tbsp. lemon juice
3/4 tsp. curry powder
1/2 can water chestnuts, sliced
2 pkg. broccoli, cooked
Slivered almonds

Remove skin and bones from chicken. Combine soups, butter, mayonnaise, lemon juice, curry powder and water chestnuts in mixing bowl. Place a layer of chicken, broccoli and half the soup mixture in a large casserole; repeat until all ingredients are used. Sprinkle slivered almonds over top. Bake in preheated 350-degree oven for 30 minutes or until heated through and bubbly. Serve over cooked rice. Yield: 12 servings.

Broxie C. Stuckey
Gordo HS, Gordo, Alabama

SHAMROCK CHICKEN

2 chickens, disjointed
3 c. water
1 onion, sliced
4 celery tops
2 bay leaves
2 tsp. monosodium glutamate
2 tsp. salt
1/2 tsp. peppercorns

Place chicken pieces in Dutch oven; add remaining ingredients. Bring to a boil, then cover tightly. Reduce heat; let simmer for 45 minutes to 1 hour or until chicken is tender. Remove from heat. Place chicken on a serving platter; keep warm. Strain and reserve broth.

Parsley-Lemon Sauce

1/4 c. butter or chicken fat
1/4 c. flour
3 c. reserved chicken broth
3 egg yolks
4 tbsp. lemon juice
1/2 c. finely chopped parsley

Melt butter in saucepan; blend in flour until smooth. Add broth gradually; cook, stirring constantly, until mixture comes to a boil and thickens. Beat egg yolks and lemon juice together; add to broth, stirring rapidly. Cook until mixture returns to a boil. Remove from heat; stir in parsley. Spoon part of the sauce over chicken; serve remaining sauce separately. Yield: 8 servings.

Mrs Brenda Hurm
Jasper HS, Jasper, Indiana

IRISH FRECKLE BREAD

4 3/4 to 5 3/4 c. unsifted flour
1/2 c. sugar
1 tsp. salt
2 pkg. Fleischmann's active dry yeast
1 c. potato water or water
1/2 c. Fleischmann's margarine
2 eggs, at room temperature
1/4 c. mashed potatoes, at room
  temperature
1 c. seedless raisins

Mix 1 1/2 cups flour, sugar, salt and undissolved yeast thoroughly in large bowl. Combine potato water and margarine in saucepan; place over low heat until water is warm. Margarine does not need to melt. Add to dry ingredients gradually; beat for 2 minutes with electric mixer at medium speed, scraping bowl occasionally. Add eggs, potatoes and 1/2 cup flour; beat at high speed for 2 minutes, scraping bowl occasionally. Stir in raisins and enough remaining flour to make soft dough. Turn out onto lightly floured board; knead for 8 to 10 minutes or until smooth and elastic. Place in greased bowl, turning to grease top. Cover; let rise in warm place free from draft for about 1 hour and 15 minutes or until doubled in bulk. Punch down; turn onto lightly floured board. Divide into 4 equal pieces; shape each piece into slender loaf about 8 1/2 inches long. Place 2 loaves, side by side, in each of 2 greased 8 1/2 x 4 1/2 x 2 1/2-inch loaf pans. Cover; let rise in warm place free from draft for about 1 hour or until doubled in bulk. Bake in preheated 350-degree oven for about 35 minutes or until bread tests done. Remove from pans; cool on wire racks. Rising time will be about 1 hour and 45 minutes if plain water is used.

Photograph for this recipe on this page.

KILLARNEY LIME BUNDT CAKE

1 pkg. Duncan Hines white cake mix
1 pkg. lime gelatin
3 eggs
2/3 c. Mazola oil
2/3 c. water
1/3 c. chopped pecans (opt.)
Sugar
1/2 c. orange juice

Combine cake mix and gelatin in large mixing bowl. Add eggs, oil and water; mix together until well blended. Fold in chopped pecans. Sprinkle greased bundt pan generously with sugar; pour in cake batter. Bake in preheated 350-degree oven for 40 minutes or until cake tests done. Let cool for 10 minutes before inverting onto plate. Mix orange juice and 2/3 cup sugar together in saucepan; bring to a rolling boil. Boil for 1 minute; set glaze aside. Remove cake from pan. Brush glaze well into warm cake, using pastry brush; drizzle any remaining glaze over top.

Margaret Morgan
Austin HS, Austin, Minnesota

ST. PATRICK'S DAY GRASSHOPPER CAKE

4 sq. unsweetened chocolate, melted
Sugar
2 1/4 c. sifted flour
3 tsp. baking powder
1 tsp. salt
1/2 c. cooking oil
7 eggs, separated
1 tsp. vanilla
1/2 tsp. cream of tartar
1 env. unflavored gelatin
1/3 c. white cream de cocoa
1/2 c. cream de menthe
2 c. whipping cream, whipped

Combine chocolate, 1/2 cup boiling water and 1/4 cup sugar, mixing well. Sift flour, 1 1/2 cups sugar, baking powder and salt into large bowl. Make a well in the center of the flour mixture; add oil, egg yolks, 3/4 cup cold water and vanilla. Beat until very smooth. Stir chocolate mixture into egg yolk mixture. Beat egg whites and cream of tartar together in large bowl until very stiff peaks form. Pour chocolate batter over entire surface of egg whites in thin stream; fold in gently. Pour into greased 12-cup bundt pan. Bake in preheated 325-degree oven for 50 to 55 minutes or until cake tests done. Let cool for 10 to 15 minutes. Invert until thoroughly cooled; remove from pan. Soften gelatin in 1/4 cup cold water. Heat liqueurs together. Add gelatin; stir until dissolved. Let cool. Fold gelatin mixture into whipped cream; refrigerate for 15 minutes. Split cake into 3 layers; spread whipped cream filling between layers and on top of cake. Refrigerate until ready to serve.

Gayle Parnow
West Jr HS, Minnetonka, Minnesota

LEPRECHAUNS

1/2 c. butter, softened
1/2 c. sugar
1/2 c. dark Karo syrup
Juice and grated rind of 1/2 lemon
2 c. flour
1/2 tsp. cinnamon
1/3 tsp. cloves
1/2 tsp. allspice
1/4 tsp. salt
1/2 tsp. soda
3/4 c. minced candied fruit
1 c. finely chopped nuts

Cream butter and sugar in large mixing bowl until light and fluffy. Add syrup, lemon juice and rind; mix well. Sift flour, cinnamon, cloves, allspice, salt, and soda together; add to creamed mixture. Stir in candied fruit and nuts. Chill until firm or overnight. Roll out dough on lightly floured board to 1/8-inch thickness; cut with small cookie cutter. Bake in preheated 350-degree oven for about 20 minutes. Cool on wire racks.

Sue Scott
Eureka HS, Eureka, Illinois

CHOCOLATE MINT STICKS

 2 sq. unsweetened chocolate
 1/2 c. margarine
 2 eggs
 1 c. sugar
 1/4 tsp. peppermint extract
 1/2 c. sifted flour
 Few grains of salt
 1/2 c. chopped nuts

Melt chocolate and margarine over hot water. Beat eggs until frothy; blend in sugar, chocolate mixture and peppermint extract. Add flour, salt and nuts; mix thoroughly. Pour into greased 9-inch square pan. Bake in preheated 350-degree oven for 20 to 25 minutes. Let cool. Cover cake; refrigerate until ready to frost.

Topping

 2 tbsp. margarine, softened
 1 c. sifted confectioners' sugar
 1 tbsp. milk
 3/4 tsp. peppermint extract

Combine margarine and sugar. Add milk and peppermint extract; mix until smooth. More milk may be added, if needed. May tint green with 1 drop food coloring, if desired. Spread on cooled cake. Cut into small fingers to serve. Sticks may be frozen. Yield: 2 dozen.

Mrs Barbara P. Bell
Andrew Lewis HS, Salem, Virginia

GREEN IRISH COOKIES

 2 egg whites
 1/8 tsp. cream of tartar
 1/8 tsp. salt
 1/8 tsp. peppermint extract
 1/8 tsp. green food coloring
 1 c. sugar
 1 6-oz. package chocolate chips

Beat egg whites, cream of tartar, salt, peppermint extract and food coloring until foamy, then beat in the sugar gradually. Beat until stiff peaks form. Fold in chocolate chips; drop by spoonfuls onto waxed paper-covered cookie sheets. Bake in preheated 250-degree oven for 15 minutes. Turn off oven heat; let cookies stand in oven until oven is cool or overnight.

Esther Engelhardt
Mt Pleasant Community Sch, Mt Pleasant, Iowa

AVOCADO CHIFFON PIE

 1 tbsp. unflavored gelatin
 2 tbsp. lemon juice
 3/4 c. boiling water
 1/3 c. sugar
 1/4 tsp. salt
 1 tsp. grated orange rind
 1/2 c. orange juice
 1 med. avocado, sieved
 1 c. whipping cream, whipped
 1 baked 9-in. pie shell

Soften gelatin in lemon juice in large mixing bowl. Add boiling water, sugar, salt, orange rind and juice; stir to mix thoroughly. Chill until partially set. Fold in avocado and whipped cream; turn into pie shell. Chill for several hours or until firm.

Mrs Linda Anderson
Somonauk HS, Somonauk, Illinois

SHAMROCK PIE

 1/2 c. water
 1 pkg. unflavored gelatin
 1 c. sugar
 4 eggs, separated
 1/4 c. lime juice
 Several drops of green food coloring
 1/4 tsp. cream of tartar
 1 baked 9-in. pie shell
 2 tbsp. green decorating sugar

Combine water, gelatin, 1/2 cup sugar, egg yolks, lime juice and food coloring in saucepan; bring to rolling boil, stirring constantly. Remove from heat; place saucepan in pan of ice water. Cool until thickened. Beat egg whites until frothy. Add cream of tartar and remaining sugar gradually; beat eggs until stiff. Fold in gelatin mixture; pour into pie shell. Sprinkle decorating sugar on top; refrigerate for at least 1 hour.

Mrs Brett W. Slusser
Agra HS, Agra, Oklahoma

ST. PATRICK'S DAY PUDDING

2   7 3/4-oz. packages fig bars
1/2 c. milk
1/4 c. butter or margarine
1 egg, well beaten
1 tsp. cinnamon
1/4 tsp. ground cloves
1/4 tsp. nutmeg
1 tsp. lemon juice
1/4 tsp. grated lemon rind
1 tbsp. baking powder

Crumble fig bars into milk; let stand for 15 minutes. Stir to mix well. Cream butter; beat in egg, spices, lemon juice, lemon rind and baking powder. Stir into fig mixture. Divide fig mixture into two 3-pound shortening cans or similar containers; cover tightly with aluminum foil. Place in large kettle containing about 2 inches water. Cover tightly; steam for 30 minutes. Let cool for 10 minutes before unmolding. Serve with hard sauce or whipped cream.

Sister Tabitha Kaup
Ryan HS, Omaha, Nebraska

ST. PATRICK'S DAY SCONES

1 1/2 c. sifted flour
3 tsp. baking powder
1/2 tsp. salt
Sugar
1/3 c. shortening
1/2 c. quick-cooking oats
2/3 c. milk
1 tsp. melted butter
Cinnamon to taste

Sift flour, baking powder, salt and 2 tablespoons sugar into mixing bowl. Cut in shortening. Add oats and milk; stir just until blended. Form dough into a ball. Divide dough into 3 parts; press each part into a circle. Spread each circle with melted butter; sprinkle with 1 teaspoon sugar and cinnamon. Arrange on cookie sheet. Bake in preheated 450-degree oven for 12 to 15 minutes or until nicely browned.

Mary Bray
Clinton Sr HS, Clinton, New York

HANGING-OF-THE-GREENS PUNCH

1 pkg. lime gelatin
1   6-oz. can pineapple juice
1 sm. bottle lemon juice
3/4 1-oz. bottle almond flavoring
1 3/4 to 2 c. sugar
1 bottle ginger ale
1 bottle soda water
Few drops of green food coloring

Prepare gelatin according to package directions. Combine all ingredients; stir until sugar is dissolved. Place ice in punch bowl; pour punch over ice to serve.

Evelyn B. Willey
Gates Co HS, Gatesville, North Carolina

ST. PATRICK'S PUNCH

1 pt. milk
1 pt. lime sherbet
Few drops of green food coloring
1 qt. carbonated grapefruit beverage

Mix milk and sherbet together in punch bowl until sherbet is soft; stir in food coloring. Pour carbonated beverage slowly down side of bowl; stir carefully. Garnish with mint or green cherries. Yield: 12 servings.

Eloise C. Frazier
Little Falls Jr-Sr HS
Little Falls, New York

EASTER

All children have those very special days that they really look forward to—Christmas, birthday and Easter. Remember when you were little how exciting it used to be to wake up to find an Easter Basket at the foot of your bed? Or, the thrill of searching for the golden egg?

Easter is a time for large family gatherings—relatives from far away and neighborhood children. It's a day you certainly want to be prepared to serve a scrumptious Sunday dinner—and, to be sure, many delightful sweets for those young Easter egg hunters.

The menu we suggest is a wonderfully eye-appealing meal suitable for your family or for larger groups including special guests. Be sure to decorate your table with plenty of spring flowers and of course, some beautifully painted eggs. Or, perhaps you might like to use an Easter Bunny as the centerpiece. You might like to make place mats and cards from yellow or pink poster paper and trim them with small daisies and rabbits.

For the Easter Egg Hunt, trim your outdoor table with a bright tablecloth and surround the punch bowl with chocolate eggs, jelly beans and freshly cut flowers.

◊ Recipe on page 75.

MENU
EASTER SUNDAY DINNER

Bunny Salad
Savory Fresh Ham Roast
Spinach Loaf
Estelle's Delicious Baked Eggplant
Rice Pilaf
Rich Strawberry Shortcake
Tea

BUNNY SALAD

Lettuce leaves
5 pear halves, chilled
10 raisins
5 red cinnamon candies
10 blanched almonds
1 pt. cottage cheese

Place lettuce leaves on plate; arrange pears on lettuce, cut side down, with narrow end of each pear toward center of plate. Place 2 raisins on each pear half for eyes; place 1 cinnamon candy on each half for nose. Use 2 almonds for ears; shape tail with 1 spoon cottage cheese.

Hazel Pielemeier
Loogootee HS, Loogootee, Indiana

SAVORY FRESH HAM ROAST

2 tsp. salt
1 tsp. pepper
1 tsp. paprika
1/4 tsp. garlic salt
1 tsp. rosemary leaves
1 tbsp. steak sauce
1   12-lb. fresh leg of pork, boned
1/3 c. chopped parsley
1/3 c. chopped black olives
1/3 c. chopped green onions
3 canned pimentos, chopped

Combine salt, pepper, paprika, garlic salt, rosemary leaves and steak sauce; rub half the mixture on inside of pork. Combine remaining ingredients; stuff inside of pork with pimento mixture. Tie securely. Score fat and skin; rub remaining salt mixture on outside of pork. Place roast, fat side up, on rack in shallow baking pan. Roast in preheated 325-degree oven for 4 hours and 30 minutes or to 185 degrees on meat thermometer. Yield: 16 servings.

Karen L. LeClair
Olivet Comm Sch, Olivet, Michigan

ESTELLE'S DELICIOUS BAKED EGGPLANT

1 lg. eggplant
1 med. onion, chopped
3 tbsp. margarine or butter
3 tbsp. chopped parsley
1 can cream of mushroom soup
Salt and pepper to taste
Worcestershire sauce to taste
Round buttery crackers, crumbled

Cut slice off eggplant lengthwise; cut out pulp, leaving about 1/4 inch around sides and bottom of shell. Cook eggplant pulp in salted water until tender; drain well and chop. Saute onion in margarine until tender; add parsley. Stir in eggplant, soup, seasonings and enough cracker crumbs to make stuffing consistency; place in eggplant shell. Sprinkle with cracker crumbs; dot with additional margarine. Bake in preheated 375-degree oven for about 35 minutes.

Mrs Estelle Boles Nickell
Morgan Co HS, West Liberty, Kentucky

RICE PILAF

2 c. long grain rice
3 cans beef broth
2 beef broth cans water
3/4 c. margarine
1 can mushrooms and liquid
2 tbsp. chopped parsley
1/2 tsp. garlic salt
1/2 tsp. onion salt
1/2 tsp. seasoned pepper

Cook rice according to package directions until partially done. Combine all ingredients in large casserole; cover. Bake in preheated 350-degree oven for 1 hour and 30 minutes. Uncover; bake for 1 hour longer, stirring several times. Yield: 16 servings.

Janet Wellman
Central Middle Sch, Montevideo, Minnesota

SPINACH LOAF

2 c. chopped frozen or fresh spinach
2 eggs, well beaten
3/4 c. diced Velveeta cheese
2 tbsp. bacon drippings
1 c. toasted bread crumbs
1 tbsp. vinegar
1/2 tsp. pepper
Creole Sauce

Thaw frozen spinach. Combine all ingredients except Creole Sauce; stir gently to mix well. Place in greased 9 x 5 x 3-inch loaf dish. Bake in preheated 400-degree oven for 30 minutes. Let stand for 10 minutes; turn out on serving platter. Slice; serve with Creole Sauce.

Creole Sauce

4 slices bacon, diced
2 tbsp. chopped onion
2 tbsp. chopped green pepper
2 tbsp. flour
1 c. strained tomatoes or tomato sauce
1/4 tsp. salt
Pinch of pepper
1 tsp. Worcestershire sauce
1/8 tsp. mace

Fry bacon, onion and green pepper until lightly browned, stirring frequently. Add flour and tomatoes; cook until thick, stirring constantly. Add remaining ingredients; cook for 5 minutes longer.

Mrs Sue Stilley
Forestburg HS, Forestburg, Texas

RICH STRAWBERRY SHORTCAKE

2 c. flour
2 tbsp. sugar
3 tsp. baking powder
1/2 tsp. salt
1/2 c. margarine
1 egg, beaten
2/3 c. light cream
Soft butter
3 to 4 c. sweetened strawberries
1 c. heavy cream, whipped

Sift dry ingredients together into bowl; cut in margarine until mixture resembles coarse crumbs. Combine egg and light cream; add all at once to margarine mixture, stirring just until dry ingredients are moistened. Turn out on floured surface; knead gently for 30 seconds. Pat or roll out 1/2 inch thick. Cut 6 shortcakes with floured 2 1/2-inch round or fluted cutter. Place on ungreased baking sheet. Bake in preheated 450-degree oven for about 10 minutes. Split shortcakes; spread butter on bottom layers; add layer of strawberries. Place tops over strawberries; add layer of strawberries. Top with whipped cream. Other fruits may be used instead of strawberries.

Mrs Suzanne LeBlanc
Saugerties Jr HS, Saugerties, New York

SHRIMP DIP

1 8-oz. package cream cheese
1 carton sour cream
2 tbsp. A-1 sauce
2 tbsp. lemon juice
2 tbsp. chili sauce
1 tsp. salt
Dash of hot sauce
Dash of Worcestershire sauce
2 lb. cleaned cooked shrimp, chopped

Soften cream cheese in bowl. Add remaining ingredients except shrimp; blend well. Add shrimp; mix.

Elizabeth Muennink
Cedar Bayou Jr Sch, Baytown, Texas

SCANDINAVIAN SWEET SOUP

1/2 c. Minute tapioca
1/2 tsp. salt
1 c. sugar
1 tbsp. vinegar
1 stick cinnamon

1 c. currants
1 c. raisins
1 c. chopped pitted prunes
1 c. chopped apples
2 c. grape juice

Pour 2 1/2 cups water into saucepan; bring to a boil. Add tapioca gradually, stirring frequently. Add remaining ingredients except grape juice; bring to a boil. Reduce heat; simmer until fruits are tender. Add grape juice. May be served hot or cold.

Liz Daby
East Peoria Comm HS, East Peoria, Illinois

THREE-LAYER CANAPE PIE

1   8-oz. package cream cheese
1   1/2-oz. package blue cheese
1 tbsp. minced parsley
2   2 1/4-oz. cans deviled ham
2 tbsp. minced sweet pickle
4 hard-cooked eggs, chopped
1 tbsp. chopped pimento
1/4 tsp. salt
Dash of pepper
2 tbsp. mayonnaise

Soften cream cheese and blue cheese in bowl. Blend cream cheese and blue cheese; stir in parsley. Spread evenly in 8-inch pie pan. Combine deviled ham and pickle; spread over cheese layer. Combine remaining ingredients; spread over ham layer. Chill overnight; serve with crackers.

Mrs Sharon A. Sharp
J. J. Pearce HS, Richardson, Texas

EASTER BONNET SALAD

2   3-oz. packages lime gelatin
4 c. boiling water
Lettuce leaves
1 c. mayonnaise

Maraschino cherries
3 tbsp. orange juice

Dissolve gelatin in boiling water. Pour 3 cups gelatin into 7-inch round flat mold which has been rinsed with cold water; chill until set. Chill remaining gelatin until thickened; whip with rotary beater until light and fluffy. Place in deep 5-inch round mold for crown of bonnet. Chill until firm. Unmold plain gelatin; place on bed of lettuce. Unmold whipped gelatin; place on plain gelatin for crown of bonnet. Place 1/4 cup mayonnaise in pastry tube; pipe onto bonnet to resemble ribbon trim. Garnish with cherries. Mix remaining mayonnaise with orange juice; serve with salad. Yield: 6-8 servings.

Mrs Marcy Lackovic
Ryan HS, Omaha, Nebraska

SUNSHINE SALAD

1   3-oz. package lemon gelatin
1   3-oz. package orange gelatin
2 c. boiling water
1 1/2 c. cold water
1 No. 2 can crushed pineapple
2 bananas, diced
40 miniature marshmallows
2/3 c. sugar
2 tbsp. flour
1 egg, beaten
1 c. whipped cream

Dissolve gelatins in boiling water; stir in cold water. Chill until thickened. Drain pineapple; reserve juice. Add pineapple, bananas and marshmallows to gelatin; mix well. Place in shallow, oblong baking dish; chill until firm. Mix sugar, flour, egg and 1 cup reserved pineapple juice in double boiler; cook until thickened, stirring constantly. Cool; fold in whipped cream. Place on top of salad. Grate cheese on top of dressing, if desired.

Kathleen Burchett
Area Supvr of Home Economics
Jonesville, Virginia

EASTER BEEF IN AN EGG SHELL

1   4 to 5-lb. beef eye of round roast
1 tbsp. prepared mustard
1 tbsp. soy sauce
Chou Paste
Butter
2 tbsp. flour
1/3 c. white table wine
Salt and pepper to taste

Place roast on large sheet of heavy-duty foil. Mix mustard and soy sauce; spread over roast. Fold sides of foil over beef, making double fold; fold ends upward and double back. Place in shallow baking pan. Roast in preheated 300-degree oven for 3 hours; chill. Open foil; reserve liquid for sauce. Place roast in shallow baking pan; pat dry with paper towels. Spread with Chou Paste, covering top, sides and ends of roast; decorate top as desired. Place on low shelf of oven; bake at 425 degrees for about 30 minutes or until brown. Melt any fat left on foil in saucepan; add enough butter, if needed, to make 2 tablespoons fat. Blend in flour. Pour wine into measuring cup; add reserved liquid. Add enough water to make 1 cup liquid; stir into saucepan. Simmer until thickened; season with salt and pepper. Serve with roast. Yield: 8 servings.

Chou Paste

3/4 c. water
1/4 tsp. salt
6 tbsp. butter
3/4 c. sifted flour
3 eggs

Place water, salt and butter in saucepan; bring to boiling point. Add flour all at once; cook over moderate heat, stirring, until mixture forms ball. Remove from heat; cool slightly. Beat in eggs, one at a time; cool.

Photograph for this recipe on this page.

BAKED HAM ROLL-UPS

1 1/2 c. ground ham
1/3 c. finely chopped celery
5 tbsp. mayonnaise
8 slices bread, crusts removed
1/4 c. melted butter
1 can Cheddar cheese or cream of
    mushroom soup
1/2 soup can milk

Combine ham, celery and mayonnaise; mix well. Brush 1 side of each slice of bread with butter; spread with ham mixture. Roll up bread slices as for jelly roll; secure with toothpicks. Arrange rolls on cookie sheet; brush with remaining butter. Bake in preheated 425-degree oven for about 12 minutes. Mix soup and milk in saucepan; heat through. Serve with roll-ups.

Rosalie Wentzell
Stettler Jr HS, Stettler, Alberta, Canada

HAM AND EGG-FILLED CREPES

1 c. cold water
1 1/2 c. milk
4 eggs
1/2 tsp. salt
2 c. flour
1/4 c. melted margarine
1 can cream of chicken soup
1 c. sour cream
1 c. cubed cooked ham
4 hard-boiled eggs, chopped
1 tbsp. chopped chives
1/4 tsp. dry mustard
1/4 c. grated Parmesan cheese

Place water, 1 cup milk, eggs, salt, flour and margarine in blender container; cover. Process at high speed for 1 minute. Scrape side of container; blend for about 3 seconds longer. Pour into container; cover. Refrigerate for 2 hours. Cook on greased griddle over medium-high heat until brown on both sides, using 3 tablespoons batter for each crepe; keep warm. Combine 1/2 can soup, sour cream, ham, boiled eggs, chives and mustard; place 3 tablespoons on each crepe. Roll as for jelly roll; place in shallow, oblong baking pan, seam side down. Mix remaining soup and remaining milk; pour over crepes. Sprinkle with cheese. Bake in preheated 350-degree oven for about 20 minutes. Yield: 16 crepes.

Ethel E. Teves
East Bakersfield HS, Bakersfield, California

EGGS BENEDICT

1 env. hollandaise sauce mix
6 rounds thinly sliced ham or
    Canadian bacon
6 rounds toast or Holland rusk
6 eggs

Prepare hollandaise sauce mix according to package directions. Fry ham in skillet until heated through; place 1 slice on each slice of toast. Keep warm. Poach eggs; place 1 egg on each slice of ham. Place toast stacks on individual serving plates; cover with hollandaise sauce. Garnish with parsley.

Angela Johansen
Sioux Falls Public Schools
Sioux Falls, South Dakota

OLD SUGAR-CURED KENTUCKY HAM

1 20-lb. sugar-cured Kentucky ham,
    2 yrs. old
1/2 1-lb. box light brown sugar
1/4 box whole cloves

Soak ham in large container in cold water for about 24 hours; drain. Scrape off mold; clean with cloth. Return to container; cover with water. Bring to a boil. Reduce heat; cover. Simmer for 2 hours. Remove from heat; do not remove cover. Cover completely with papers, rugs or other heavy covers to insulate for 12 hours. Remove ham from water. Cut off skin; score ham. Spread brown sugar on top of ham; place whole cloves in scored squares. Place ham in baking pan. Bake in preheated 250-degree oven for 1 hour; cool.

Mrs Anna Lee Morris
Paul G. Blazer HS, Ashland, Kentucky

MAGIC EASTER EGGS

1/2 c. butter
1 tsp. vanilla extract
1 tsp. salt
1/2 15-oz. can Borden's Eagle Brand
  sweetened condensed milk
6 c. sifted confectioners' sugar

Cream butter, vanilla and salt in medium mixing bowl; blend in sweetened condensed milk until smooth. Add sugar gradually, blending well after each addition; blend until mixture is very stiff. Turn onto clean board; knead in all remaining sugar carefully. Mixture should be smooth and not sticky. Cut mixture into desired number of pieces; mold each piece into egg shape with palms of hands. Place on waxed paper-lined cookie sheet; chill for several hours or overnight. Coconut eggs may be made by kneading in 3/4 cup flaked coconut after all sugar has been kneaded into fondant. Almond eggs may be made by substituting 1 teaspoon almond extract or one 8-ounce can almond paste for vanilla extract. Peanut butter eggs may be made by substituting 3/4 cup peanut butter for butter, increasing milk to 1 can and decreasing sugar to 4 cups. Do not substitute any other milk for sweetened condensed milk.

Dipping Chocolate

1/2 lb. semisweet chocolate
1/3 to 1/2 slab household paraffin wax

Place chocolate and wax in top of double boiler; place over hot water. Cook over medium heat, stirring with wire whisk, until chocolate and paraffin are melted. Never melt paraffin over direct heat. Remove double boiler from heat. Insert double-pronged kitchen fork into bottom of fondant egg or place egg on flat wire skimmer. Dip into chocolate; let excess chocolate drip for moment. Place egg carefully on waxed paper-lined cookie sheet. Stir chocolate thoroughly with wire whisk before dipping each egg. Place over low heat and reheat if chocolate begins to cool and thicken; let chocolate coating dry thoroughly before adding decoration.

Buttercream Frosting

1/3 c. butter
1 tsp. vanilla extract
3 c. sifted confectioners' sugar
1 tbsp. egg white
Food coloring
2 tsp. heavy cream (opt.)

Cream butter in medium mixing bowl until fluffy; blend in vanilla. Add sugar gradually, mixing well after each addition; mixture will be very stiff. Beat in egg white until smooth and creamy. Add enough food coloring for desired shade; add only enough cream to make of suitable consistency to press through decorating tube, if mixture needs slight thinning. Place in decorating tube; press onto eggs in desired designs.

Photograph for this recipe on this page.

EASTER EGG HUNT PARTY

Easter Basket Rainbow Delight

Greek Easter Cookies

Peanut Butter Eggs

Easter Egg Candy

Green Sherbet Punch

EASTER BASKET RAINBOW DELIGHT

1 pkg. macaroon mix
1 pt. whipping cream
3 tbsp. sugar
1 tsp. vanilla
1 c. chopped pecans
4 pt. sherbet, varied flavors

Prepare macaroon mix according to package directions; place in greased 9-inch square pan. Bake according to package directions; cool. Cut into 1/2-inch squares. Whip cream with sugar and vanilla until stiff. Fold macaroons and pecans into whipped cream; spread 2/3 of the mixture in 9 x 13-inch pan. Refrigerate until chilled. Soften sherbets; spoon in layers over macaroon mixture. Top with remaining macaroon mixture; freeze. Use 4 different flavors of sherbet to give color to dish. Eighteen baked macaroons, crushed, may be substituted for macaroon mix. Yield: 16 servings.

Bonita Kindschi Wiersig
Anson Jones Sch, Bryan, Texas

GREEK EASTER COOKIES

4 c. flour
1 lb. butter, melted
2 egg yolks
Powdered sugar

Sift flour 3 times; place in bowl. Stir in butter and egg yolks; shape into small logs. Place about 2 inches apart on cookie sheet. Bake in preheated 350-degree oven until brown; sprinkle with powdered sugar.

Lynda Henderson
Washington Jr HS, Ogden, Utah

PEANUT BUTTER EGGS

2 eggs, well beaten
1/8 tsp. salt
1 1/2 to 2 c. peanut butter
4 to 5 c. powdered sugar
1 tsp. vanilla
1 Hershey bar
1 6-oz. package semisweet
*   chocolate morsels*

Mix first 5 ingredients in order listed; form into egg shapes. Melt Hershey bar and chocolate morsels in double boiler. Dip eggs into chocolate; place on waxed paper until set.

Mrs Betty G. Brant
Shanksville Stonycreek Sch
Shanksville, Pennsylvania

EASTER EGG CANDY

1 c. hot mashed potatoes
2 tbsp. butter
1 c. shredded coconut
1 tsp. vanilla
3 1-lb. boxes confectioners' sugar
1 8-oz. package dot chocolate

Combine potatoes and butter; stir in coconut and vanilla. Add sugar gradually, mixing well after each addition. Form into egg shapes, using 1 tablespoon mixture for each egg; place on waxed paper. Let harden for 1 to 3 days. Melt chocolate over hot water; dip eggs into chocolate, using 2 spoons. Place on waxed paper to harden. Unsweetened chocolate or chocolate bits with 1/8 cake paraffin may be melted over hot water if dot chocolate is unavailable. Chopped nuts, candied fruits or peanut butter may be used instead of coconut.

Mrs Nannie C. Edwards
Oxford Area HS, Oxford, Pennsylvania

GREEN SHERBET PUNCH

2 46-oz. cans pineapple juice
2 6-oz. cans frozen limeade
2 qt. ginger ale
2 qt. lime sherbet
1 bottle green maraschino cherries

Chill pineapple juice. Prepare limeade according to can directions; mix with pineapple juice. Add sugar, if desired. Add ginger ale; spoon sherbet into punch. Garnish with cherries.

Mrs Ann Davis
Gentry High School, Gentry, Arkansas

EASY EASTER BREAD

1 pkg. yeast
1/4 c. warm water
1 3-oz. package instant lemon
   pudding mix
1/4 c. margarine
1/2 tsp. salt
3/4 c. scalded milk
4 to 4 1/2 c. flour
4 eggs
1 tbsp. water
Multicolored sprinkles

Dissolve yeast in warm water. Mix pudding mix, margarine and salt in bowl; pour milk over pudding mixture. Mix until margarine is melted and pudding is dissolved; cool to lukewarm. Add 1 1/2 cups flour; mix well. Beat in yeast and 3 eggs with electric mixer; add enough remaining flour gradually to make soft dough. Turn out on floured surface; let rest for 10 minutes. Knead for 10 minutes; place in greased bowl. Let rise for 1 hour. Divide into 6 equal parts; shape each part into rope. Make 2 braids, using 3 ropes for each; place in circle in 2 greased 9-inch round cake pans. Let rise for 1 hour. Beat remaining egg with water; brush on braids. Shake sprinkles over braids. Bake in preheated 375-degree oven for 25 minutes.

Mrs Charlotte Van Arum
Greece Olympia HS, Rochester, New York

BRAN MUFFINS

2 c. boiling water
2 c. Nabisco 100% Bran
1 c. shortening
2 1/2 c. sugar
4 eggs
5 c. flour
5 tsp. soda
1 1/2 tsp. salt
1 qt. buttermilk
4 c. Kelloggs All-Bran
1 lb. raisins

Add boiling water to 100% bran; let stand. Cream shortening and sugar; add eggs, one at a time, mixing well after each addition. Stir in bran mixture. Sift flour, soda and salt together; combine buttermilk and All-Bran. Add buttermilk mixture and flour mixture alternately to creamed mixture; stir in raisins. Place in large container; cover. Place in refrigerator for as long as desired; do not stir. Spoon into greased muffin cups. Bake in preheated 350-degree oven for about 15 minutes or until lightly browned. Yield: 60 muffins.

Mrs Irene B. Knudsen
Del Norte HS, Crescent City, California

EASTER CARROT BARS

1 pkg. coconut macaroon mix
4 eggs
2 c. sugar
1 1/2 c. vegetable oil
3 jars carrot baby food
2 c. flour
1 tsp. vanilla
Frosting
Chopped nuts

Mix macaroon mix with 3/4 cup water; set aside. Beat eggs slightly. Add remaining ingredients; mix well. Spread 1/2 of the carrot mixture in 15 1/2 x 10 1/2-inch jelly roll pan; spoon macaroon mixture over mixture in pan. Spread remaining carrot mixture over top. Bake in preheated 350-degree oven for

---

45 minutes; cool. Spread with Frosting; sprinkle with nuts.

Frosting

1 3-oz. package cream cheese
1/4 c. butter
1 3/4 c. powdered sugar
1 tsp. vanilla

Mix all ingredients well.

Mrs Carol Edwards
Blair HS, Blair, Wisconsin

DELICIOUS CHEESECAKE PIE

16 graham crackers
1/4 c. melted butter
3 3-oz. packages cream cheese
2 eggs
2 tsp. vanilla
Sugar
1 c. sour cream

Roll graham crackers with rolling pin until fine crumbs are formed; reserve some of the crumbs for topping. Mix remaining crumbs with butter; pat into 8-inch pie pan. Bake in preheated 350-degree oven for 5 minutes; cool. Reduce oven temperature to 300 degrees. Mash cream cheese until soft. Add eggs; blend until smooth. Add 1 teaspoon vanilla and 1/2 cup sugar. Place in pie shell. Bake for 15 minutes; cool for 5 minutes. Blend sour cream, 2 tablespoons sugar and remaining vanilla; pour over cream cheese mixture. Sprinkle with reserved crumbs. Bake for 5 minutes longer; chill for 24 hours before serving.

Mrs Ellamae Peery
Anaheim HS, Anaheim, California

CHOCOLATE FUDGE CREAM PUFFS

3/4 c. margarine or butter
1/2 c. flour
4 eggs
3/4 c. sugar
2 sq. unsweetened chocolate, melted

1 tsp. vanilla
Fudge sauce

Combine 1/4 cup margarine and 1/2 cup water in saucepan; bring to a rolling boil. Stir in flour; cook over low heat, stirring, for about 1 minute or until mixture forms ball. Remove from heat. Add 2 eggs; beat until smooth. Drop by tablespoonfuls, 3 inches apart on ungreased cookie sheet. Bake in preheated 400-degree oven for 35 to 40 minutes; cool. Cut off tops; remove inside dough. Cream remaining margarine and sugar until light and fluffy. Add chocolate and vanilla; beat until smooth. Add remaining eggs, one at a time, beating for 5 minutes after each addition; chill. Spoon into cream puffs; spoon fudge sauce over top of each.

Sue Scott
Eureka HS, Eureka, Illinois

LAYERED ANGEL FOOD CAKE X

1 angel food cake
1 3-oz. package strawberry gelatin
1 3-oz. package lime gelatin
1 3-oz. package orange-pineapple gelatin
1 pkg. frozen strawberries, thawed and drained
1/2 gal. vanilla ice cream
1 No. 2 can crushed pineapple, drained
1 can mandarin oranges, drained

Divide angel food cake into 3 sections. Place in 3 bowls; crumble into small pieces. Sprinkle 1 package gelatin into each bowl; mix until gelatin sticks to cake. Place strawberry gelatin cake in large tube pan; add strawberries. Add 1/3 of the ice cream; add lime gelatin cake. Spread pineapple over cake; add 1/2 of the remaining ice cream. Add orange-pineapple gelatin cake; add oranges. Spread remaining ice cream over top; freeze for 1 to 2 days. Slice; serve.

Willetta R. Wallace
Whiteville Sr HS, Whiteville, North Carolina

EASTER EGG AND CHICKS

Vanilla ice cream
Nabisco Fancy Crest Cakes
Small gumdrops
Semisweet chocolate pieces
Candy corn
Pink-tinted whipped cream
Green-tinted flaked coconut
Small candy eggs

Fill 1-quart melon mold with ice cream; freeze until firm. Make chicks from Nabisco Fancy Crests Cakes, using a cake for base. String 3 gumdrops on a toothpick; insert in cake. Insert another cake on side into toothpick on top of gumdrops. Use chocolate pieces for eyes and piece of candy corn for beak. Unmold ice cream onto large plate; pipe with whipped cream across top and sides of mold. Sprinkle plate with coconut; decorate with candy eggs. Stand chicks on plate with Easter egg. Yield: 6-8 servings.

Photograph for this recipe on this page.

EASTER COCONUT POUND CAKE

6 eggs
1 c. shortening
1/2 c. margarine, softened
3 c. sugar
1/2 tsp. almond extract
1/2 tsp. coconut or vanilla extract
3 c. sifted cake flour
1 c. milk
2 c. grated fresh coconut
Confectioners' sugar
Green-tinted shredded coconut
Jelly beans

Separate eggs, placing egg whites in large bowl and egg yolks in another large bowl. Let egg whites come to room temperature. Add shortening and margarine to egg yolks; beat with electric mixer at high speed until well blended. Add sugar gradually, beating until light and fluffy. Add extracts; beat until blended. Beat in flour alternately with milk, beginning and ending with flour, with mixer at low speed. Add coconut; beat until well blended. Beat egg whites just until stiff peaks form; fold into batter gently until well combined. Turn into greased 10-inch tube or bundt pan. Bake in preheated 300-degree oven for 2 hours or until cake tester inserted in center comes out clean. Cool in pan on wire rack for 15 minutes. Remove from pan; cool. Sprinkle with confectioners' sugar; place green coconut and jelly beans around outer edge. Canned flaked coconut may be used instead of fresh coconut and 2 5/8 cups all-purpose flour may be substituted for cake flour.

Sandra Adkins
Mogadore HS, Mogadore, Ohio

NAPOLEON CREMES

Butter
1/4 c. sugar
1/4 c. cocoa
1 tsp. vanilla
1 egg, slightly beaten
2 c. fine graham cracker crumbs
1 c. flaked coconut
3 tbsp. milk
1 3 3/4-oz. package instant
  vanilla pudding mix
2 c. sifted confectioners' sugar
1 6-oz. package semisweet
  chocolate morsels

Combine 1/2 cup butter, sugar, cocoa and vanilla in top of double boiler; cook over simmering water until butter melts. Stir in egg; cook, stirring, for about 3 minutes or until thick. Blend in crumbs and coconut; press into buttered 9-inch square pan. Cream 1/2 cup butter well. Stir in milk, pudding mix and confectioners' sugar; beat until fluffy. Spread evenly over crust. Melt chocolate and 2 tablespoons butter in top of double boiler over simmering water; cool. Spread over pudding layer; chill. Cut into 2 x 3/4-inch bars. Yield: About 44 bars.

Mrs Jean Mason
High Plains Sch, Seibert, Colorado

LEMON LOVE NOTES

Butter
Flour
1 c. powdered sugar
2 tbsp. lemon juice
Grated rind of 1 lemon
2 eggs, beaten
1 c. sugar
1/2 tsp. baking powder
1/2 tsp. vanilla
1 1/2 tsp. milk

Blend 1/2 cup butter, 1 cup flour and 1/4 cup powdered sugar; pat into 9-inch square pan. Bake in preheated 350-degree oven for 14 minutes; cool. Mix lemon juice, grated rind, eggs, sugar, 2 tablespoons flour and baking powder; place on crust. Bake for 25 minutes longer; cool. Mix remaining powdered sugar, vanilla, 1 tablespoon butter and milk until smooth; spread on baked mixture. Cut into bars.

Esther Engelhardt
Mt Pleasant Comm Schools, Mt Pleasant, Iowa

ICE CREAM PARFAIT MOLD

2 1-lb. packages frozen strawberries
Milk
2 3-oz. packages strawberry gelatin
2 pt. vanilla ice cream
1 c. whipping cream, whipped
Green coconut (opt.)

Thaw strawberries. Drain; reserve syrup. Add enough milk to reserved syrup to make 1 3/4 cups liquid; bring to a boil. Add gelatin; stir until dissolved. Cut each pint of ice cream into 8 pieces. Add to gelatin mixture; stir until ice cream is melted. Chill until partially set; fold in strawberries. Pour into oiled melon mold; chill until firm. Unmold; decorate Easter egg fashion with whipped cream and green coconut. Cut in slices to serve. Yield: 8-10 servings.

Photograph for this recipe on page 62.

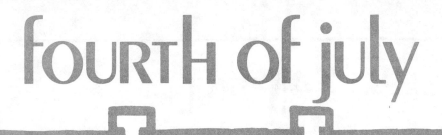

fourth of july

**Grand picnic—great food
Everyone's in the mood
The birth of our Nation
Brings this celebration**

And, so it goes . . . For almost two centuries, Americans have been gathering for splendid outdoor feasts. Planning weeks in advance, community, civic and church groups across the country prepare barbecues and picnics for large groups of young and old.

Of course, of all the day's events and entertainment, eating is certain to be the most popular. So, why not try some of these recipes . . . designed to win for you the biggest applause of the day.

Recipe on page 89.

MENU

Bang–Up
4th Of July Picnic

Carnival Salad
Spinach Salad and Dressing
Red-White and Blue Delight
Firecrackers For
An Old-Fashioned Fourth
Garlic-Fried Chicken
Texas Meat Loaf
Old-Fashioned Baked Beans
Zebra Bread
Freezer Ice Cream
Red Plum Cake
Fresh Coconut Cake
Strawberry-Lemonade Punch

CARNIVAL SALAD

1 lb. macaroni, cooked
1/2 lb. Cheddar cheese, cubed
1 1/2 c. finely diced celery
1/2 c. diced red sweet pepper
1 c. coarsely chopped sweet pickles
1/2 c. grated red onion
French dressing

Combine all ingredients, using enough French dressing to moisten as desired. Refrigerate at least overnight. Stir occasionally to distribute dressing over ingredients.

Nancy Stearley
Bloomfield HS, Bloomfield, Indiana

SPINACH SALAD AND DRESSING

1 c. mayonnaise
1 c. sour cream
3 hard-cooked eggs, chopped
1 med. red onion, minced
1 med. unpeeled red apple, minced
1/4 lb. blue cheese, crumbled
5 c. spinach leaves, lightly packed

Combine mayonnaise, sour cream, eggs, onion, apple and blue cheese; mix well. Cover; let stand in refrigerator for 12 to 24 hours. Combine dressing with spinach; toss lightly. Yield: 6-8 servings.

Mrs Alex Pozniak
Marion L. Steele HS, Amherst, Ohio

RED-WHITE AND BLUE DELIGHT

2 sm. packages raspberry gelatin
1 pkg. unflavored gelatin
1 c. sugar
1 c. half and half
1 8-oz. package cream cheese,
*   softened*
1/2 c. slivered almonds
1 can blueberries

Dissolve 1 package raspberry gelatin in 2 cups hot water; pour into 9 x 13-inch pan. Chill until firm. Soften unflavored gelatin in 1/2 cup cold water. Place sugar and half and half in saucepan; bring to boiling point. Do not boil. Remove from heat; add softened gelatin and cream cheese. Beat at low speed until smooth. Add almonds; let cool. Pour over firm raspberry layer; chill until firm. Dissolve remaining raspberry gelatin in 1 cup hot water; add blueberries and juice. Let cool. Pour over cheese layer; chill until firm.

Nona J. Verloo
State Dept of Ed, Sacramento, California

FIRECRACKERS FOR AN OLD-FASHIONED FOURTH

1 recipe potato salad
12 slices boiled ham
Parsley

Place 2 rounded tablespoons potato salad in center of each slice of boiled ham. Roll up; secure with toothpicks. Stick a small sprig of parsley in one end of each roll for a fuse.

Mrs Phyllis Fry
Orrville HS, Orrville, Ohio

GARLIC-FRIED CHICKEN

Chicken breasts or legs
Salt to taste
Freshly ground pepper to taste
Garlic powder to taste
Flour
Oil

Sprinkle each piece of chicken with salt, pepper and garlic powder. Place in plastic bag with flour; shake bag until chicken is well coated. Heat oil in skillet to 400 degrees. Fry chicken until richly browned on one side; turn and fry other side. Remove pieces; drain on absorbent toweling.

Waunice A. Aldridge
Milton HS, Alpharetta, Georgia

TEXAS MEAT LOAF

1 lb. ground beef
1 can tomatoes, chopped
2 eggs
1/2 c. chopped olives
Onions
2 c. fine bread crumbs
Catsup
1 tsp. chili powder
1 tsp. salt
1/8 tsp. pepper
1 sm. can mushroom bits
1/2 to 1 tsp. mustard
1 tbsp. white Karo syrup

Place ground beef in large mixing bowl; mix in tomatoes, eggs and olives. Chop 1 large onion; mix into beef mixture. Add bread crumbs, 1/4 cup catsup, chili powder, salt, pepper and mushroom bits. Mix well; shape into loaf. Place in baking dish. Combine 2 tablespoons catsup, mustard, syrup and 2 tablespoons finely chopped onion; spread over meat loaf. Cover. Bake in preheated 350-degree oven for 2 minutes. Remove cover; bake for 30 minutes longer. Place meat loaf on serving platter; let stand for 30 minutes before slicing. Yield: 6 servings.

Missy Davis
Penelope Sch, Penelope, Texas

OLD-FASHIONED BAKED BEANS

2 lb. dried navy beans
1 tsp. soda
1 med. onion, sliced
1 tbsp. salt
4 tsp. cider vinegar
1 tsp. prepared mustard
2/3 c. brown sugar
3/4 c. molasses
1/4 c. catsup
Pinch of pepper
3/4 lb. salt pork, sliced

Wash beans thoroughly; place in 4-quart saucepan. Add enough water to cover 2 inches above beans; let soak overnight. Drain off water; cover with fresh cold water. Add soda; bring to a boil. Drain again and rinse well. Cover with cold water; bring to a boil. Place onion slices in bean pot or deep casserole; add remaining ingredients except salt pork. Add hot beans and enough boiling water to barely cover beans. Place strips of salt pork over top; cover. Bake in 250-degree oven for 9 to 10 hours or until beans are tender, adding more boiling water as liquid evaporates. Remove cover; bake for 1 hour longer to let salt pork become crisp and brown. Serve piping hot, plain or with catsup or chili sauce. Yield: 10-12 servings.

Marie Heltzel
Union Co HS, Lake Butler, Florida

ZEBRA BREAD

2 c. biscuit mix
1/4 c. sesame seed
1/2 tsp. salt
2/3 c. milk

Combine biscuit mix, sesame seed and salt in bowl. Stir milk in vigorously; beat for 20 strokes. Turn out on floured board; knead 8 to 10 times. Divide dough into 3-inch balls; flatten each ball into 1/8 to 1/4-inch thick circle. Grill circles 5 inches from medium-hot coals for 3 to 4 minutes on each side. Cut in half; butter with an herb butter, if desired. Parmesan cheese, bacon bits, chives, chopped onions, peppers or mushrooms may be added for variation of flavor.

Cora Caldwell
Gooding HS, Gooding, Idaho

RED PLUM CAKE

2 c. sugar
3/4 c. Wesson oil
3 eggs
2 sm. jars red plum baby food
2 tsp. vanilla
1 tbsp. red food coloring
2 c. flour

1 tsp. cinnamon
1 tsp. nutmeg
1/2 tsp. soda
1/2 tsp. salt
1 c. chopped nuts
Lemon juice
1/2 c. confectioners' sugar

Combine sugar, oil, eggs, baby food, vanilla and food coloring in mixer bowl; mix until blended. Add flour, cinnamon, nutmeg, soda and salt; beat for 3 to 4 minutes. Stir in nuts; pour batter into bundt pan. Bake in preheated 350-degree oven for 1 hour. Let cool for 10 minutes before removing from pan. Stir enough lemon juice into confectioners' sugar to make a creamy glaze. Pour glaze over warm cake.

Oleta Hayden
Milford HS, Milford, Texas

FRESH COCONUT CAKE

3/4 c. butter
Sugar
4 eggs, separated
3 c. flour
3 1/2 tsp. baking powder
1 tsp. vanilla
1 c. milk
3 egg whites
1 coconut, grated fine

Cream butter with 2 cups sugar until light and fluffy; add beaten egg yolks. Sift flour and baking powder together; add vanilla to milk. Add flour mixture to butter mixture alternately with milk, beginning and ending with the flour mixture. Fold in 4 stiffly beaten egg whites carefully. Divide batter into 3 greased and floured pans. Bake in preheated 350-degree oven for 30 minutes or until done. Let cool. Beat remaining 3 egg whites until soft peaks form; add 1 cup sugar gradually, beating constantly. Beat until stiff. Reserve part of the coconut to decorate top and side of cake; fold remaining coconut into the egg white mixture. Stack layers together with frosting; frost side and top

of cake. Sprinkle reserved coconut on top of cake; pat onto side.

Ruth F. Thompson
El Paso Pub Schools, El Paso, Texas

FREEZER ICE CREAM

1 lg. or 2 sm. packages vanilla
    pudding mix
Milk
3 c. sugar
1 tbsp. vanilla
1/2 to 3/4 tsp. salt
6 eggs, well beaten

Prepare pudding mix according to package directions, using 3 cups milk; cook until thick. Add sugar gradually; add vanilla and salt. Add pudding mixture to beaten eggs, beating constantly; pour into freezer container. Add milk until container is 2/3 full. Freeze according to manufacturer's directions. Cream may be substituted for the milk used to fill container 2/3 full, if desired. Yield: 1 1/2 gallons.

Jean Searcy
Silver Lake HS, Silver Lake, Kansas

STRAWBERRY-LEMONADE PUNCH

1 12-oz. can frozen pink lemonade
    concentrate
1 6-oz. can frozen orange juice
    concentrate
1 10-oz. package frozen sliced
    strawberries
1 12-oz. bottle ginger ale,
    chilled
Vodka (opt.)

Combine lemonade, orange juice, strawberries and 3 cups water in container; refrigerate until ready to use. Pour lemonade mixture into punch bowl; add ginger ale slowly. Add vodka; stir well.

Mrs Jane K. Marsh
Delta Sr Secondary Sch
Delta, British Columbia, Canada

BABKA

2 c. unsifted flour
1/4 c. sugar
1 pkg. Fleischmann's active dry
  yeast
1/2 c. milk
1/4 c. Fleischmann's margarine
3 eggs, at room temperature
1/4 c. mixed candied fruits
1/4 c. seedless raisins
Rum Syrup

Mix 3/4 cup flour, sugar and undissolved yeast thoroughly in large bowl. Combine milk and margarine in saucepan; place over low heat until liquid is very warm. Margarine does not need to melt. Add to dry ingredients gradually; beat for 2 minutes with electric mixer at medium speed, scraping bowl occasionally. Add eggs and 1/2 cup flour; beat at high speed for 2 minutes, scraping bowl occasionally. Add remaining flour and beat at high speed for 2 minutes. Cover; let rise in warm place, free from draft, for about 1 hour or until bubbly. Stir in candied fruits and raisins. Turn into greased and floured 2-quart Turk's Head pan or tube pan; let rise, uncovered, in warm place, free from draft, for 30 minutes. Bake in preheated 350-degree oven for about 40 minutes or until done. Prick surface with fork immediately; pour Rum Syrup over cake. Let stand until syrup is absorbed. Remove from pan; cool on wire rack. Frost with confectioners' sugar frosting, if desired. Yield: 1 cake.

Rum Syrup

1/2 c. sugar
1/3 c. water
2 tsp. rum extract

Combine sugar, water and rum extract in saucepan; bring to a boil.

Photograph for this recipe on page 83.

KULICH

2 1/4 to 2 3/4 c. unsifted flour
1/4 c. sugar
1 tsp. salt
1 tsp. grated lemon peel
1 pkg. Fleischmann's active dry yeast
1/2 c. milk
1/4 c. water
2 tbsp. Fleischmann's margarine
1 egg, at room temperature
1/4 c. chopped Planters blanched
  almonds
1/4 c. seedless raisins
Confectioners' sugar frosting
Colored sprinkles (opt.)

Mix 3/4 cup flour, sugar, salt, lemon peel and undissolved yeast thoroughly in large bowl. Combine milk, water and margarine in saucepan; place over low heat until liquids are very warm. Margarine does not need to melt. Add to dry ingredients gradually; beat for 2 minutes with electric mixer at medium speed, scraping bowl occasionally. Add egg and 1/2 cup flour; beat at high speed for 2 minutes, scraping bowl occasionally. Stir in enough remaining flour to make soft dough. Turn out onto lightly floured board; knead for 8 to 10 minutes or until smooth and elastic. Place in greased bowl, turning to grease top. Cover; let rise in warm place, free from draft, for about 1 hour or until doubled in bulk. Punch dough down; turn onto lightly floured board. Knead in almonds and raisins. Divide in half. Shape each half into ball; press each into greased 1-pound coffee or shortening can. Cover; let rise in warm place, free from draft, for about 1 hour or until doubled in bulk. Bake in preheated 350-degree oven for about 30 to 35 minutes or until done. Remove from cans; cool on wire racks. Frost tops with confectioners' sugar frosting; decorate with colored sprinkles. Yield: 2 cakes.

Photograph for this recipe on page 83.

PORTUGUESE EASTER BREAD

6 1/2 to 7 1/2 c. unsifted flour
1 c. sugar
1 tsp. salt
2 pkg. Fleischmann's active dry yeast
1 c. milk
1/4 c. water
1/4 c. Fleischmann's margarine
3 eggs, at room temperature
8 hard-cooked eggs

Mix 2 cups flour, sugar, salt and undissolved yeast thoroughly in large bowl. Combine milk, water and margarine in saucepan; place over low heat until liquids are very warm. Margarine does not need to melt. Add to dry ingredients gradually; beat for 2 minutes with electric mixer at medium speed, scraping bowl occasionally. Add 3 eggs and 3/4 cup flour; beat at high speed for 2 minutes, scraping bowl occasionally. Stir in enough remaining flour to make soft dough. Turn out onto lightly floured board; knead for 8 to 10 minutes or until smooth and elastic. Place in greased bowl, turning to grease top. Cover; let rise in warm place, free from draft, for about 1 hour or until doubled in bulk. Punch dough down; turn out onto lightly floured board. Divide into 8 equal pieces. Remove about 1/4 of each piece and set aside. Shape larger pieces into round balls. Press large pieces of dough down into circles about 1/2 inch thick on greased baking sheets; place 1 hard-cooked egg in center of each. Divide each of the remaining 8 pieces of dough in half; shape each into 6-inch rope. Cross 2 ropes in an X over each egg; seal ends underneath dough. Cover; let rise in warm place, free from draft, for about 1 hour or until doubled in bulk. Bake in preheated 350-degree oven for 20 to 25 minutes or until done. Remove from baking sheets; cool on wire racks. Yield: 8 individual breads.

Photograph for this recipe on page 83.

FRUIT AND PORK KABOBS

1 3-lb. cooked boneless pork loin,
   cut into 1-in. cubes
3 apples, cut into wedges
6 apricots, halved and seeded
3 green bananas, cut into
   1 1/2-in. pieces
1 10-oz. jar Concord grape jam
2 tbsp. honey
1/4 tsp. curry powder
1/8 tsp. ground ginger

Arrange pork, apples, apricots and bananas on skewers. Combine jam, honey, curry and ginger in small saucepan; heat, stirring, until jam is melted. Grill kabobs 3 to 5 inches from heat, basting with grape sauce. Turn; grill, basting several times, until pork and fruits are thoroughly heated. Serve with curried rice. Yield: About 6 kabobs.

Photograph for this recipe on page 84.

GREAT GRAPE ICE CREAM

2 c. sugar
5 c. light cream
3 c. heavy cream
1/2 tsp. salt
3 tsp. vanilla extract
4 10-oz. jars Concord grape
   preserves
2 tsp. lemon extract

Mix sugar and creams until sugar is dissolved. Add salt and vanilla extract; pour into ice cream can of ice cream maker. Freeze ice cream according to manufacturer's directions. Stir in preserves and lemon extract when ice cream is almost frozen, blending well. Food coloring may be added to intensify grape color, if desired. Freeze until consistency of whipped cream; ripen according to manufacturer's directions. Yield: About 4 quarts.

Photograph for this recipe on page 84.

SPARKLING GRAPE REFRESHER

1 c. water
1 c. sugar
1 qt. Concord grape juice
2 c. apple juice
2 c. orange juice
2/3 c. lime juice
1 28-oz. bottle ginger ale
Ice Mold

Mix water and sugar in saucepan; bring to boiling point, stirring constantly until sugar is dissolved. Cool. Chill juices and ginger ale. Combine sugar syrup and fruit juices in punch bowl just before serving; add ginger ale. Float Ice Mold on surface of punch, fruit side up. Yield: About 3 1/2 quarts.

Ice Mold

Lime slices
Orange slices

Arrange lime and orange slices in 4-cup ring mold in attractive design. Pour water into mold to partially cover slices; freeze. Add water to fill mold 3/4 full; freeze.

Photograph for this recipe on page 84.

PATIO LUAU

Cheese Tidbits

Tropical Upside-Down Salads

Island Chop Suey

Sweet and Sour Carrot Pennies

Strawberry-Banana Split Pie

Singing Bamboo Punch

CHEESE TIDBITS

1 c. margarine, softened
2 c. grated sharp Cheddar cheese
2 c. flour
2 c. Rice Crispies
1/4 tsp. red pepper
1/2 tsp. salt

Combine all ingredients; mix well. Form into small balls; place on cookie sheet. Press down with fork in crisscross fashion. Bake in preheated 325-degree oven for 20 minutes.

Mrs Ruth M. Wilson
MacArthur Jr HS, Beaumont, Texas

TROPICAL UPSIDE-DOWN SALADS

1 8 1/4-oz. can sliced pineapple
3 maraschino cherries
1 3-oz. package orange gelatin
2/3 c. evaporated milk
2 tbsp. mayonnaise
1 8 3/4-oz. can fruit cocktail,
   drained
1/3 c. flaked coconut
1/4 c. chopped nuts

Drain pineapple; reserve juice. Add enough water to juice to make 1 1/2 cups liquid. Cut each pineapple slice into 3 equal pieces; cut each cherry in half. Place 2 pineapple pieces and 1 cherry half in bottom of each of six 6-ounce custard cups. Bring pineapple liquid to a boil. Add gelatin; stir until dissolved. Let cool. Add milk and mayonnaise; blend well, using rotary beater. Chill until partially congealed. Stir in remaining ingredients; mix well. Spoon about 1/2 cup gelatin mixture into each cup; chill for 2 to 3 hours or until firm. Invert to serve.

Sara Yowell
Ramay Jr HS, Fayetteville, Arkansas

ISLAND CHOP SUEY

1 8-oz. can or 1/2 lb. fresh
   mushrooms
1 sm. can bamboo shoots
1 can bean sprouts
1 1/4 lb. veal steak, cubed
1/2 lb. pork steak, cubed
3 c. finely chopped celery

2 c. finely chopped onions
1 sm. can water chestnuts, drained
   and sliced
4 tsp. flour
1 tsp. salt
2 tbsp. water
3 tbsp. soy sauce

Drain and reserve juice from mushrooms, bamboo shoots and bean sprouts; add enough water to juice to measure 1 3/4 cups liquid. Saute veal and pork in small amount of fat until browned. Add celery, onions and reserved liquid; cook over low heat for 35 minutes. Stir in water chestnuts, mushrooms, bamboo shoots and bean sprouts. Combine flour, salt, water and soy sauce; stir to make a smooth paste. Stir into meat mixture; cook until thick.

Mrs Cheryl Assenheimer
Troy Jr HS, Avon Lake, Ohio

SWEET AND SOUR CARROT PENNIES

2 lb. carrots, sliced
1 onion, sliced
1 tsp. Worcestershire sauce
3/4 c. vinegar
Salt and pepper to taste
1 green pepper, slivered
1 can tomato soup
1/4 c. sugar
1 tsp. prepared mustard
1/2 c. salad oil

Cook carrots in small amount of salted water until just tender. Do not overcook. Drain and cool. Combine remaining ingredients to make a marinade. Stir carrots into marinade; let stand for 24 hours. Will keep for at least 2 weeks.

Mrs Bob Shandley
Leakey HS, Leakey, Texas

STRAWBERRY-BANANA SPLIT PIE

2 c. graham cracker crumbs
1 c. melted margarine
2 c. confectioners' sugar

1 egg, beaten
5 bananas
1 No. 2 can crushed pineapple,
   drained
2 c. frozen sliced strawberries,
   thawed and drained
1 lg. carton Cool Whip
1 c. chopped pecans
Red maraschino cherries

Combine cracker crumbs and 1/2 cup melted margarine; press into 8 x 12-inch pan. Mix confectioners' sugar with remaining melted margarine and egg; pour on top of crust. Cut bananas into long thin slices; place on top of sugar mixture. Add layers of pineapple and strawberries. Spread top with Cool Whip; sprinkle with pecans. Decorate with cherries; chill until ready to serve.

Judy Lowe
Bellevue HS, Bellevue, Texas

SINGING BAMBOO PUNCH

3 c. peach nectar
1/3 c. honey
2 qt. orange-pineapple juice
1 qt. lemon-lime carbonated beverage

Stir peach nectar into honey gradually; stir in juice. Chill until ready to serve. Add carbonated beverage just before serving.

Brenda Stoeck
James Madison Sr HS, Houston, Texas

EXOTIC PEACH SALAD

1 c. miniature marshmallows
1 sm. can crushed pineapple
1 can coconut
1 carton sour cream
Peach halves

Mix marshmallows, pineapple, coconut and sour cream together. Spoon into peach halves to serve.

Mary Rogers
Benjamin Russell HS, Alexander City, Alabama

CHINESE-BROILED BREAST STEAKS OF TURKEY

1 turkey breast
1 tsp. grated fresh ginger
1 tsp. dry mustard
1 tsp. monosodium glutamate
1 tbsp. honey
1/2 c. soy sauce
1/4 c. salad oil
3 cloves of garlic, minced

Have butcher bone and cut turkey breast crosswise into 1 to 1 1/2 inch-thick steaks; chill until ready to use. Combine remaining ingredients in glass or pottery bowl; let stand at room temperature for 24 hours. Pour over turkey steaks; cover. Refrigerate for several hours or overnight. Drain steaks; reserve marinade. Cook steaks over hot coals for about 8 minutes on each side, brushing occasionally with reserved marinade, if desired. One teaspoon ground ginger may be used instead of fresh ginger. Frozen turkey breast or turkey breast roll, cut while frozen, then thawed, may be substituted for fresh turkey breast.

Photograph for this recipe on this page.

GRILLED BARBECUED CHICKEN

4 chicken quarters
Salt
2 c. red wine vinegar
1 c. oil
1 tbsp. Tabasco sauce
Dash of garlic salt

Sprinkle chicken quarters generously with salt. Mix wine vinegar, oil, Tabasco sauce, garlic salt and 3 tablespoons salt. Place chicken on grill, skin side down; brush with sauce. Grill for 10 minutes; turn. Grill until chicken is done, brushing with sauce frequently and turning chicken every 10 minutes.

Mrs Claude L. Fox, Jr
LaFayette HS, Oxford, Mississippi

RED-WHITE AND BLUEBERRY PANCAKES

1 pt. strawberries, sliced
1 c. fresh blueberries
Sugar
2 c. complete pancake mix
1 1/3 c. water
Melted butter
Sour cream
Brown sugar

Place strawberries and blueberries in bowl; sprinkle lightly with sugar. Set aside. Place pancake mix and water in bowl; stir lightly until fairly smooth. Pour batter onto hot, lightly greased griddle for each pancake; turn pancakes when edges look cooked, turning only once. Brush pancakes with butter. Stack 2 or 3 pancakes on each plate; top with fruit topping and a dollop of sour cream. Sprinkle with brown sugar. Frozen blueberries, thawed and drained, may be substituted for fresh blueberries.

Photograph for this recipe on page 76.

BLACKBERRY COBBLER

1 qt. canned blackberries, sweetened
1 can refrigerator biscuits
1 pt. vanilla ice cream

Pour blackberries and juice into large saucepan; heat to boiling point. Cut each biscuit into 4 equal pieces. Add the biscuit quarters to blackberries, one at a time, until all are added. Cover; cook until biscuits are done. Serve with vanilla ice cream.

Mrs Linda Cherry
Griggsville HS, Griggsville, Illinois

FOURTH OF JULY BANG-UP DESSERT

1 can fruit pie filling
1 sm. box cake mix
1/2 c. butter or margarine, melted
1/4 c. chopped nuts
1/4 c. (packed) brown sugar

Preheat oven to 350 degrees. Grease sides and bottom of 8 x 8 x 2-inch baking pan generously. Pour pie filling into pan; spread evenly. Sprinkle dry cake mix evenly over fruit filling; drizzle butter over top. Sprinkle nuts and brown sugar over top. Bake for 45 minutes to 1 hour; serve hot. May top with whipped cream or ice cream, if desired.

Barbara Jean Bracken
Belcourt HS, Belcourt, North Dakota

ORANGE POP ICE CREAM

2 qt. orange soda
2 cans sweetened condensed milk
1 No. 1 1/2 can crushed pineapple
*   with juice*

Combine all ingredients; mix well. Pour into freezer container; freeze according to manufacturer's directions. Strawberry soda and strawberries may be substituted for the orange soda and pineapple, if desired.

Margaret Raburn
Mustang HS, Mustang, Oklahoma

FESTIVE BANANA SPLIT CAKE

2 c. graham cracker crumbs
1/2 c. melted margarine
1 box confectioners' sugar
1 c. margarine, softened
2 eggs
1 tsp. vanilla
1 sm. can crushed pineapple, drained
4 lg. bananas, sliced
1 lg. container whipped dairy
*   topping*
Chopped nuts

Combine cracker crumbs and melted margarine; press into 9 x 13-inch pan. Mix confectioners' sugar, softened margarine, eggs and vanilla together until fluffy; spread over crust. Spread pineapple over sugar mixture; arrange banana slices over pineapple. Spread whipped topping over bananas; sprinkle with nuts. Garnish with cherries, if desired.

Peggy Pickens
Waverly HS, Waverly, Illinois

labor day

Summer's almost over
The season's at its best
Work, Work, Work, Work
We need a day of rest

For most sections of America, this Working Man's Holiday comes at the end of summer—just before school, football and harvest seasons begin anew. Across the Nation, families scurry to their favorite beaches, lakes, ponds or camping sites for one more taste of the outdoor life before autumn begins.

And, since so many of our activities on this long weekend will be centered around the water, we recommend an Old Fashioned Fish Fry—maybe even those your family fishermen caught themselves. Our menu is easily prepared, leaving very little "labor" for you, and can be readily adapted to a large backyard crowd of family, friends and neighbors.

Keep your decorations simple—use late summer flowers and greenery or a dried arrangement to signify the coming of fall. Of course, one of the most colorful and attractive centerpieces can be made using fresh yellow and green vegetables such as corn, squash, avocados, cucumbers, etc. Be sure to use a large paper tablecloth and have plenty of paper napkins—they'll really be used when you serve those great fried fish.

◁ Recipe on page 97.

MENU
Old–Fashioned
Labor Day Fish Fry

Relish Tray
Red Cabbage Salad
Fish In Beer Batter
Munchy Onion Rings
Creamy Cheese Potatoes
Laborer's Blueberry Cake
Iced Tea

RED CABBAGE SALAD

1 tbsp. butter
1 tbsp. flour
1/2 c. sugar
1/2 c. vinegar
1 tsp. salt
1 tsp. pepper
1 tsp. dry mustard
1 head red cabbage, shredded

Mix all ingredients except cabbage in saucepan; cook, stirring, until thick. Place cabbage in salad bowl. Pour mustard mixture over cabbage; mix well.

Marjane Telck
Rock Springs Jr HS, Rock Springs, Wyoming

FISH IN BEER BATTER

1 c. flour
1 c. beer
1 egg
1 tsp. salt
1 tsp. baking powder
Fish

Place first 5 ingredients in bowl; beat lightly. Dip fish into batter to coat; cook in pan containing hot shortening or butter until brown.

Mrs Marilyn Fritch
Hawthorne Jr HS, Wauwatosa, Wisconsin

CREAMY CHEESE POTATOES

1 1/4 c. milk
1 8-oz. package cream cheese, softened
1 tbsp. snipped chives
1/2 tsp. instant minced onion
1/4 tsp. salt
4 c. cubed cooked potatoes
Paprika

Blend milk into cream cheese in medium saucepan; place over low heat. Stir in chives, onion and salt. Add potatoes; stir carefully to coat. Turn into 1 1/2-quart casserole; sprinkle with paprika. Bake in preheated 350-degree oven for 30 minutes. Yield: 5-6 servings.

Jane A. Bower
Del Norte HS, Crescent City, California

MUNCHY ONION RINGS

3 or 4 onions
1/2 tsp. salt
1 egg
1 c. flour
1/2 tsp. soda
1 c. buttermilk

Slice onions 1/4 inch thick; separate into rings. Soak in ice water for 2 hours. Drain; dry. Mix remaining ingredients in bowl. Dip onions in batter; fry in hot, deep fat until brown.

Marian Morris
Plains HS, Plains, Texas

LABORER'S BLUEBERRY CAKE

1/2 c. butter
1 c. flour
1 c. sugar
1/4 tsp. salt
1 tbsp. baking powder
2/3 c. milk
1 can blueberry pie filling

Melt butter in baking dish. Mix remaining ingredients except pie filling; pour into baking dish. Mix. Pour pie filling into center of flour mixture; do not stir. Bake in preheated 350-degree oven for about 45 minutes or until brown.

Mary R. Abney
Bay Springs HS, Bay Springs, Mississippi

FRESH HERB AND KRAUT RELISH

5 c. drained sauerkraut
1/4 c. chopped parsley
1 tbsp. fresh chopped chives
1/4 tsp. dillweed
1/4 tsp. savory
1/2 c. mayonnaise

Mix sauerkraut with parsley, chives, dill-weed, savory and mayonnaise; chill. Garnish with parsley, if desired. Yield: 8 servings.

Photograph for this recipe on page 90.

LEMON-MUSTARD FRANKETTE APPETIZERS

8 to 10 frankfurters
2/3 c. lemon juice
1 tsp. salt
2/3 c. salad oil
4 tsp. prepared mustard
2 tsp. sugar
1/2 tsp. pepper
1/4 c. flour
1 1/2 c. water
3/4 c. pickle relish

Cut each frankfurter into 6 to 8 pieces. Combine lemon juice, salt, oil, mustard, sugar and pepper in saucepan; bring to a boil. Pour over frankfurters; let stand for about 1 hour. Drain mustard sauce into saucepan. Blend flour and water; stir into sauce. Simmer for 10 to 12 minutes or until thickened, stirring constantly. Add pickle relish; simmer for 1 minute longer. Add frankfurters; heat through. Place in chafing dish; serve with wooden picks.

Mrs Loretta C. Bennett
Thomas Jefferson HS, Alexandria, Virginia

GREEN BEANS IN SOUR CREAM DRESSING

1 onion, thinly sliced
3 cans Blue Lake beans, drained
1 can water chestnuts
1 tbsp. salad oil
1 tbsp. vinegar
Coarsely ground pepper to taste
Salt to taste
1 c. sour cream
1/2 c. mayonnaise
1 tsp. lemon juice
1/4 tsp. dry mustard
1 tbsp. horseradish

Place onion over beans in container. Drain water chestnuts; slice. Place over onion. Add oil, vinegar, pepper and salt; refrigerate for 1 hour or longer. Drain well. Mix remaining ingredients and salt. Add to bean mixture; mix well. Refrigerate for at least 12 hours before serving.

Mrs Martha Dunlap
Corsicana HS, Corsicana, Texas

RASPBERRY-PINEAPPLE ASPIC

1 3-oz. package black raspberry
   gelatin
1 c. boiling water
1/2 pt. sour cream
1 sm. can crushed pineapple
1 can red raspberries
1 c. broken walnuts

Dissolve gelatin in boiling water; cool. Add sour cream; stir until well mixed. Add un-drained pineapple, undrained raspberries and walnuts; pour into 10 x 6 x 1 3/4-inch baking dish. Chill until firm. Frozen raspberries, thawed, may be used instead of canned raspberries.

Mrs Ellamae Peery
Anaheim HS, Anaheim, California

PECAN-COTTAGE CHEESE SALAD

1 c. chopped celery
1 c. chopped green pepper
1/2 tsp. salt
1 c. chopped salted pecans
1 tbsp. unflavored gelatin
1/4 c. water

1/4 c. hot pineapple juice
2 c. crushed pineapple
1 pt. creamed cottage cheese
3/4 c. salad dressing
1/2 c. powdered sugar
1/2 c. heavy cream, whipped

Mix celery, green pepper, salt and pecans. Soften gelatin in water for 5 minutes. Add pineapple juice; stir until gelatin is dissolved. Stir in pineapple; cool. Mix cottage cheese, salad dressing and sugar in large bowl; fold in whipped cream. Add celery mixture; mix well. Stir in gelatin mixture; chill until firm. Yield: 6 servings.

Judith A. Evans
Desert Jr HS, Wamsutter, Wyoming

COLD GERMAN POTATO SALAD

2 lb. potatoes
1 sm. onion, chopped
1/4 c. cooked crumbled bacon
2 tbsp. chopped sour pickle
2 to 4 tbsp. chopped celery
1 hard-cooked egg, chopped
1 beef bouillon cube
3/4 c. boiling water
1/2 tsp. pepper
3 tbsp. oil
3 tbsp. vinegar
1 tsp. salt

Cook potatoes in boiling water until tender but firm; drain. Peel; cut into vertical slices. Cool. Add onion, bacon, pickle, celery and egg to potatoes. Dissolve bouillon cube in boiling water; stir in pepper, oil, vinegar and salt. Pour over potato mixture; toss with forks until completely mixed. Chill until ready to serve.

Mary Evelyn Mitchell
Palm Beach Gardens HS
Palm Beach Gardens, Florida

POTATO SALAD SCALLOP

3 tbsp. butter or margarine
3 tbsp. flour

1 c. milk
1/2 c. mayonnaise or salad dressing
1 med. onion, chopped
1 1/2 c. chopped celery
1 1/2 tsp. salt
1/4 tsp. pepper
6 med. cooked potatoes, diced

Melt butter in small saucepan; blend in flour. Stir in milk slowly; cook over medium heat, stirring constantly, until thickened. Remove from heat. Blend in mayonnaise, onion, celery, salt and pepper; fold in potatoes. Spoon into 6 individual ramekins or 1 1/2-quart baking dish. Bake in preheated 350-degree oven for 30 minutes or until lightly browned; serve hot or cold. Sliced pimentos may be added with celery and onions. Yield: 6-8 servings.

Eunice Anderson
C. M. Russell HS, Great Falls, Montana

SOUR CREAM-POTATO SALAD

6 c. hot diced cooked potatoes
1/2 c. Wishbone Italian dressing
1/2 c. chopped green onions and tops
1 tsp. celery seed
1 1/2 tsp. salt
1/2 tsp. pepper
4 hard-cooked eggs
1 c. sour cream
1/2 c. mayonnaise
1/4 c. vinegar
1 tsp. prepared mustard
3/4 c. diced cucumber

Place potatoes in bowl; pour Italian dressing over potatoes. Chill. Add onions, celery seed, salt and pepper; toss lightly. Separate whites from yolks of eggs; chop. Add to potatoes; chill. Mash egg yolks. Add sour cream, mayonnaise, vinegar and mustard; mix well. Pour over potatoes; toss lightly. Let stand for 20 minutes. Add cucumber just before serving; garnish with parsley.

Dorotha Hurst
Baytown Jr HS, Baytown, Texas

CHURN-METHOD STRAWBERRY ICE CREAM

2 pt. fresh California strawberries
2 c. sugar
6 egg yolks
1/2 tsp. salt
3 c. scalded milk
1 tbsp. vanilla extract
3 c. heavy cream
12 drops of red food coloring (opt.)

Wash and hull strawberries. Place in blender container; process until pureed. May be pressed through sieve. Mix strawberry puree with 1 cup sugar; let stand in refrigerator for at least 1 hour. Beat egg yolks, remaining sugar and salt in bowl; stir in milk slowly. Pour into medium saucepan; cook over medium heat, stirring, until mixture coats metal spoon. Remove from heat. Add vanilla; cool. Stir in cream and food coloring; chill. Combine custard with strawberry puree; pour into 4-quart electric or hand-churn ice cream freezer. Freeze according to manufacturer's instructions.

Photograph for this recipe on this page.

GRILLED BARBECUED CHICKEN

3/4 c. catsup
1 tbsp. prepared mustard
2/3 c. drained sweet pickle relish
2 tbsp. soy sauce
2 tbsp. brown sugar
1 clove of garlic, crushed
1/8 tsp. pepper
2 chickens, cut into serving pieces

Blend catsup and mustard in small bowl. Add remaining ingredients except chicken; mix thoroughly. Set aside. Test temperature of charcoal briquet fire by cautiously holding hand, palm side down, just above grill. Hand should be kept in position for 4 seconds for medium heat needed for barbecuing chickens. Grill chickens about 8 inches from coals for 35 minutes, turning with tongs occasionally. Brush both sides with sauce. Grill for about 25 minutes or until chickens are tender, brushing and turning frequently. Raise grill or separate coals to lower temperature of charcoal fire. Tap outer gray layer from coals and push coals closer together to raise temperature. Add briquets to outer edge of hot coals if coals are needed.

Photograph for this recipe on this page.

MACARONI-OLIVE-SOUR CREAM SALAD

Salt
1 8-oz. package elbow macaroni
1/2 c. sour cream
1/2 c. mayonnaise
1/3 c. milk
1/2 tsp. dry mustard
1 tsp. crushed basil leaves
1 tbsp. lemon juice
1/3 c. chopped onion
1 c. thinly sliced fresh carrots
3/4 c. diced seeded peeled cucumbers
1/2 c. sliced red radishes
3/4 c. sliced pimento-stuffed olives
Pepper

Add 1 tablespoon salt to 3 quarts rapidly boiling water; add macaroni gradually so that water continues to boil. Cook, uncovered, stirring occasionally, until tender; drain in colander. Rinse with cold water; drain again. Blend sour cream, mayonnaise, milk, mustard, basil and lemon juice in large bowl. Add macaroni, vegetables and olives; toss until combined. Season with salt and pepper to taste. Cover; chill for several hours.

Photograph for this recipe on this page.

APRICOT PARFAITS

2 30-oz. cans apricot halves
2 c. half and half
1/2 c. milk
Sugar
1/3 c. light corn syrup
1/8 tsp. salt
2 tsp. grated lemon peel
2 1/2 tbsp. lemon juice
2 tbsp. cornstarch
3 tbsp. orange liqueur or
    orange juice
Red maraschino cherry halves (opt.)
Sprigs of fresh mint (opt.)

Drain apricots; reserve 1 cup syrup. Reserve 3 apricot halves for garnish; chill until needed. Puree remaining apricots in electric blender or press apricots through sieve. Reserve 1 cup puree for sauce. Mix half and half, milk, 3/4 cup sugar, corn syrup and salt in saucepan; bring to a simmer, stirring occasionally. Remove from heat; cool. Stir in lemon peel, 1 1/2 tablespoons lemon juice and remaining apricot puree. Pour into refrigerator trays; freeze for several hours or until firm. Spoon half the sherbet into electric blender container; blend until smooth. Return to refrigerator tray. Repeat blending with remaining sherbet; return to tray. Freeze for about 4 hours or until firm. Mix cornstarch and 1/3 cup sugar in medium saucepan; blend in reserved puree, reserved apricot syrup and orange liqueur. Bring to a boil, stirring constantly; reduce heat. Simmer for about 3 minutes, stirring frequently. Remove from heat; stir in remaining lemon juice. Cool; chill. Layer sherbet and apricot

sauce in eight 8-ounce parfait glasses. Cut reserved apricot halves into thirds lengthwise; garnish each parfait with a slice of apricot, then with a cherry half and small sprig of mint.

Photograph for this recipe on page 96.

KRAUT-BARBECUED LAMB

1 c. sauerkraut juice
1 med. onion, sliced
2 cloves of garlic, halved
1/4 tsp. celery seed
1/4 tsp. pepper
1 leg of lamb
1/3 c. honey
1 tsp. lemon juice

Combine sauerkraut juice, onion, garlic, celery seed and pepper. Place lamb in shallow pan; pour sauerkraut juice mixture over lamb. Cover; chill for 1 day, turning lamb occasionally. Skewer lamb with rotisserie spit; place spit about 8 inches above grey-hot coals. Roast for 30 minutes per pound or until meat thermometer registers 175 degrees for medium doneness. Blend honey and lemon juice; brush on lamb during last 30 minutes of roasting.

Photograph for this recipe on page 90.

LAZY DAY STEW

2 lb. ground beef
2 lg. onions, chopped
1 No. 2 can tomatoes
1 c. barbecue sauce
2/3 c. green peas
2/3 c. corn
1 c. pineapple juice
1 c. grated cheese

Cook ground beef and onions in large saucepan until lightly browned; drain off fat. Add remaining ingredients except cheese; simmer for about 40 minutes, adding tomato juice or water if moisture evaporates. Add cheese; cook until melted. Serve hot.

Mrs Minnie Torbush
Howard Middle Sch, Alexandria, Virginia

SUMMER MACARONI AND CHEESE

Salt
1 1-lb. package elbow macaroni
2 pt. sour cream
1 lb. creamed cottage cheese
1 c. thinly sliced scallions
1/2 tsp. pepper
2 tsp. Worcestershire sauce
1 c. grated Cheddar cheese
2 whole scallions

Add 2 tablespoons salt to 4 to 6 quarts rapidly boiling water; add macaroni gradually so that water continues to boil. Cook, uncovered, stirring occasionally, until tender; drain in colander. Combine macaroni, sour cream, cottage cheese, sliced scallions, 1 teaspoon salt and remaining seasonings; mix well. Turn into 3-quart casserole; cover. Bake in preheated 350-degree oven for 30 minutes. Uncover; sprinkle Cheddar cheese around edge of casserole. Bake for 10 to 15 minutes longer; garnish with whole scallions. Yield: 8-10 servings.

Photograph for this recipe on page 90.

BURNT SUGAR CAKE

2 1/2 c. sugar
1/2 c. hot water
1/2 c. butter
2 eggs, separated
2 1/2 c. Swans Down cake flour
1 c. cold water
2 tsp. baking powder
1 tsp. vanilla extract

Place 1 cup sugar in heavy skillet; cover. Cook over very low heat for 20 to 30 minutes or until golden brown. Stir in hot water slowly, several drops at a time at first; cook, stirring, until sugar is dissolved. Cool. Cream remaining sugar with butter until fluffy. Add egg yolks; beat vigorously. Sift flour 3 times, then measure. Add cold water to creamed mixture alternately with 2 cups flour; beat for 5 minutes. Add remaining flour, baking powder, vanilla and 2 teaspoons caramelized

syrup; beat well. Beat egg whites until stiff peaks form; fold into batter. Pour into 2 oiled and paper-lined layer pans. Bake in preheated 350-degree oven for 35 minutes. Refrigerate remaining syrup, covered, for future use.

Mrs Lila Akes
Central Decatur Comm Sch, Leon, Iowa

ANGEL DELIGHT CAKE

1 angel food cake
2 3-oz. packages strawberry
*   gelatin*
2 1/2 c. boiling water
2 10-oz. packages frozen
*   strawberries*
2 tbsp. sugar
1 pt. whipping cream, whipped

Tear cake into bite-sized pieces. Dissolve gelatin in boiling water; stir in strawberries and sugar. Chill until thickened; fold in whipped cream. Place half the cake in 9 x 13-inch pan; add half the strawberry mixture. Repeat layers; refrigerate until firm.

Cheryl Drewel
Roosevelt HS, Seattle, Washington

OLD-FASHIONED DRIED APPLE
STACK CAKE

1 c. sorghum molasses
1 c. vegetable shortening
2 eggs
5 1/2 c. all-purpose flour
1 tsp. soda
1/2 tsp. salt
2 tsp. baking powder
2 tsp. allspice
2 tsp. cinnamon
1 tsp. nutmeg
1 tsp. ginger
1/2 c. buttermilk
Cooked dried apples

Cream molasses and shortening until fluffy; add eggs, one at a time, beating well after each addition. Sift dry ingredients together twice; add to creamed mixture alternately with buttermilk. Chill dough, if necessary. Roll out on floured surface very thin; cut circles 6 inches in diameter. Place on greased cookie sheet. Bake in preheated 400-degree oven for 7 to 9 minutes or until lightly browned; cool thoroughly. Stack together with apples between each layer; cover top and .sides with apples. May be made ahead and stored in refrigerator to develop flavor. Yield: One 12-15 layer cake.

Juanita M. Rogers
Paul G. Blazer HS, Ashland, Kentucky

FRENCH COCONUT PIE

3 eggs
1 1/2 c. sugar
1/2 c. soft butter or margarine
1 tbsp. lemon juice
1 tsp. vanilla extract
1 3 1/2-oz. can flaked coconut
1 unbaked 9-in. pie shell

Beat eggs in bowl with fork; stir in sugar, butter, lemon juice, vanilla and coconut. Pour into pie shell. Bake in preheated 350-degree oven for about 45 minutes or until knife inserted halfway between center and edge comes out clean; cool.

Martha Atlas
South Panola HS, Batesville, Mississippi

HARVESTTIME PUMPKIN PIE

1 c. (packed) brown sugar
1/3 c. chopped pecans
2 tbsp. soft margarine
1 unbaked 9-in. pie shell
2 eggs
1 c. canned pumpkin
1 tbsp. flour
1 tsp. cinnamon
1/4 tsp. ginger
1/4 tsp. cloves
1/2 tsp. salt

1/3 c. sherry
1/2 c. whipping cream, whipped

Combine 1/3 cup brown sugar with pecans and margarine; sprinkle over pie shell. Place eggs, remaining sugar and remaining ingredients except cream in bowl; beat well. Place in pie shell over pecan mixture. Bake in preheated 450-degree oven for 10 minutes. Reduce temperature to 325 degrees; bake for 40 minutes longer. Cool; garnish with whipped cream and additional chopped pecans.

Mary Anne Guender
Garnet Valley HS, Concordville, Pennsylvania

PEACH CUSTARD PIE

2 1/2 to 3 c. chopped fresh peaches
2 eggs, well beaten
2 tbsp. melted butter
1 to 1 1/2 c. sugar
2 soda crackers, crushed
1 unbaked 9-in. pie crust

Combine peaches, eggs, butter, sugar and cracker crumbs; let stand for 10 minutes. Pour into crust. Bake in preheated 400-degree oven for 15 minutes. Reduce oven temperature to 375 degrees; bake for 35 to 45 minutes longer.

Mrs Cheryl Assenheimer
Troy Jr HS, Avon Lake, Ohio

FROSTY PUNCH

1 qt. sweetened rhubarb juice
1 qt. pineapple juice
1 6-oz. can frozen lemonade
2 sm. packages lemonade mix
2 qt. water
1 qt. ginger ale
1 pt. lemon sherbet

Mix all ingredients except ginger ale and sherbet; chill. Add ginger ale and sherbet just before serving. Yield: 1 1/2 gallons.

Mrs Clarence Anderson
Pierson Jr HS, Pierson, Iowa

HALLOWEEN

**Our children all dressed as ghosts
To play a fun trick on their host
Each wearing a mask
Set out for the task
The SCARIEST each hoping to boast**

Witches, skeletons, scarecrows, pirates and devils . . . They're all coming over to your house—so, you better be ready with those delicious spooky treats—delectable little surprises in Halloween shapes and colors. And, of course, you'll want to carry the orange and black color scheme throughout the decorations with black cats, orange pumpkins, black witches and orange punch. In setting the tone for Halloween, don't forget to make things spooky by dimming the lights and hanging skeleton bones and grotesque masks from the ceilings.

To make sure you get no tricks, you'll want to be sure to prepare some of these fantastic ghostly goodies. And, while the masked little devils are dining—eerie tales of horror and suspense.

◁ Recipe on page 109.

MENU

Children's Hobgoblin Party

Devil's Party Mix
Ghostly Potato Doughnuts
Cinnamon Apples
Flying Witch Cake
Molasses Popcorn Balls
Taffy Treats
Goblin's Perky Punch

DEVIL'S PARTY MIX

6 tbsp. butter or margarine
4 tsp. Worcestershire sauce
1 tsp. onion powder
1/2 tsp. garlic powder
2 c. wheat cereal
2 c. corn cereal
3/4 c. dry roasted peanuts
2 c. pretzels
2 c. Cheese Nips crackers

Melt butter in large, shallow pan over low heat; stir in Worcestershire sauce, onion powder and garlic powder. Add remaining ingredients; cook, stirring, until all pieces are coated. Bake in preheated 250-degree oven for 45 minutes, stirring every 15 minutes. Spread on absorbent paper to cool; store in airtight containers. Yield: 6 1/4 cups.

Mrs Eileen Yeakley
Martinsville Jr HS, Martinsville, Indiana

GHOSTLY POTATO DOUGHNUTS

1 c. mashed potatoes
1 c. potato water
3/4 c. shortening
1 tsp. salt
1/2 c. sugar
1 env. yeast
3/4 c. warm water
2 eggs, beaten
5 to 6 c. flour
Oil
6 c. powdered sugar
1 c. boiling water

Mix potatoes, potato water, shortening, salt and sugar. Dissolve yeast in warm water; add to potato mixture. Stir in eggs and enough flour for stiff dough. Knead on floured surface until smooth; cover. Let rise for 1 hour and 30 minutes. Pat dough out to 3/4 inch thick; cut with doughnut cutter. Let rise until doubled in bulk. Cook doughnuts in 3 to 4 inches oil at 375 degrees in deep fat fryer until golden brown; drain on paper toweling. Mix powdered sugar and boiling water; spread doughnuts with glaze while warm.

Helen Giles
Susan B. English Sch, Seldovia, Alaska

CINNAMON APPLES

8 med. apples
8 wooden skewers
2 c. sugar
2/3 c. light corn syrup
1 c. water
1/2 tsp. red food coloring
6 drops of oil of cinnamon

Wash apples; remove stems. Stick 1 skewer in each apple. Combine sugar, corn syrup, water and coloring in saucepan; cook, stirring, until mixture comes to a boil. Cook over medium heat to hard-crack stage. Add oil of cinnamon; remove from heat. Dip each apple into syrup, tilting saucepan to coat easier; let excess syrup drip back into saucepan. Place apples on buttered cookie sheet or rack to cool. Make lollipops with remaining syrup.

Mrs May Charlesworth
Northeast HS, Pasadena, Maryland

MOLASSES-POPCORN BALLS

1 c. light corn syrup
1 c. molasses
1 tsp. vinegar
1 tsp. soda
1 tbsp. hot water
4 qt. popcorn

Mix corn syrup, molasses and vinegar in saucepan; cook until mixture forms brittle ball when dropped into cold water. Dissolve soda in hot water; stir into molasses mixture. Pour over popcorn; mix well. Form into balls of desired size.

Mrs Eunice Cole Salomonson
Conrad Ball Jr HS, Loveland, Colorado

FLYING WITCH CAKE

1 pkg. yellow cake mix
2 eggs
Orange food coloring
3 sq. unsweetened chocolate
3 tbsp. sugar
1 pkg. orange butter frosting
1 1/2 tsp. butter

Mix cake mix with 1 1/4 cups water and eggs; reserve 1 cup batter. Add enough food coloring to remaining batter for desired shade. Melt 1 1/2 squares chocolate in double boiler. Add sugar and 3 tablespoons water; mix until sugar is dissolved. Blend into reserved batter. Spoon batters alternately into 2 greased and floured 8-inch square pans; marbleize with knife. Bake in preheated 350-degree oven for about 30 minutes or until done. Cool in pans on racks for 10 minutes. Remove from pans; cool on racks. Prepare orange butter frosting according to package directions; spread between layers and on top and sides of cake. Cut paper pattern of witch; trace outline of witch on frosting with tip of knife. Melt remaining chocolate with butter in double boiler; spread within outline.

Mildred Taylor Marsh
Jones HS, Orlando, Florida

TAFFY TREATS

1/3 c. sugar
1 1/3 c. ground nuts
2/3 c. evaporated milk
1/2 c. butter or margarine
1/3 c. powdered sugar
1/2 tsp. salt
1/3 c. (packed) brown sugar
1 egg
1 tsp. vanilla extract
2 c. sifted flour
1 pkg. caramels

Combine sugar, 1/3 cup nuts and 1/3 cup evaporated milk in top of double boiler; cook over boiling water, stirring, until thick. Cool. Cream butter, powdered sugar, salt and brown sugar. Add egg and vanilla; mix well. Add flour gradually, mixing well after each addition; shape into 1-inch balls. Make depression in each ball; place 1/4 teaspoon nut mixture in each depression. Roll, sealing nut mixture inside; place on lightly greased cookie sheet. Bake in preheated 350-degree oven for 15 to 18 minutes. Remove from oven; stick toothpick in center of each cookie. Cool. Mix remaining evaporated milk and caramels in top of double boiler; cook over boiling water, stirring, until caramels are melted. Dip each cookie into caramel mixture, coating well; roll bottom half of each cookie in remaining ground nuts.

Mrs Beverly Beekler Carrington
Larkin HS, Elgin, Illinois

GOBLIN'S PERKY PUNCH

Candy pumpkins
Candy corn
1   46-oz. can orange fruit drink
1 lg. can pineapple juice
2 No. 2 cans apricot nectar
1/4 c. lemon juice
1 qt. Seven-Up

Place 1 pumpkin and several pieces of candy corn alternately in each section of ice cube tray; fill with water. Freeze overnight. Chill remaining ingredients. Mix orange drink, pineapple juice, apricot nectar, and lemon juice in punch bowl; add Seven-Up just before serving. Add ice cubes to punch; serve punch in cups with ice cube in each cup.

Mrs Judy Vrklan
Arlington-Green Isle Public Schools
Arlington, Minnesota

HOT CHEESE DIP

1/2 c. mayonnaise
1/2 lb. Velveeta cheese, sliced
3 tbsp. milk
1 tbsp. lemon juice
1 jalapeno pepper

1/4 onion, cut in sm. pieces
1/2 tsp. sugar
1 clove of garlic

Place mayonnaise and Velveeta cheese in saucepan; cover. Place over very low heat for about 8 minutes or until cheese is melted. Place remaining ingredients in electric blender container; pour cheese mixture over ingredients in blender. Process at high speed for 40 seconds or until blended. Serve hot with crackers, chips or vegetable sticks.

Ruth H. Burch
Foster Jr HS, Tulsa, Oklahoma

ZESTY MEATBALLS WITH DIP

2 eggs, slightly beaten
1/3 c. milk
2/3 c. mashed potato flakes
2 tbsp. instant minced onion
1 tsp. salt
1/8 tsp. pepper
1/8 tsp. garlic powder
1 tsp. Worcestershire sauce
1 lb. ground beef

Combine eggs, milk and potato flakes in bowl; let stand for about 1 minute. Add remaining ingredients; mix well. Shape into 1-inch meatballs. Cook in skillet until brown and well done; keep warm in oven until ready to serve. Serve with toothpicks.

Dip

1 c. chive or onion sour cream
1 tbsp. brown gravy mix
2 tsp. milk

Combine all ingredients in saucepan. Heat through, stirring constantly; do not boil. Serve with meatballs.

Mrs Thelma Maxey
Lorenzo HS, Lorenzo, Texas

BEWITCHING TURNIP SALAD

3 med. turnips
3 med. carrots
1/2 cauliflower
1 sm. green pepper
2 tsp. salt
1/2 c. vinegar
1/3 c. sugar
1/4 c. salad oil
2 tsp. curry powder
1/4 tsp. pepper

Pare and slice turnips and carrots. Separate cauliflower into flowerets; cut green pepper into strips. Combine turnips, carrots, cauliflower and green pepper in saucepan; add 2 cups water and 1 teaspoon salt. Bring to a boil; reduce heat. Cover; simmer for 5 minutes. Drain; cool. Combine remaining salt and remaining ingredients. Pour over vegetables; toss lightly. Refrigerate for several hours before serving. Yield: 8 servings.

Mrs Robert E. Koch
Brookens Jr HS, Urbana, Illinois

FALL CINNAMON APPLESAUCE SALAD

1 3-oz. package lemon gelatin
1/4 c. red cinnamon candies
1 1/2 c. boiling water
1 c. unsweetened applesauce
1 1/2 tsp. lemon juice
Pinch of salt
1/4 c. broken pecans
1 3-oz. package cream cheese, softened
2 tbsp. milk
1 tbsp. mayonnaise
Lettuce

Dissolve gelatin and candies in boiling water. Stir in applesauce, lemon juice, and salt; chill until thickened. Add pecans; place in 9 x 5-inch loaf pan. Blend cream cheese, milk and mayonnaise; spoon on top of gelatin mixture. Swirl through salad with knife to marbleize; chill until firm. Serve on bed of lettuce.

Nona Verloo
Bureau of Homemaking Ed, State Dept of Ed
Sacramento, California

CORN SHOCK SALAD WITH MINI-CHEESE PUMPKINS

2 3-oz. packages lemon gelatin
1/2 c. shredded carrots
1/2 c. shredded cabbage
1 c. crushed pineapple
9 or 10 cone-shaped drinking cups
1 15-oz. can asparagus spears
Chopped Lettuce
Process cheese spread
Whole cloves
Yellow food coloring

Dissolve gelatin according to package directions; stir in carrots, cabbage and pineapple. Chill until partially thickened. Place cone-shaped cups in water glasses to hold erect; spoon gelatin mixture into cups. Chill until set. Run boning knife between salad and cup; place salads on platter, flat side down to resemble corn shocks. Place asparagus spears vertically against each cone; place chopped lettuce around base. Form cheese into pumpkin shapes, using 2 teaspoons for each; place clove on top for stem. Dip toothpick in yellow coloring; make grooves for pumpkin. Place pumpkins around corn shocks.

Angela Johansen
Sioux Falls Public Schools
Sioux Falls, South Dakota

HEARTY HALLOWEEN STEW

3 or 4 potatoes
1 onion, chopped
3 carrots, sliced
1 or 2 stalks celery, chopped
1 tsp. salt
1 lb. ground beef
1 can English peas
1 can whole kernel corn
1 can tomatoes, cut up
1 sm. can tomato sauce
3/4 c. catsup
2 tbsp. mustard
Dash of hot sauce
1 or 2 jalapeno peppers
1 tsp. garlic salt
1 clove of garlic, chopped
1/8 tsp. pepper
1 tbsp. chili powder
1 tsp. thyme
1 c. uncooked macaroni

Peel potatoes; cut into small chunks. Place potatoes, onion, carrots and celery in 6-quart saucepan; add about 2 quarts water. Add salt. Bring to a boil; reduce heat. Simmer until vegetables are tender. Cook beef in skillet until brown; drain. Add to potato mixture. Add peas, corn, tomatoes, tomato sauce, catsup, mustard, hot sauce, jalapeno peppers, garlic salt, garlic, pepper, chili powder and thyme; simmer for 30 minutes, adding water, if needed. Cook macaroni according to package directions; drain. Add to beef mixture; simmer for 10 to 15 minutes longer. Remove jalapeno peppers before serving. Yield: About 5 quarts.

Mrs Juanita Pitts
Linden-Kildare HS, Linden, Texas

HOT HAMBURGER STROGANOFF SANDWICHES

1 lb. hamburger
1 onion, chopped fine
1 clove of garlic, minced
2 1/2 tbsp. flour
1 8-oz. can sliced mushrooms
1 can cream of chicken soup
1/2 c. sour cream
8 hamburger buns

Cook hamburger and onion in skillet until brown, breaking up hamburger with spoon. Add garlic and flour; blend well. Add undrained mushrooms and soup; stir well. Cook until thick, stirring occasionally. Blend in sour cream; remove from heat. Fill hamburger buns with beef mixture; wrap in foil. Place on cookie sheet. Bake in preheated 350-degree oven for 15 minutes. One-half teaspoon garlic powder may be used instead of garlic clove. Yield: 8 servings.

Cheryl Lalli
Model Middle Sch, Erie, Pennsylvania

WITCHES' RICE-SAUSAGE CASSEROLE

1 lb. sausage
1 c. chopped celery
1/2 c. chopped onion
2 c. cooked rice
1 can cream of mushroom soup
1 soup can milk

Cook sausage in skillet until brown; remove from skillet. Saute celery and onion in drippings in skillet until golden brown; drain off excess drippings. Stir in sausage, rice, soup and milk; place in casserole. Bake in preheated 350-degree oven for 30 minutes. Yield: 10 servings.

Mrs Dorothy M. Ham
Brantley Co HS, Nahunta, Georgia

ORIGINAL KORNY DOGS

1 c. flour
3/4 c. cornmeal
3 tsp. baking powder
1 tsp. salt
2 tbsp. sugar
1 c. milk
2 eggs
1/4 c. melted fat
10 metal skewers
1 pkg. beef wieners, at room
  temperature

Mix dry ingredients in large bowl. Add milk; mix well. Add eggs, one at a time, beating well after each addition; stir in melted fat. Stick skewer into end of each wiener; coat with batter. Cook in deep, hot fat until brown; serve with mustard if desired.

Mrs Ruth F. Thompson, Retired
El Paso Public Sch, El Paso, Texas

BEEF IN COSTUME FOR HALLOWEEN

1   4-lb. pumpkin
1 lb. lean ground beef

1 c. chopped onions
Cooking oil
1/3 c. chopped red pepper
1/3 c. chopped green pepper
1 clove of garlic, minced
1 tsp. salt
1/4 tsp. thyme
1/4 tsp. pepper
1   7 1/2-oz. can pitted ripe olives
1   8-oz. can tomato sauce
2 eggs, beaten

Cut top from pumpkin; scrape out pumpkin seeds and fibers. Simmer pumpkin and top in enough salted water to cover for about 20 to 25 minutes or until almost tender; drain. Cook beef and onions in 1 tablespoon oil until brown. Add red and green pepper and garlic; cook for 1 minute longer. Remove from heat; stir in remaining ingredients. Spoon into pumpkin; place lid on top. Place pumpkin in baking pan; brush with oil. Bake in preheated 350-degree oven for about 1 hour. Let stand for about 10 minutes; cut into wedges to serve. May use lettuce basket to lower pumpkin into boiling water and to remove easily without breaking skin. Yield: About 8 servings.

Photograph for this recipe on this page.

107

CREAMY CARROT FUDGE

1 1/2 c. grated carrots
3 1/2 c. sugar
1/2 c. sweetened condensed milk
1/2 c. water
1/2 tsp. lemon flavoring

Mix carrots, sugar, milk and water in saucepan; cook to soft-ball stage. Remove from heat. Add lemon flavoring; mix well. Cool. Beat until creamy; pour into buttered pan in layer. Cool; cut into squares.

Esther Engelhardt
Mt Pleasant Jr HS, Mt Pleasant, Iowa

HALLOWEEN MIDNIGHT COOKIES

1 pkg. refrigerator cookie dough
1 1/2 c. Grape Nuts
4 bars chocolate candy

Cut cookies according to package directions; place close together in lightly greased square pan. Sprinkle 1/2 of the Grape Nuts over cookies. Break chocolate bars into small chunks; scatter over Grape Nuts. Top with remaining Grape Nuts. Bake in preheated 350-degree oven for 20 to 25 minutes; cool. Cut into squares. Yield: 2 dozen.

Josephine Castillo
Brownsville HS, Brownsville, Texas

GOBLIN FROSTIES

4 med. oranges
8 licorice candy drops
Whole cloves
1 1/2 qt. lime sherbet
4 maraschino cherries with stems

Cut off thin slice of peel from bottom end of each orange with sharp knife to steady. Cut off 1/3 of the orange crosswise from top to make hat. Scoop out pulp from orange; make face on orange, using licorice for eyes and cloves for nose and mouth. Fill shells with sherbet, mounding above rim. Place hats on top of sherbet at an angle. Stick cherry in hat with toothpick; anchor end of toothpick in sherbet. Place in freezer until served.

Elna P. Larson
Ondossagon Sch, Ashland, Wisconsin

HALLOWEEN TREATS

1 c. sugar
1 c. light corn syrup
1 c. peanut butter
6 c. Rice Krispies
1 c. chocolate chips
1 c. butterscotch chips

Mix sugar and corn syrup in 3-quart pan; cook over moderate heat until mixture begins to bubble. Remove from heat; stir in peanut butter and Rice Krispies. Press into buttered 13 x 9 x 2-inch pan; let harden. Mix chocolate and butterscotch chips in top of double boiler; place over hot water until melted, stirring to blend. Spread over cereal mixture; chill. Cut into 2 x 1-inch bars. Yield: 48 bars.

Opal Pruitt
Western HS, Buda, Illinois

SPOOKY LIGHT DOUGHNUTS

4 tsp. baking powder
1/2 tsp. nutmeg
1 tsp. salt
3 1/2 c. flour
1 egg
2 egg yolks
1 c. milk
1 c. sugar
3 tbsp. melted butter, cooled
Cinnamon-sugar

Sift baking powder, nutmeg, salt and flour together. Beat egg and egg yolks in bowl. Add milk, sugar and butter; mix well. Add sifted ingredients; stir until combined. Knead lightly on floured surface; roll out 1/4 inch thick. Cut with doughnut cutter. Fry in deep fat at 370 degrees, until brown, turning once; do not pierce with fork. Roll in cinnamon-sugar while warm.

Mary K. Rattan
Ector HS, Odessa, Texas

JACK-O'-LANTERN CAKE

1 box angel food cake mix
3/4 c. white corn syrup
2 egg whites
Pinch of salt
1 tsp. vanilla
Orange food coloring
1 tube brown decorating icing

Prepare and bake cake according to package directions; cool. Pour corn syrup into small saucepan; bring to boiling point. Beat egg whites in bowl with electric mixer until stiff; add salt. Pour corn syrup over egg whites slowly, beating constantly; beat until very stiff peaks form. Fold in vanilla and desired amount of food coloring. Round off edge of cake at top and bottom; spread with frosting. Make ridges from bottom to top of cake with spoon to resemble pumpkin; make eyes and mouth with tube icing. Twist sheets of brown paper; place in hole for stem.

Mrs Ann J. Hilliard
Plant City Sr HS, Plant City, Florida

ALL-SOULS' CAKE

5 1/2 to 6 1/2 c. unsifted flour
Sugar
1/2 tsp. salt
2 pkg. Fleischmann's active dry yeast
1/2 c. milk
1/2 c. water
2/3 c. Fleischmann's margarine
4 eggs, at room temperature
1 tsp. anise extract
1 tsp. orange extract
1 egg, beaten

Mix 1 cup flour, 1/2 cup sugar, salt and undissolved yeast thoroughly in large bowl. Combine milk, water and margarine in saucepan; place over low heat until liquids are warm. Margarine does not need to melt. Add to dry ingredients gradually; beat with electric mixer at medium speed for 2 minutes, scraping bowl occasionally. Add 4 eggs, anise and orange extracts and 1 cup flour; beat at high speed for 2 minutes, scraping bowl occasionally. Stir in enough remaining flour to make soft dough. Cover; let rise in warm place free from draft for about 1 hour or until doubled in bulk. Stir down. Turn out onto lightly floured board; divide in half. Shape each half into ball, reserving about 1/4 cup dough from each half for trim. Place balls in 2 well-greased 8-inch round cake pans. Make four 3-inch bone shapes, four 1 1/2-inch tears and 1 round ball about 1 inch in diameter from each half of reserved dough. Place ball on top center of dough; arrange tears and bones around side. Cover; let rise in warm place free from draft for about 1 hour or until doubled in bulk. Brush lightly with beaten egg, keeping egg from dripping onto side of cake pan; sprinkle dough with sugar. Bake in preheated 375-degree oven on lowest rack position for about 25 to 30 minutes or until done. Remove from pans; cool on wire racks.

Photograph for this recipe on page 100.

SPOOK CAKE DELIGHT

3 c. sifted flour
6 tbsp. cocoa
2 c. sugar
2 tsp. soda
1 tsp. salt
2 tsp. vanilla extract
2 tsp. vinegar
10 tbsp. melted shortening
2 c. water
Orange confectioners' frosting

Sift flour with cocoa, sugar, soda and salt into large bowl. Mix vanilla, vinegar, shortening and water; add to flour mixture gradually, mixing well. Place in 2 greased and floured layer pans. Bake in preheated 350-degree oven for 30 to 35 minutes; cool. Remove from pans; frost with orange frosting.

Marilyn J. McDonald
Lanark Comm Unit Sch, Lanark, Illinois

EASY CARROT CAKE

4 eggs
2 c. flour
2 c. sugar
2 tsp. soda
1 tsp. salt
1 1/4 tsp. cinnamon
1 1/4 c. salad oil
2 7-oz. jars carrot jr. baby food

Place all ingredients in bowl; beat until well combined. Pour into greased 9 x 13-inch pan. Bake in preheated 350-degree oven for 25 minutes. Cool; remove from pan.

Frosting

1 3-oz. package cream cheese,
*   softened*
1/4 c. margarine, softened
2 c. powdered sugar
1/2 c. chopped nuts
2 tsp. vanilla

Place all ingredients in bowl; mix well. Spread on cake.

JoAnn Less
Camanche HS, Camanche, Iowa

FESTIVE ORANGE SLICE CAKE

Butter
2 c. sugar
4 eggs
1 lb. dates, chopped
1 lb. orange candy slices, cut up
2 c. chopped pecans
1 c. shredded coconut
3 1/2 c. flour
1 1/2 c. buttermilk
1 tsp. soda
1 c. orange juice
2 c. confectioners' sugar

Cream 1 cup butter and sugar; add eggs, one at a time, beating well after each addition. Mix dates, candy, pecans and coconut with 1/2 cup flour; set aside. Add 1/2 cup buttermilk to sugar mixture; beat well. Add soda to remaining buttermilk. Sift remaining flour; add to sugar mixture alternately with buttermilk. Fold in date mixture; turn into oiled and floured tube pan. Bake in preheated 250-degree oven for 2 hours and 30 minutes. Mix orange juice, confectioners' sugar and 2 tablespoons butter in saucepan; heat, stirring, until sugar and butter are melted. Pour over hot cake; cool. Remove from pan.

Mrs Faye H. Lynch
Hickman Co Jr HS, Centerville, Tennessee

BLACK BOTTOM WITCHES' PIE

18 chocolate wafers
1/2 c. sugar
1/4 c. melted butter
1 6-oz. package chocolate bits
1/2 c. heavy cream
1/2 tsp. vanilla extract
1/2 pt. chocolate ice cream
1 qt. orange sherbet

Crush wafers; place in bowl. Add sugar and melted butter; mix well. Press into 9-inch pie plate; chill. Place chocolate bits and cream in saucepan; cook over low heat, stirring occasionally, until melted. Stir in vanilla; chill until thickened. Stir chocolate ice cream until smooth; spoon into crust. Spread 3/4 of the chocolate sauce over ice cream; return to freezer until firm. Soften sherbet; spoon over chocolate sauce. Drizzle remaining chocolate sauce on top. Freeze until firm. Yield: 8 servings.

Mrs Deborah Wheeler
Cabot HS, Cabot, Vermont

GHOST AND GOBLIN PIE

1 1/3 c. fine gingersnap crumbs
1/3 c. melted butter
1 pkg. vanilla pudding mix
1 env. unflavored gelatin
2 egg yolks
1 1/2 c. milk
2 sq. unsweetened chocolate, melted
3 egg whites
1/8 tsp. cream of tartar

1/4 c. sugar
2 tbsp. rum
1/2 c. heavy cream, whipped
9 gingersnap halves

Mix gingersnap crumbs with butter; press into 8-inch pie plate. Bake in preheated 300-degree oven for 10 minutes; cool. Mix pudding mix with gelatin in saucepan. Beat egg yolks with milk; stir into pudding mixture. Cook, stirring, until thick. Add half the pudding mixture to chocolate; mix until smooth. Spoon into crust; chill. Chill remaining pudding mixture until thickened. Beat egg whites with cream of tartar until stiff, adding sugar gradually; fold in thickened pudding mixture and rum. Place on chocolate layer in pie plate; chill until set. Top with whipped cream; insert gingersnap halves into whipped cream. Chill until served. Yield: 8 servings.

Betty L. Fowler
Kilgore HS, Kilgore, Texas

ORANGE POPCORN BALLS

1 1/2 c. sugar
1 1/4 c. water
1 c. orange marmalade
1/2 tsp. salt
1/2 c. light corn syrup

1 tsp. vinegar
5 qt. popcorn

Combine sugar, water, marmalade, salt, corn syrup and vinegar in saucepan; bring to a boil, stirring until sugar dissolves. Cook to hard-ball stage or to 250 degrees on candy thermometer. Pour over popcorn slowly; mix thoroughly. Shape into 2 1/2-inch balls with buttered hands. Black popcorn balls may be made by substituting one 6-ounce package licorice sticks, cut in small pieces, for orange marmalade. Yield: 15 balls.

Photograph for this recipe on this page.

HALLOWEEN HOT CHOCOLATE MIX

1 16-oz. jar non-dairy coffee creamer
1 c. powdered sugar
1 8-qt. box instant nonfat dry milk
1 2-lb. can instant chocolate drink powder

Mix all ingredients well; place in large container. Cover tightly. Place 1/3 cup chocolate mixture in cup; add enough hot water to fill cup. Stir well. Top with marshmallows, if desired.

Gudrun Harstad
Detroit Lakes Sr HS
Detroit Lakes, Minnesota

PERKY PUNCH

3 1 1/2-qt. bottles cranberry juice
5 qt. pineapple juice
4 c. water
2 2/3 c. (packed) brown sugar
4 tbsp. whole cloves
4 tbsp. whole allspice
24 2-in. sticks whole cinnamon

Pour cranberry juice, pineapple juice, water and brown sugar into 50-cup percolator; stir until sugar is dissolved. Place filter paper in percolator basket; add cloves, allspice and cinnamon sticks. Percolate as for coffee.

Mrs Ellen Goolsbey
Appleton HS East, Appleton, Wisconsin

THANKSGIVING

With the harvest season over and winter fast approaching, we celebrate the oldest of the truly American holidays, by setting aside an annual day of thanksgiving for the abundance of the past year.

As in the first years of our country's settlement, we observe this occasion with a large family feast of foods much like those prepared by colonial women . . . delicious cranberries, squash, yams, corn, pumpkins and of course . . . the turkey. The menu we are suggesting contains many recipes which can be prepared in advance, leaving time for you to enjoy the plans of the day . . . parades, football games or just a long walk in the woods while the leaves are so pretty.

Cornucopias are the traditional centerpiece. You can easily create a very personal horn of plenty by using fresh fruits and berries, autumn vegetables and nuts.

◁ Recipe on page 126.

MENU

Thanksgiving Dinner

Quick and Easy
Chicken-Mushroom Soup
Colonial Cranberry Salad
Easy Baked Turkey
Corn Bread Stuffing
Squash Supreme
Broccoli Puff Casserole
Scalloped Celery
Layered Sweet Potato Casserole
Three-Day Yeast Rolls
Pumpkin Chiffon Tarts
Carrot-Pineapple Cake
Coffee

QUICK AND EASY
CHICKEN-MUSHROOM SOUP

1 can cream of mushroom soup
1 can chicken broth
2 c. water
2 tbsp. butter
1 tsp. salt
1 can boned chicken
1 tbsp. chopped chives
1 tsp. curry powder
1 c. cream
1 c. cooked rice

Combine all ingredients in large saucepan; heat through.

Mrs Van Jones
Marlin HS, Marlin, Texas

COLONIAL CRANBERRY SALAD

1 c. sugar
2 c. fresh cranberries
1   6-oz. package strawberry gelatin
2 tbsp. lemon juice
1 tbsp. brandy (opt.)
1   3-oz. package cream cheese, cubed
1/2 c. chopped nuts
1 c. chopped celery
1 c. chopped apples

Combine 1 cup water, sugar and cranberries in saucepan; bring just to a boil. Remove from heat; cover and let cool for about 5 minutes. Combine 1 cup boiling water and gelatin; stir until dissolved. Add 1 cup cold water, cranberry mixture and lemon juice; chill until partially congealed. Fold in remaining ingredients; chill until firm.

Candy Pickens
Kemp Jr-Sr HS, Kemp, Texas

SCALLOPED CELERY

3 c. diced celery
1/4 c. slivered almonds
1/2 c. water chestnuts, sliced
5 tbsp. butter
3 tbsp. flour
1 c. chicken broth
3/4 c. half and half
Salt and pepper to taste
1/2 c. mushrooms
1/2 c. shredded sharp Cheddar cheese
1/2 c. bread crumbs

Parboil celery in salted water for 5 minutes; drain well. Combine celery, almonds and water chestnuts in 1 1/2-quart casserole. Melt 3 tablespoons butter in saucepan; stir in flour to make a smooth paste. Stir in broth and half and half slowly; simmer over low heat until thick. Season with salt and pepper. Stir mushrooms into sauce; pour over celery. Sprinkle with cheese. Melt remaining butter; stir into bread crumbs. Sprinkle over cheese. Bake in preheated 350-degree oven for 30 minutes or until bubbly. Yield: 6 servings.

Eunice Anderson
C. M. Russell HS, Great Falls, Montana

CORN BREAD STUFFING

1 recipe sugarless southern corn bread
2 c. day-old bread crumbs
1 tsp. salt
1/2 tsp. pepper
1/4 c. minced parsley
1 tbsp. mixed herbs
1 lg. onion, chopped
1/2 c. melted margarine
1 c. finely chopped celery
1 lg. apple, chopped

Crumble corn bread and bread crumbs into large bowl; sprinkle with salt, pepper, parsley and herbs. Cook onion in margarine for about 15 minutes. Stir onion mixture, celery and apple into bread mixture. Yield: Stuffing for 10 to 12-pound turkey.

Barbara J. Ebner
Middletown Area HS, Middletown, Pennsylvania

EASY BAKED TURKEY

1 frozen turkey, thawed
Salt and pepper to taste
3 tbsp. paprika
1/8 c. hot water
1 c. peanut oil

Season inside and outside of turkey with salt and pepper. Dissolve paprika in water; blend in peanut oil. Baste turkey generously with oil mixture; brush inside of heavy brown grocery bag with remaining oil mixture, greasing well. Place turkey in bag, breast side up; tie end of bag. Place bag in baking pan. Bake in preheated 325-degree oven for 15 minutes per pound.

Mrs Variel Garner
Moody HS, Moody, Texas

SQUASH SUPREME

2 c. cooked yellow squash
1 tbsp. grated onion
1 can cream of chicken soup
1 c. sour cream
1 carrot, grated
Salt and pepper to taste
1 bag Pepperidge Farm Stuffing Mix
Butter

Mash squash; stir in onion, soup, sour cream, carrot, salt and pepper. Sprinkle layer of stuffing mix in buttered casserole. Add squash mixture; cover with layer of stuffing mix. Dot generously with butter. Bake in preheated 350-degree oven for 30 to 40 minutes. This dish freezes well.

Jane Wheeler
University HS, Waco, Texas

BROCCOLI PUFF CASSEROLE

1 10-oz. package frozen chopped
    broccoli
1 can cream of mushroom soup
1/2 c. shredded sharp processed
    American cheese
1/4 c. milk

1/2 c. mayonnaise
1 egg, beaten
1 tbsp. melted margarine
1/4 c. fine dry bread crumbs

Cook broccoli according to package directions, omitting the salt; drain thoroughly. Place broccoli in 10 x 6 x 1 1/2-inch baking dish. Combine soup and cheese; add milk, mayonnaise and egg gradually, stirring until well blended. Pour over broccoli. Combine margarine and bread crumbs; sprinkle evenly over soup mixture. Bake in preheated 350-degree oven for 45 minutes or until bubbly and crumbs are lightly browned. Garnish with parsley.

Mrs Mary J. Higgins
East Cobb Middle Sch, Marietta, Georgia

LAYERED SWEET POTATO CASSEROLE

6 to 8 med. sweet potatoes
3/4 c. (packed) brown sugar
1/4 c. butter
1 can whole cranberry sauce
1/2 c. orange juice

Boil sweet potatoes in jackets until done; peel and cut into slices. Place half the slices in a layer in buttered casserole. Add half the brown sugar; dot with half the butter. Add a layer of cranberry sauce. Repeat layers; pour orange juice over top. Bake in preheated 350-degree oven until heated through.

Broxie C. Stuckey
Gordo HS, Gordo, Alabama

THREE-DAY YEAST ROLLS

2 pkg. yeast
1 c. margarine
3/4 c. sugar
2 cggs, beaten
7 c. sifted flour
2 tsp. salt

Dissolve yeast in 1/4 cup warm water. Melt margarine in 1 cup boiling water in saucepan; add sugar, 1 cup cold water and eggs, mixing well. Stir yeast into margarine mixture. Combine flour and salt in large mixing bowl. Add yeast mixture; stir well. Turn dough into large greased bowl. Cover; place in refrigerator until ready to use. May be kept for 3 days. Remove from refrigerator; turn out on lightly floured board. Knead dough until smooth and elastic. Shape into rolls; place on greased baking pan. Let rise until doubled in bulk. Bake in preheated 425-degree oven for 25 minutes or until browned.

Mrs Joy Barkowsky
Stanton Jr HS, Hereford, Texas

PUMPKIN CHIFFON TARTS

    3/4 c. (packed) brown sugar
    1 env. unflavored gelatin
    1/2 tsp. salt
    1 tsp. cinnamon
    1/2 tsp. nutmeg
    1/4 tsp. ginger
    3 eggs, separated
    3/4 c. milk
    1 1/4 c. canned or cooked mashed
        pumpkin
    1/3 c. sugar
    7 or 8 baked 4-in. tart shells,
        cooled

Combine brown sugar, gelatin, salt and spices in saucepan. Combine slightly beaten egg yolks and milk; stir into gelatin mixture. Cook, stirring constantly, until mixture comes to a boil. Remove from heat; stir in pumpkin. Chill until partially congealed. Beat egg whites until soft peaks form. Add sugar gradually; beat until stiff peaks form. Fold pumpkin mixture gently into egg whites. Turn into tart shells; chill until firm. Garnish with whipped cream and chopped candied ginger. The secret of the fluffy filling is not to let the gelatin mixture get too stiff before folding it into the egg white meringue.

Mrs Hal Nave, Jr.
Fulton HS, Knoxville, Tennessee

CARROT-PINEAPPLE CAKE

    1 1/2 c. oil
    2 c. sugar
    3 eggs
    1 c. drained crushed pineapple
    2 c. grated carrots
    2 1/2 c. flour
    1 tsp. soda
    1/2 tsp. salt
    1 tsp. cinnamon
    1 tsp. vanilla
    1 c. finely chopped nuts
    Topping

Cream oil, sugar and eggs together. Add pineapple and carrots; mix well. Sift flour, soda, salt and cinnamon together. Add to carrot mixture; stir in vanilla and nuts. Beat well; pour into cake pan. Bake in preheated 350-degree oven for 45 minutes or until cake tests done. Let cool; remove from pan. Spread Topping over cooled cake.

Topping

    1 lb. confectioners' sugar, sifted
    1/2 c. margarine, softened
    1 3-oz. package cream cheese,
        softened
    1 tsp. vanilla

Combine sugar, margarine and cream cheese; mix until smooth. Add vanilla; mix well.

Elva Powers
Omak Sr HS, Omak, Washington

COCKTAIL SAUSAGE BALLS

    1 lb. hot bulk sausage
    3 c. biscuit mix
    1 8-oz. jar Cheez Whiz

Combine sausage, biscuit mix and cheese; shape into cocktail-size meatballs. Place in baking pan. Bake in preheated 300-degree oven for about 25 minutes or until lightly brown. May be made ahead and frozen.

Mrs Dorothy Smith
Palacios Sr HS, Palacios, Texas

117

OLIVE CHEESECAKE SPREAD

1 c. sour cream
1/4 c. finely chopped green pepper
1/4 c. finely chopped celery
2 tbsp. chopped stuffed olives
1 tsp. lemon juice
1/2 tsp. Worcestershire sauce
Dash of paprika
2 or 3 drops of bottled hot pepper
    sauce
2/3 c. round cheese cracker crumbs

Combine all ingredients except cracker crumbs; mix well. Line 2 1/2-cup bowl with plastic wrap; spread 1/2 of the sour cream mixture in bowl. Add 1/4 cup crumbs. Repeat layers, then cover and chill overnight. Turn out on plate; remove plastic wrap. Sprinkle with remaining crumbs. Serve with crackers or fresh vegetables.

Barbara Mosher
Wilson Central Sch, Wilson, New York

SWEET AND SOUR MEATBALLS

1 lb, finely ground beef chuck
1 egg, beaten
Salt and pepper to taste
1 sm. jar grape jelly
1 jar chili sauce

Combine beef, egg and seasonings; mix well. Shape into small balls; brown in skillet. Keep warm until ready to use. Combine jelly and chili sauce in chafing dish. Add meatballs; keep warm over low heat. Additional seasonings may be mixed into meatballs, if desired.

Mrs Frances Baratz
Clark Lane Jr HS, Waterford, Connecticut

APPETIZER MEATBALLS IN CRANBERRY SAUCE

2 c. soft bread crumbs
1/2 c. milk
1 tbsp. soy sauce
1/2 tsp. garlic salt
1/4 tsp. onion salt
1 lb. hamburger
1 6-oz. can water chestnuts,
    drained and finely chopped
1 1-lb. can jellied cranberry
    sauce
1 12-oz. bottle chili sauce
2 tbsp. (firmly packed) brown sugar
1 tbsp. bottled lemon juice

Combine bread crumbs, milk, soy sauce, garlic salt and onion salt. Add hamburger and water chestnuts; mix well. Form mixture into 1-inch balls; place on 15 1/2 x 10 x 1-inch baking pan. Bake in preheated 350-degree oven for 18 to 20 minutes or until done. Remove from pan; place on paper towels to absorb fat. Mix remaining ingredients together in large saucepan; cook over moderate heat until mixture is smooth and cranberry sauce is melted, stirring frequently. Heat meatballs in sauce; serve in chafing dish or electric casserole. Use toothpicks for serving. Meatballs may be frozen. Yield: 5 dozen.

Mrs M. Judelle Jones
Turlock HS, Turlock, California

CABBAGE BORSCHT

2 lb. soup bones
2 qt. cold water
2 carrots, cut (opt.)
1 med. head cabbage, finely chopped
2 med. potatoes, cubed
1 med. onion, minced
1 sm. bay leaf
10 whole allspice
1/2 star anise (opt.)
1 1/2 tbsp. chopped parsley
1 tsp. salt
Dash of pepper
1 to 1 1/2 c. tomatoes
1/2 c. heavy cream or evaporated milk

Boil soup bones in water in kettle for at least 1 hour and 30 minutes. Add more water as needed to make 2 quarts water before adding vegetables. Add carrots, cabbage, potatoes and onion; stir in seasonings. Cook until vegetables are crisp-tender. Add tomatoes; bring just to a boil. Stir in cream just before serving.

E. Klassen
Georges P. Vanier Sch
Donnelly, Alberta, Canada

MACARONI-TURKEY SALAD

1 tbsp. salt
1 8-oz. package elbow macaroni
1 c. sour cream
1/3 c. mayonnaise
1/4 c. lemon juice
1 tsp. seasoned salt
1/2 tsp. dillweed
1/4 tsp. white pepper

2 c. julienne-cut cooked turkey
1 c. cooked cut green beans
1/4 c. chopped onion
1 4-oz. can pimentos, drained and halved
1 6-oz. jar marinated artichoke hearts, drained
Crisp salad greens

Add salt to 3 quarts rapidly boiling water; add macaroni gradually so that water continues to boil. Cook, uncovered, stirring occasionally, until tender; drain in colander. Rinse with cold water; drain again. Blend sour cream, mayonnaise, lemon juice, seasoned salt, dillweed and pepper in large bowl. Add macaroni; toss well. Arrange turkey, beans, onion, pimentos and artichoke hearts over macaroni mixture; chill. Toss just before serving; place greens around bowl. Yield: 4-6 servings.

Photograph for this recipe on this page.

CRANBROSIA SALAD

2 c. fresh cranberries, chopped or
    ground
1 c. sugar
2 env. unflavored gelatin
3/4 c. pineapple juice
1 c. drained mandarin oranges
1 c. drained pineapple chunks
1 lg. banana, cubed
1 c. coconut
1 c. sour cream
1 c. whipping cream, whipped

Combine cranberries and sugar; mix thoroughly to dissolve sugar. Sprinkle gelatin over pineapple juice to soften. Place over medium heat; stir constantly until gelatin is dissolved. Add to cranberry mixture; stir well. Stir in fruits; fold in sour cream. Fold in whipped cream; chill until firm. Cool Whip may be substituted for whipped cream, if desired.

Mrs Lois W. Gerald
Whiteville Sr HS, Whiteville, North Carolina

FROZEN CRANBERRY SALAD

2 3-oz. packages cream cheese,
    softened
2 tbsp. mayonnaise
2 tbsp. sugar
1 can whole cranberry sauce
1 sm. can crushed pineapple
1 c. chopped pecans
1 c. whipped cream

Combine cream cheese, mayonnaise and sugar; blend well. Stir in cranberry sauce, pineapple and pecans. Fold in whipped cream; place in oblong Pyrex casserole. Freeze until ready to serve. Remove from freezer 10 to 15 minutes before serving for easier cutting. Serve frozen. Unused portion may be returned to freezer.

Lynn Lankford
Taylor HS, Taylor, Texas

THANKSGIVING WALDORF SALAD

2 bananas, peeled and sliced
2 fresh pears, cored and diced
1/2 c. sliced celery
1/4 c. broken walnuts
2 tbsp. salad dressing
2 tbsp. sour cream
1 tbsp. lemon juice
1 tsp. sugar or honey
1/8 tsp. ginger

Place bananas, pears, celery and walnuts in salad bowl. Combine remaining ingredients in small bowl; mix well. Pour over fruit, tossing lightly to coat. Serve in lettuce-lined salad bowls, if desired. Yield: 4 servings.

Helen B. Boots
Lakeland Village Sch
Medical Lake, Washington

THANKSGIVING

Minted Fruit Cups
Seafood Royale
Corn Soufflé
Orange-Chocolate-Nut Truffles
Frozen Pumpkin Squares
Hot Buttered Cranberry Punch

ORANGE-CHOCOLATE-NUT TRUFFLES

3 1/2 c. semisweet chocolate bits
2 c. confectioners' sugar
2/3 c. heavy cream
4 tbsp. orange juice
2 tsp. orange peel
2 c. chopped walnuts

Melt chocolate in 4 tablespoons water in top of double boiler over hot but not boiling water, stirring frequently. Turn chocolate into medium bowl. Add sugar, cream, orange juice and orange peel; stir until combined. Beat to mix well. Place plastic wrap directly on surface; refrigerate overnight. Place a sheet of waxed paper on a damp surface; sprinkle walnuts on waxed paper. Drop chocolate by teaspoonfuls onto walnuts. Roll to cover completely. Refrigerate until ready to serve.

Susan C. Forsythe
Danville Sr HS, Danville, Pennsylvania

FROZEN PUMPKIN SQUARES

1 1-lb. can pumpkin
1 c. sugar
1 tsp. salt
1 tsp. ginger
1 tsp. cinnamon
1/2 tsp. nutmeg
1 c. chopped pecans, toasted
1/2 gal. vanilla ice cream, softened
36 vanilla wafers or gingersnaps

Combine pumpkin, sugar, salt, ginger, cinnamon and nutmeg; stir in pecans. Combine pumpkin mixture and ice cream in chilled bowl. Line bottom of 13 x 9-inch pan with half the ice cream mixture. Cover with layer of cookies; add remaining ice cream mixture. Freeze for about 5 hours or until firm. Cut into squares; serve with pecan halves or whipped cream, if desired. Yield: 18 servings.

Irene Seibert
No Poseyville Sch, Poseyville, Indiana

HOT BUTTERED CRANBERRY PUNCH

1 1-lb. can jellied cranberry
    sauce
1/3 c. (firmly packed) light brown
    sugar
1/4 tsp. cinnamon
1/4 tsp. allspice
1/8 tsp. ground cloves
1/8 tsp. nutmeg
1/8 tsp. salt
2 c. water

2 c. unsweetened pineapple juice
Butter

Crush cranberry sauce in saucepan with fork; mix in sugar, cinnamon, allspice, cloves, nutmeg and salt. Add water gradually, beating until smooth with rotary beater. Stir in pineapple juice. Heat to boiling point, then simmer for 5 minutes. Pour into punch cups; float a pat of butter in each cup. Yield: 6 cups.

Mrs Martha Jo Mims
Mississippi State College for Women
Columbus, Mississippi

SEAFOOD ROYALE

1/3 c. butter
1/3 c. flour
2 tsp. prepared mustard
1 tbsp. grated onion
1 tbsp. Worcestershire sauce
1/2 tsp. paprika
1/2 tsp. salt
Dash of red pepper
3 c. milk
1 6-oz. package Gruyere cheese,
    cubed
1/2 c. slivered ripe olives
1 6 1/2-oz. can crab meat
1 6 1/2-oz. can lobster
1 3/4 c. canned shrimp
1 med. avocado
1 tbsp. lemon juice

Preheat oven to 350 degrees. Melt butter in saucepan over low heat; blend in flour, mustard, onion, Worcestershire sauce, paprika, salt and red pepper. Add milk; cook until thickened, stirring constantly. Add cheese; stir until melted. Remove from heat; blend in olives and seafood. Place in casserole. Bake for 25 minutes or until bubbly. Peel avocado; slice and place on top of seafood mixture. Brush avocado slices with lemon juice; bake for 5 minutes longer. Yield: 6-8 servings.

Barbara Goedicke
Lindsay Thurber Comprehensive HS
Red Deer, Alberta, Canada

121

CORN SOUFFLE

1/2 c. butter, softened
1/2 c. flour
1 can cream-style corn
3 eggs, separated
Milk
1/2 tsp. salt
Soda crackers

Mix butter and flour together in souffle dish or casserole. Add corn; mix well. Stir beaten egg yolks into corn mixture; pour milk over corn mixture just to cover. Add salt; mix thoroughly. Fold in stiffly beaten egg whites; crumble crackers over top. Bake in preheated 350-degree oven for 1 hour. Yield: 4-6 servings.

Diane Scott
Lincoln East HS, Lincoln, Nebraska

MINTED FRUIT CUPS

1 can pineapple chunks, chilled
1/2 lb. Tokay grapes
1/4 c. after-dinner mints
Ginger ale or Seven-Up

Drain pineapple; halve and seed grapes. Combine pineapple and grapes in large bowl. Add mints; mix well. Place in 6 sherbet glasses; top each glass with 2 to 3 tablespoons ginger ale. Each glass may be garnished with fresh mint and a maraschino cherry.

Roby C. Reitz
Springhouse Jr HS, Allentown, Pennsylvania

HAM AND CHEESE CASSEROLE

1 c. diced cooked ham
1 c. rice, cooked
1 c. grated Cheddar cheese
1 c. medium white sauce
Salt and pepper to taste

Combine ham, rice, 1/2 cup cheese, white sauce, salt and pepper; place in greased casse-

role. Bake in preheated 350-degree oven for 20 minutes. Top with remaining cheese; serve immediately.

Mrs Lynn Wagner
Newton HS, Newton, Mississippi

NEWPORT CRAB

1 c. chopped celery
1/4 c. chopped onion
1/4 c. chopped green pepper
1 can mushrooms
Butter
3 tbsp. flour
1/2 c. milk
1/2 tsp. salt
Pepper to taste
1 c. mayonnaise
1/2 tsp. Worcestershire sauce
2 c. crab meat
3 c. cooked rice
Buttered crumbs

Saute celery, onion, green pepper and mushrooms in 1/3 cup butter; set aside. Melt 3 tablespoons butter in saucepan; stir in flour to make a smooth paste. Add milk, salt and pepper, stirring constantly; cook until thick. Stir in mayonnaise; do not boil. Add Worcestershire sauce and crab meat; mix well. Place rice in casserole. Combine vegetable mixture and crab mixture; pour over rice. Top with buttered crumbs. Bake in preheated 300-degree oven for 30 minutes or until bubbly.

June Miller
Lincoln Jr HS, Newport, Oregon

THANKSGIVING TURKEY WITH ONION-APPLE STUFFING

1   12 to 16-lb. frozen turkey
6 med. yellow onions
3 qt. day-old bread crumbs or cubes
2 tbsp. ground sage
1 tsp. poultry seasoning
2 to 3 tsp. salt
1/4 tsp. pepper
4 c. diced unpeeled red apples

Leave turkey in plastic bag. Place in heavy brown paper sack; close end. Thaw at room temperature, allowing 1 hour per pound of turkey. Remove from sack; remove plastic bag. Remove neck and giblets from cavities. Rinse turkey; wipe dry. Cook neck and giblets until done in enough water for mixing with dressing and for giblet gravy. Cook onions in enough boiling water to cover for about 15 minutes or until crisp-tender. Drain; chop fine. Add bread crumbs, sage, poultry seasoning, salt, pepper and apples; mix well. Stir in enough giblet broth to moisten crumbs; stuff into neck and body cavities of turkey. Secure skin over neck opening; fasten down legs by tying or tucking under skin band. Twist wings akimbo. Place turkey, breast side up, on rack in shallow baking pan; brush with butter, margarine or cooking oil, if desired. Insert meat thermometer into thickest part of thigh, if used; bulb should not touch bone. Roast in preheated 325-degree oven for 4 hours and 30 minutes to 5 hours and 30 minutes or to 180 to 185 degrees on thermometer. Place tent of foil loosely over turkey if browning too fast; remove occasionally to baste turkey. Remove foil last 30 minutes of roasting for browning. Turkey is done when drumstick and thigh may be moved easily. Prepare gravy as desired from giblets and remaining broth. Yield: 12-16 servings.

Photograph for this recipe on this page.

MAKE-AHEAD MASHED POTATOES FOR A CROWD

5 lb. potatoes, cooked and mashed
2 c. sour cream
2 3-oz. packages cream cheese
Salt and pepper to taste

Combine all ingredients, mixing well; place in casseroles. Refrigerate until ready to use. Bake in preheated 350-degree oven for 30 minutes. May store in refrigerator for a week.

Elaine Engan
Sauk Rapids Jr HS, Sauk Rapids, Minnesota

RICH TURKEY-VEGETABLE AND NOODLE SOUP

Bones and skin of 1 turkey
1 chicken bouillon cube
2 tsp. salt
12 peppercorns
4 whole cloves
1 stalk celery, chopped
1 carrot, chopped
1/2 c. chopped onion
1 c. cubed potatoes
1 c. sliced carrots
1 c. sliced celery
1   10-oz. package frozen baby lima
*   beans*
1 c. uncooked noodles
2 c. cut-up turkey

Place bones and skin in large kettle; barely cover with cold water. Add bouillon cube, 1 teaspoon salt, peppercorns, cloves, chopped celery, chopped carrot and 1/4 cup onion; bring to a boil. Reduce heat; cover. Simmer for 2 to 3 hours, adding water, as needed, to keep ingredients covered. Strain broth; meas-ure 2 quarts. Pour into large saucepan; bring to a boil. Add remaining onion and salt, veg-etables and noodles; simmer for 15 minutes or until vegetables are tender. Add turkey; heat through. Yield: 6 servings.

Photograph for this recipe on this page.

CHICKEN AND RICE

Margarine
2 1/2 c. water
1 c. rice
1 can sliced or whole mushrooms,
*   drained (opt.)*
1 pkg. dry onion soup mix
1 chicken, disjointed or 4 chicken
*   breasts*

Grease baking dish with small amount of margarine. Add water, rice and mushrooms. Sprinkle onion soup on top; dot with mar-garine. Arrange chicken pieces on top; cover. Bake in preheated 350-degree oven for 1 hour and 30 minutes.

Denise Kalmus
Middletown HS, Middletown, Ohio

124

SPINACH-BROCCOLI BUFFET CASSEROLE

2   10-oz. packages frozen chopped
     spinach
2   10-oz. packages frozen chopped
     broccoli
2 c. sour cream
1 pkg. dry onion soup mix
Salt to taste
1/2 c. grated Cheddar cheese

Cook spinach and broccoli according to package directions; drain well. Combine sour cream and soup mix; stir into spinach and broccoli. Season with salt. Place in casserole. Bake, covered, in preheated 325-degree oven for 40 minutes. Remove from oven; top with cheese.

Elaine Hillyer
Chinook Jr HS, Bellevue, Washington

ORANGE SWEET POTATOES

1 can sweet potatoes, sliced
1 unpeeled orange, cut in 1/4-in.
     slices
2/3 c. sugar
1 tbsp. cornstarch
1/4 tsp. salt
1 c. orange juice
2 tbsp. butter

Arrange sweet potato slices and orange slices in casserole. Combine remaining ingredients in saucepan; simmer, stirring constantly, until thickened. Pour over potatoes; cover. Bake in preheated 400-degree oven for 25 minutes. Uncover; bake for 20 minutes longer.

Mrs Frances A. Feltham
Stroudsburg HS, Stroudsburg, Pennsylvania

SWEET POTATO FLUFF

2 c. cooked sweet potatoes
1/2 c. melted margarine
1 1/4 c. sugar
3 eggs

1 sm. can evaporated milk
Juice and rind of 1 orange
1 sm. can Angel Flake coconut
1 1/2 c. miniature marshmallows
1/2 c. chopped nuts

Beat potatoes, margarine, sugar, eggs, milk, orange juice and rind with electric mixer until fluffy. Add remaining ingredients; mix well. Pour into greased baking dish. Bake in preheated 350-degree oven for 45 minutes. Yield: 8-10 servings.

Louise O. Gurley
Sun Valley HS, Monroe, North Carolina

PRUNE SPICE CAKE

1 1/2 c. sugar
2 c. flour
1 tsp. soda
1 tsp. cinnamon
1/2 tsp. nutmeg
1/2 tsp. salt
3 eggs
2 sm. jars baby food prunes
1 c. salad oil
1 c. chopped nuts
Glaze

Sift sugar, flour, soda, cinnamon, nutmeg and salt together. Add eggs, prunes and oil; mix well. Stir in nuts; pour into well-greased tube or bundt pan. Bake in preheated 300-degree oven for 50 to 60 minutes or until cake tests done. Let cool for 10 minutes; remove from pan. Spoon hot Glaze over hot cake.

Glaze

1/4 c. margarine
1/2 c. sugar
1/4 c. buttermilk
1/8 tsp. soda
1/8 tsp. vanilla

Combine all ingredients in small saucepan. Bring to a boil; boil for 2 minutes.

Jodie R. Cannon
R. O. Gibson Jr HS, Las Vegas, Nevada

DELECTABLE THANKSGIVING AMBROSIA

2 Florida grapefruit
3 Florida oranges
2 Florida tangerines
1/3 to 1/2 c. sugar
1/2 c. shredded coconut

Cut slice from top of grapefruit; cut off peel from grapefruit in strips from top to bottom, cutting deep enough to remove white membrane. Cut off slice from bottom of grapefruit. Go over grapefruit again, removing any white membrane. Cut along side of each dividing membrane from outside to middle of core; remove sections over bowl to retain juice. Remove seeds. Cut off peel from orange round and round in spiral fashion; remove sections as for grapefruit. Peel tangerines; separate into sections. Cut sections in half; remove seeds. Place half the fruits and all the juices in serving dish; sprinkle with half the sugar and coconut. Repeat layers; chill for at least 1 hour before serving. Yield: 8 servings.

Photograph for this recipe on page 112.

ALMOND-PUMPKIN CUSTARD

8 eggs
3/4 c. sugar
1 1-lb. can pumpkin
2 c. half and half
1 tsp. almond extract
1 tsp. salt
1/2 tsp. cinnamon
1/2 tsp. nutmeg
1/2 tsp. allspice
1 tbsp. finely chopped candied
*   ginger (opt.)*
1/2 c. sliced almonds
1/4 c. (packed) light brown sugar

Beat eggs with sugar until light and fluffy. Blend in pumpkin, half and half, almond extract, salt, spices and ginger. Reserve 1 tablespoon almonds; mix in remaining almonds. Sprinkle bottom of lightly greased 1 1/2-quart ring mold with brown sugar. Turn pumpkin mixture into mold; place in pan of hot water. Bake in preheated 350-degree oven for about 55 minutes or until knife inserted in center comes out clean. Remove from oven; let cool for about 15 minutes. Invert onto serving dish. Garnish with reserved almonds. May serve warm or chilled; top with ginger-flavored whipped cream, if desired. One and 1/2 teaspoons spice mix may be substituted for the cinnamon, nutmeg and allspice. Custard may be baked in individual molds. Sprinkle 1/2 tablespoon brown sugar in each of 8 lightly greased 6-ounce custard cups; reduce baking time to 45 minutes. Yield: 8 servings.

Mrs Karen Williams
Elk River Jr HS, Elk River, Minnesota

PUMPKIN-FROSTED DREAM CAKE

1 pkg. spice cake mix
3 env. Dream Whip
4 eggs
1 pkg. butterscotch instant pudding
*   mix*
1 1/2 c. cold milk
1 c. canned pumpkin
Chopped nuts

Combine cake mix, 1 envelope dry Dream Whip, eggs and 1 cup cold water in large mixer bowl; beat until ingredients are moistened. Beat at medium speed for 4 minutes; pour into 2 greased and floured 9-inch layer pans. Bake in preheated 350-degree oven for 30 minutes or until cake tests done. Let cool for 15 minutes; turn out on wire racks to cool completely. Combine 1 envelope dry Dream Whip, pudding mix and milk in deep mixing bowl; beat slowly until well blended. Increase speed; beat for about 8 minutes or until soft peaks form. Fold in pumpkin carefully. Split cake layers; frost each layer with fluffy pumpkin frosting. Stack layers on serving plate. Prepare remaining envelope of

Dream Whip according to package directions; frost side of cake. Sprinkle nuts over top.

Myrtle Knutson
Fairview Jr HS, St Paul, Minnesota

DELICIOUS DATE-NUT CAKE

2 1/2 c. chopped dates
2 tsp. soda
4 tbsp. butter
2 1/2 c. sugar
2 c. sifted flour
2 eggs, beaten
2 tsp. vanilla
1/2 tsp. salt
1 c. chopped nuts

Combine 2 cups dates, 2 cups hot water, soda and butter; let stand for 5 minutes. Combine 2 cups sugar, flour, eggs, vanilla, salt and nuts; mix well. Add to date mixture; pour into greased 8 x 12-inch pan. Bake in preheated 350-degree oven for 30 minutes. Remove from oven; let cool. Combine remaining 1/2 cup dates, 1/2 cup water and 1/2 cup sugar in saucepan; cook until thick, stirring constantly. Spread warm icing on warm cake. Serve topped with whipped cream.

Catherine A. Carter
State Div of Voc and Tech Ed
Springfield, Illinois

PUMPKIN CHIFFON CAKE

2 c. cake flour
1 1/2 c. sugar
3 tsp. baking powder
1 tsp. salt
1 tsp. cinnamon
1/2 tsp. cloves
1/2 tsp. nutmeg
1/2 c. salad oil
8 eggs, separated
1/2 c. water

3/4 c. pumpkin
1/2 tsp. cream of tartar

Sift flour, sugar, baking powder, salt, cinnamon, cloves and nutmeg into mixing bowl. Make a well in center; add salad oil, egg yolks, water and pumpkin; beat until very smooth. Set aside. Beat egg whites until foamy; add cream of tartar. Beat until stiff peaks form. Pour batter slowly into egg whites, folding in gently. Pour batter into ungreased 10-inch tube pan. Bake in preheated 325-degree oven for 55 minutes. Increase oven temperature to 350 degrees; bake for 10 minutes longer.

Laura M. Chaney
Fernando Rivera Sch, Daly City, California

PUMPKIN BREAD WITH TOPPING

3 c. sugar
1 c. oil
4 eggs
2 c. pumpkin
3 1/2 c. flour
2 tsp. soda
1 1/2 tsp. salt
1 tsp. cinnamon
1 tsp. nutmeg
1 c. nuts (opt.)
1 pkg. Dream Whip
1 c. drained crushed pineapple

Beat sugar, oil, eggs, 2/3 cup water and pumpkin together. Sift dry ingredients together; beat into egg mixture. Stir in nuts. Pour into 2 small well-greased and floured loaf pans. Bake in preheated 350-degree oven for 1 hour. Let cool; turn out of pans. Prepare Dream Whip according to package directions; stir in pineapple. Slice bread; serve with a dollop of pineapple topping. Batter may be poured into 4 well-greased and floured 1-pound coffee cans, filling 1/2 full.

Mrs Patsy Evans
Bridge City HS, Bridge City, Texas

DUTCH OLIEBOLLENS

Sugar
2 pkg. yeast
1 tbsp. salt
7 1/2 c. flour
1 tbsp. baking powder
2 c. milk
1/2 c. shortening
2 eggs
1/2 tbsp. lemon extract
1 c. raisins
1 c. chopped apples

Mix 1/2 cup sugar, yeast, salt, 2 1/2 cups flour and baking powder together in large bowl. Heat milk and shortening to 120 to 130 degrees. Pour hot milk mixture into flour mixture; beat with electric mixer at medium speed for 2 minutes. Add eggs, lemon extract and 1/2 cup flour; mix at medium speed for 2 minutes. Add raisins and apples; mix well. Add remaining flour a small amount at a time, mixing well after each addition. Knead for 5 to 10 minutes or until dough is elastic. Cover; let rise until doubled in bulk. Punch down; shape into small balls. Cover; let rise until doubled in bulk. Fry in deep fat at 335 degrees until golden brown. Roll in sugar. Yield: 4 1/2-5 dozen.

Linda Zylstra
Willapa Valley HS, Menlo, Washington

PEACH-NOODLE KUGEL WITH STREUSEL TOPPING

1 8-oz. package wide noodles
3 tbsp. butter
Sugar
1/2 tsp. salt
3 eggs, beaten
2 c. milk
1 c. seedless raisins
1 16-oz. can peaches
3 tbsp. melted margarine
1/4 c. dry bread crumbs
1/4 c. rolled oats

Cook noodles according to package directions; drain well. Place in large bowl; toss with butter. Combine 1/2 cup sugar, salt, eggs and milk in bowl; mix well. Add raisins; combine with noodles. Pour into greased 12 x 8-inch casserole; arrange peaches on top. Combine 3 tablespoons sugar and remaining ingredients for topping; sprinkle over noodle mixture. Bake in preheated 350-degree oven for 35 to 40 minutes. Let stand for 10 to 15 minutes before cutting to serve.

Mrs Earl T. Charlesworth
North East HS, Pasadena, Maryland

OLD-FASHIONED PECAN PIE

3 eggs
2 tbsp. melted butter
3 tbsp. flour
1/4 tsp. vanilla
1/8 tsp. salt
1/2 c. sugar
1 1/2 c. syrup
2/3 c. chopped pecans
1 unbaked pie shell

Beat eggs; blend in butter, flour, vanilla, salt, sugar and syrup. Add pecans; pour into pie shell. Bake in preheated 425-degree oven for 10 minutes. Reduce oven temperature to 325 degrees; bake 40 to 45 minutes longer.

Barbara J. Vargo
Holton HS, Holton, Michigan

LIGHT PUMPKIN PIE DELUXE

1 recipe 3-crust pie pastry
3 c. pumpkin
1 c. (firmly packed) light brown
*   sugar*
1 c. sugar
1/2 tsp. nutmeg
1/2 tsp. mace
1/2 tsp. ginger
1/2 tsp. cinnamon

1/2 tsp. salt
3 eggs, slightly beaten
1 c. whipping cream, whipped

Roll out pastry on floured board; place in three 9-inch pie pans. Flute edges; prick shells generously. Bake in preheated 400-degree oven for only 5 minutes or until lightly browned. Remove from oven; reduce oven temperature to 350 degrees. Combine pumpkin, sugars, spices and salt. Mix eggs and whipped cream together; add to pumpkin mixture, blending until smooth. Pour filling into partially baked hot pastry shells. Sprinkle tops lightly with nutmeg, if desired. Bake until a knife inserted in center comes out clean.

Mrs Mildred I. Green
Central Cabarrus HS, Concord, North Carolina

APPLE PAN PIE

Never-Fail Pastry
5 lb. apples, peeled and sliced
Sugar
3/4 c. brown sugar
1/4 tsp. salt
1/2 tsp. nutmeg
1 tsp. cinnamon
1/4 c. butter
Milk
1 c. confectioners' sugar

Roll out half the pastry on a floured board; fit into 15 1/2 x 10 1/2 x 1-inch jelly roll pan. Arrange half the apples on the pastry. Combine 3/4 cup sugar, brown sugar, salt, nutmeg and cinnamon, mixing well; sprinkle half the mixture over apples. Top with remaining apples; sprinkle with remaining sugar mixture. Dot with butter. Roll out remaining pastry; place over top of pan. Seal edges; cut vents. Brush pastry with milk; sprinkle with sugar. Bake in preheated 400-degree oven for 50 minutes. Combine confectioners' sugar with 2 tablespoons milk; drizzle over top of pie. Yield: 24 servings.

Never-Fail Pastry

5 c. sifted flour
4 tbsp. sugar
1/2 tsp. salt
1/2 tsp. baking powder
1 1/2 c. lard
2 egg yolks

Combine flour, sugar, salt and baking powder in mixing bowl; cut in lard. Place egg yolks in measuring cup; beat with fork to mix well. Add enough water to measure 1 scant cup. Sprinkle over flour mixture; toss with fork to make a soft dough.

Marilyn Wendel
Brookville HS, Brookville, Indiana

PECAN-PUMPKIN PIE

3 eggs, slightly beaten
1/2 c. sugar
Brown sugar
2 tbsp. flour
1/2 tsp. salt
1 tsp. cinnamon
1/2 tsp. nutmeg
1/2 tsp. allspice
1 1/2 c. pumpkin
1 1/2 c. half and half, heated
1 unbaked 9-in. pie shell
1 tbsp. butter or margarine
3/4 c. pecan halves

Combine eggs, sugar, 1/2 cup firmly packed brown sugar, flour, salt, cinnamon, nutmeg and allspice. Add pumpkin; mix well. Add half and half gradually; mix well. Turn into pie shell. Bake in preheated 450-degree oven for 10 minutes. Reduce oven temperature to 350 degrees; bake for 20 minutes longer. Melt butter; stir in 2 tablespoons brown sugar. Add pecan halves; stir to coat thoroughly. Remove pie from oven; spoon pecan mixture quickly over top. Bake for 20 to 30 minutes longer or until knife inserted in center comes out clean.

Sister Mary Benedict
Mt St Benedict Sch, Crookston, Minnesota

FRESH CRANBERRY DELIGHT

*1/4 lb. graham crackers, finely
    crushed
1/4 c. melted butter or margarine
Sugar
1 can sweetened condensed milk
Lemon juice
1 tsp. vanilla
1/2 lb. cranberries, ground
1 orange, peeled and diced
1 banana, coarsely chopped
Whipped cream or dessert topping*

Preheat oven to 350 degrees. Combine graham cracker crumbs, butter and 1/4 cup sugar. Line pie plate or 8-inch square baking dish with crumb mixture. Bake for 10 minutes; let cool. Combine milk with 2 tablespoons lemon juice and vanilla; spread over graham cracker crust. Combine cranberries with orange, banana, 2 tablespoons lemon juice and 1/3 cup sugar. Spread evenly over milk mixture; cover with whipped cream. Chill until ready to serve. May be frozen.

*Wilma Jean Good
Trimble Technical HS, Fort Worth, Texas*

FLAMING PLUM PUDDING CAKE

*2 c. sugar
1 c. oil
3 eggs
2 c. self-rising flour
1 tsp. nutmeg
1 tsp. cinnamon
1 tsp. allspice
1 jar prune jr. baby food
1/2 c. chopped nuts
1 lg. sugar cube
Lemon extract*

Mix sugar and oil. Add eggs; beat well. Sift flour and spices together; stir into oil mixture. Add prunes; mix well. Add nuts; mix. Pour into greased and floured tube or bundt pan. Bake in preheated 300-degree oven for 1 hour. Cool; remove from pan. Place piece of foil in center of cake. Soak sugar cube in lemon extract; place in foil. Ignite. Serve hard sauce with cake, if desired.

*Mrs Gladys Herring
Corsicana HS, Corsicana, Texas*

FAVORITE CRANBERRY PUDDING

*1/2 c. hot water
1/2 c. molasses
2 tsp. soda
1 1/3 c. flour
2 c. cranberries, halved
1 c. sugar
1/2 c. butter
1/2 c. cream
1 tsp. vanilla*

Combine hot water and molasses; stir in soda. Add flour; beat well. Stir in cranberries; place in greased mold. Steam for 1 hour and 15 minutes. Combine remaining ingredients in double boiler. Cook until thickened, stirring constantly. Serve hot over hot pudding.

*Mary Wyczawski
New Ulm Jr HS, New Ulm, Minnesota*

BUTTER CRUNCH TOFFEE

*1 c. butter or margarine
1 c. sugar
1 tbsp. water
1 tbsp. light corn syrup
3/4 c. broken nuts
4 sq. semisweet chocolate, melted
1 1/2 c. finely chopped nuts*

Melt butter over low heat in heavy 2-quart saucepan. Remove from heat; add sugar. Stir until well blended. Return to low heat; stir until mixture reaches a full rolling boil. Add water and corn syrup; mix well. Cook over low heat, stirring constantly, to 290 degrees or soft-crack stage. Remove from heat; stir in 3/4 cup nuts immediately. Pour into lightly buttered 13 x 9 x 2-inch pan; spread out with spatula quickly. Let cool; remove from pan. Place on waxed paper; spread top with melted chocolate. Sprinkle with finely chopped nuts. Let stand until chocolate is set, then break into pieces. Yield: 1 1/4 pounds.

Donna Marie Gigurich
Canton Sr HS, Canton, Illinois

DATE ROLL CANDY

2 c. sugar
1/2 c. milk
2 tbsp. butter
1 c. chopped dates
1 tsp. vanilla
1/2 c. chopped nuts
Confectioners' sugar

Boil sugar, milk and butter together in saucepan to 236 degrees on candy thermometer or to soft-ball stage. Add dates; cook for 3 minutes longer. Remove from heat. Add vanilla and nuts; let cool to 110 degrees or until lukewarm. Beat until creamy. Turn out of pan onto waxed paper dusted lightly with confectioners' sugar; shape into long strip, using sugared hands. Wrap in waxed paper; place in refrigerator until chilled. Cut into slices. This candy may also be poured into a pan and cut into squares.

Mrs Lola Spangler
Richland Center HS
Richland Center, Wisconsin

QUICK CRANBERRY SHERBET

1 pkg. cranberry-orange gelatin
1 c. sugar
1 c. cooked cranberries, pureed
2 c. buttermilk
Pinch of salt

Dissolve gelatin in 1 cup hot water; stir in remaining ingredients. Place in freezer con-tainer; freeze according to manufacturer's instructions. May be frozen in refrigerator freezer, processed in blender and returned to freezer before serving. Yield: 1 1/2 quarts.

Mrs Larry L. Clark
Cowley Co. Community College
Arkansas City, Kansas

ROMMERGRAT

1/2 c. butter
3/4 c. flour
4 c. milk
1/4 c. (about) sugar
1/2 tsp. salt

Melt butter in saucepan; remove 2 table-spoons butter and keep warm. Stir in flour to make a smooth paste. Stir in half the milk; bring to a boil. Heat remaining milk; add to flour mixture, stirring constantly. Stir in sugar and salt. Cook and stir until thick-ened and smooth. Pour into serving bowl; keep warm. Pour on reserved melted butter. May be served with sugar, cinnamon, brown sugar and raisins, if desired.

Beth Tveiten
Gonvick HS, Gonvick, Minnesota

SPICY PERCOLATOR PUNCH

2 c. cranberry juice
2 1/2 c. pineapple juice
1/2 c. water
1/3 c. (packed) brown sugar
3 2-in. sticks cinnamon
1 1/2 tsp. whole cloves
1/2 tsp. whole allspice

Place cranberry juice, pineapple juice, water and brown sugar in percolator. Place cinna-mon, cloves and allspice in basket; perk as for coffee.

Mrs Eileen Beauregard
Sequoyah HS, Doraville, Georgia

131

BLACK MAGIC CAKE

2 sq. unsweetened chocolate
1/4 c. water
Sugar
6 lg. eggs, separated
1/2 tsp. salt
1/2 tsp. cream of tartar
1/2 c. Florida orange juice
1 1/2 c. sifted cake flour
1 tbsp. grated orange rind
1/2 tsp. soda
Orange Butter Frosting
Shadow Glaze

Combine chocolate with water and 2 table-spoons sugar in top of double boiler. Place over simmering water; stir occasionally until melted and smooth. Remove from water; cool. Beat egg whites with salt and cream of tartar in large bowl with electric mixer until soft peaks form. Beat in 1/2 cup sugar gradually; continue to beat until stiff peaks form. Beat egg yolks in another mixing bowl, using the same beaters, until light and lemon colored. Beat in 1 cup sugar gradually; continue beating until thick enough to form a ribbon when beaters are raised. Blend in orange juice, at low speed or by hand, alternately with flour. Pour over egg whites; fold in gently but thoroughly. Divide into 2 equal portions. Fold orange rind into half the batter. Stir soda into melted chocolate; fold into remaining batter. Place alternate spoonfuls of orange and chocolate batter in ungreased 10-inch tube pan. Run knife through batter to marble; do not mix. Bake in preheated 325-degree oven for 1 hour or until cake springs back when touched lightly with finger; invert to cool. Turn cake out of pan; frost with Orange Butter Frosting. Drizzle Shadow Glaze along edge of cake. Yield: 12-16 servings.

Orange Butter Frosting

1/2 c. soft butter or margarine
1 egg
1 tsp. grated orange rind
6 c. sifted confectioners' sugar
1/4 c. Florida orange juice

Cream butter. Beat in egg and orange rind; beat in confectioners' sugar alternately with orange juice. Frosting should be soft because cake is very delicate.

Shadow Glaze

1/4 c. light corn syrup
1/2 c. semisweet chocolate pieces
1 tbsp. water

Combine all ingredients in small saucepan; stir over low heat until melted and smooth. Cool slightly.

Photograph for this recipe on page 133.

SORCERER'S PUNCH

3 6-oz. cans frozen Florida orange
    juice concentrate
1/2 c. sugar
1/2 c. water
12 whole cloves
2 2-in. pieces of stick cinnamon
1 qt. sweet cider

Thaw orange juice concentrate; prepare according to can directions. Combine sugar, water and spices in saucepan. Simmer for 10 minutes; strain. Return syrup to saucepan. Add orange juice and cider; heat through. Yield: Twenty-eight 1/2-cup servings.

Photograph for this recipe on page 133.

YULE LOG

1 tsp. vanilla extract
1/2 tsp. almond extract
8 drops of green food coloring
4 drops of yellow food coloring
1   4 1/2-oz. container Cool Whip,
    thawed
Chocolate Sponge Roll
Chocolate Glaze
2 tbsp. (about) chopped almonds or
    pistachio nuts
Candied cherries, halved or quartered

Blend vanilla, almond extract and food colorings into Cool Whip. Fill Chocolate Sponge Roll with Cool Whip mixture. Roll up again, leaving edge of cake underneath; place on serving platter. Spread Chocolate Glaze over top and sides of cake roll; sprinkle with almonds. Decorate with cherry pieces. Refrigerate until ready to serve.

Chocolate Sponge Roll

3/4 c. sifted Swans Down cake flour
1/2 tsp. baking powder
1/2 tsp. salt
5 eggs, at room temperature
Sugar
2 or 2 1/2 sq. Baker's unsweetened
    chocolate
1/4 c. cold water
1/4 tsp. soda
Confectioners' sugar

Sift flour with baking powder and salt. Beat eggs in large bowl with electric mixer at high speed or with rotary beater, adding 3/4 cup sugar gradually and beating until mixture becomes fluffy, thick and light colored. Fold in flour mixture gradually. Melt chocolate in saucepan over very low heat; add cold water, 2 tablespoons sugar and soda immediately, stirring until thick and smooth. Blend quickly into batter. Grease bottom and sides of 15 x 10-inch jelly roll pan. Line bottom with waxed paper; grease waxed paper. Pour batter into prepared pan. Bake in preheated 350-degree oven for 18 to 20 minutes or until cake tester inserted into center comes out clean. Turn cake out onto cloth which has been sprinkled lightly with confectioners' sugar. Remove paper quickly; trim off crisp edges of cake. Roll up, rolling cloth up in cake, starting with short side. Place on rack to cool. Unroll; remove cloth.

Chocolate Glaze

1 sq. Baker's unsweetened chocolate
1 tbsp. butter
3/4 c. unsifted confectioners' sugar
Dash of salt
2 tbsp. (about) hot milk

Melt chocolate with butter in saucepan over low heat; remove from heat. Add sugar and salt; add milk, small amount at a time, until mixture is of glaze consistency. Blend well. Spread over cake while warm; spread with spatula. Yield: 1/2 cup.

Photograph for this recipe on page 134.

◊ Recipe on page 159.

CHRISTMAS

The jolliest time of the year
All waiting for Santa's reindeer
He'll never get lost
No matter the cost
On Christmas, St. Nick will be here

Few times of the year can compare with this season of thrill and excitement. Young and old alike are filled with anticipation—waiting impatiently for friends, relatives and SANTA.

To make your Christmas more enjoyable, be sure to prepare as many of these delicious recipes as far in advance as possible. Whether your party is to be a brunch, a breakfast, a dinner or just snacks for Old St. Nick, you want to be free to enjoy all the seasonal delights with your family.

Your house will already be gaily decorated and trimmed, so why not fix a special centerpiece for the table? . . . A bright red tablecloth with a colorful grouping of large red and white candles surrounded by holly . . . add several candy canes and silver bells and you have a delightful arrangement.

MENU
Traditional
Christmas Dinner

Syllabub
Polish Christmas Mushroom Soup
Christmas Tree Salads
Goose with Fruit Stuffing
Holiday Peas
Stuffed Artichokes Supreme
Scalloped Corn and Oysters
Christmas Pickles
Christmas Dinner Rolls
Christmas Suet Pudding
White Christmas Fruitcake
Coffee or Tea

SYLLABUB

1 qt. heavy cream
1 c. milk
1 c. sugar
1 tsp. vanilla
1/2 c. grape juice

Have all ingredients cold. Place ingredients in large bowl; beat with egg beater until frothy. Serve immediately. One-fourth cup orange juice and 1/4 cup sherry may be used instead of grape juice. Yield: About 20 servings.

Marion P. Elkin
East Duplin HS, Beulaville, North Carolina

POLISH CHRISTMAS MUSHROOM SOUP

1 oz. dried Polish mushrooms
1 tbsp. salt
1 c. evaporated milk
Boiled potatoes

Place mushrooms in bowl; cover with water. Soak overnight. Remove mushrooms with slotted spoon; cut very large mushrooms into smaller pieces. Place mushrooms in large saucepan. Strain liquid from soaked mushrooms through cheesecloth to remove sediment; pour into saucepan with mushrooms. Add 2 quarts cold water; bring to a boil. Add salt; reduce heat. Simmer for 4 to 5 hours or until mushrooms are tender, adding water to maintain 2-quart capacity. Add more salt, if needed. Add evaporated milk. Bring to boiling point; remove from heat. Place serving of potatoes in each soup bowl; ladle soup over potatoes in bowls. Yield: 8 servings.

Eleanora R. Buras
Salem HS, Salem, Massachusetts

CHRISTMAS PICKLES

1   1-qt. jar dill pickles
1 1/4 c. sugar
2 tbsp. dried onion flakes
1 tsp. celery seed
3 tbsp. vinegar

Drain pickles; discard liquid. Slice each pickle lengthwise into quarters. Repack pickle strips in jar, adding remaining ingredients alternately with pickles. Cover; let stand at room temperature for 1 day. Refrigerate; shake jar frequently to dissolve sugar. Jar will be about 2/3 full of liquid and pickle strips will be crisp.

Nancy Stearley
Bloomfield HS, Bloomfield, Indiana

GOOSE WITH FRUIT STUFFING

2 c. pitted prunes
Sherry
1   12-lb. goose
Salt and pepper to taste
2 c. white raisins
2 fresh pears
2 pkg. frozen peaches, thawed
2 c. dried apple rings, cut in half
2 c. dried apricots
1 c. dry or toasted bread crumbs
1/2 tsp. ginger
1/2 tsp. cinnamon
8 whole cloves
1/4 tsp. nutmeg
3/4 c. apricot brandy
Green or red grapes

Place prunes in bowl; add enough sherry to cover. Soak overnight. Sprinkle goose inside and out with salt and pepper. Rinse raisins in hot water. Peel pears; remove cores. Dice pears. Add fruits to prunes and sherry; stir in bread crumbs and spices. Stuff into cavity of goose; truss. Place goose, breast side up, in roasting pan. Bake in preheated 325-degree oven for 4 hours, draining off fat occasionally. Bake for 45 minutes longer, basting goose with brandy frequently. Place grapes in pan; bake for 15 minutes longer, basting goose and grapes with brandy frequently. Place goose on platter; place grapes around goose. Serve with rice. Yield: 8 servings.

Mary Alice Bird
Southwestern HS, Detroit, Michigan

CHRISTMAS TREE SALADS

1 env. unflavored gelatin
1/4 c. cold water
1 1-lb. can jellied cranberry
*   sauce*
1 c. finely shredded cabbage
1/4 c. diced celery
1/2 c. chopped walnuts

Place gelatin in heatproof custard cup. Add cold water; let stand for 2 minutes. Place cup in pan of boiling water; heat until gelatin is dissolved. Mash cranberry sauce with fork; stir in gelatin. Stir in cabbage, celery and walnuts. Spoon into cone-shaped paper cups supported in small glasses; chill until firm. Place on lettuce; peel off paper cups. Garnish with softened cream cheese. Yield: 4-6 servings.

Mrs Betty Rassette
Central HS, Salina, Kansas

STUFFED ARTICHOKES SUPREME

5 boxes frozen artichoke hearts
3 sprigs of parsley, minced
2 cloves of garlic, minced
1 c. minced yellow celery leaves
2 pkg. crackers, crushed
3 c. grated Romano cheese
1 tsp. salt
Dash of pepper
3 tbsp. Worcestershire sauce
2 or 3 dashes of hot sauce
2 tsp. sweet basil
1 tsp. allspice
2 c. olive oil
1 egg

Thaw artichoke hearts; drain. Mix parsley, garlic and celery leaves; reserve small amount for topping. Reserve some of the cracker crumbs for topping. Place grated cheese in large bowl; add remaining parsley mixture. Mix well. Add remaining cracker crumbs, salt, pepper, Worcestershire sauce, hot sauce, basil and allspice. Add olive oil, small amount at a time, to make thick, moist stuf-

fing. Add egg; mix well. Mound over artichoke hearts. Pour 1/4 cup water into oblong pan; place artichokes in pan. Top with reserved parsley mixture and cracker crumbs. Cover with foil. Bake in preheated 350-degree oven for 45 minutes. Remove foil; bake until lightly browned. Serve warm or cold; may be frozen.

Mrs Dyane Pearce
Tarkington HS, Cleveland, Texas

HOLIDAY PEAS

1 4-oz. can mushroom stems and
*   pieces*
1 10-oz. package frozen green peas
1 sm. onion, chopped
1/2 c. chopped celery
3 tbsp. butter
1 2-oz. jar pimentos, drained and
*   chopped*
1/2 tsp. salt
1/8 tsp. pepper

Drain mushrooms, reserving liquid. Cook peas according to package directions, substituting reserved liquid for equal amount of water; drain. Cook onion and celery in butter in saucepan until soft. Add mushrooms and pimentos; heat thoroughly. Add peas and seasonings; heat through.

Lettie Ann Boggs
Orrville Sr HS, Orrville, Ohio

SCALLOPED CORN AND OYSTERS

1 1-lb. can cream-style corn
1 can oyster stew
1 1/2 c. cracker crumbs
1 c. milk
1/4 c. chopped celery
1 egg, slightly beaten
1 tbsp. chopped pimento
2 tbsp. melted butter

Combine corn, oyster stew, 1 cup cracker crumbs, milk, celery, egg and pimento; pour into greased casserole. Combine butter and remaining cracker crumbs; sprinkle over corn mixture. Bake in preheated 350-degree oven for 45 minutes.

Mrs Marian Baker
Sycamore HS, Sycamore, Illinois

CHRISTMAS DINNER ROLLS

2 pkg. yeast
1 c. warm water
2 c. hot water
3/4 c. oil
1/4 c. honey
2 tsp. sea salt
2 eggs, beaten
6 c. unsifted whole wheat flour

Dissolve yeast in warm water in large bowl. Add remaining ingredients except flour; mix well. Add flour gradually; mixture will be sticky, but do not knead. Chill overnight. Shape into rolls; place in greased pan. Bake in preheated 425-degree oven for about 10 minutes.

Susan McAlexander
Abernathy HS, Abernathy, Texas

CHRISTMAS SUET PUDDING

1 c. ground suet
2 c. bread crumbs
1 c. raisins
1/2 c. chopped nuts
1 c. sugar
1/2 c. milk
1 egg, beaten
1/2 c. soda
1 tsp. cinnamon
1/2 tsp. cloves
1/2 tsp. allspice
1/2 tsp. salt
Brandy Sauce

Place all ingredients in bowl; mix well. Pour into greased pudding mold; cover loosely with aluminum foil. Steam on rack in large pan over boiling water for 2 hours, adding boiling water, as needed, to fill to rack. Serve with Brandy Sauce or whipped cream.

Brandy Sauce

1/2 c. sugar
1/8 tsp. salt
2 tbsp. cornstarch
1/2 c. boiling water
2 tbsp. butter
3 tbsp. brandy

Mix sugar, salt and cornstarch in saucepan; stir in water gradually. Cook until thick, stirring constantly; remove from heat. Stir in butter and brandy; serve warm. May substitute rum or lemon flavoring for brandy.

Barbara J. Vargo
Holton HS, Holton, Michigan

WHITE CHRISTMAS FRUITCAKE

2 c. butter
2 c. sugar
6 eggs, beaten
1 tbsp. vanilla
4 c. flour
1 lb. dates, chopped
1 lb. white raisins
1/2 c. chopped candied pineapple
1 c. chopped candied cherries
2 c. chopped nuts
1/2 tsp. salt

Cream butter and sugar thoroughly; stir in eggs and vanilla. Mix 1 cup flour with fruits and nuts. Mix remaining flour and salt; stir into butter mixture. Stir in fruit mixture. Grease tube pan; place 2 or 3 layers waxed paper on bottom and side. Place batter in tube pan. Pour 2 cups water into shallow pan; place on bottom shelf of oven beneath cake pan. Bake cake in preheated 250-degree oven for 2 hours and 30 minutes to 3 hours or until cake tests done.

Peggy O. Munter
Moore HS, Moore, Oklahoma

CHILI CHEESE BALL

2 lb. Velveeta cheese
2 8-oz. packages cream cheese
1 c. chopped nuts
1/2 tsp. garlic powder
Dash of salt
Chili powder

Place Velveeta cheese and cream cheese in large bowl; let come to room temperature. Mix cheeses well. Add nuts, garlic powder and salt; mix well. Shape into ball; roll in chili powder. Wrap in foil; chill until firm.

Mary Ella Porter
Como-Pickton HS, Como, Texas

HOLIDAY PINEAPPLE-CHEESE BALL

2 8-oz. packages cream cheese
2 tbsp. chopped green pepper
2 tbsp. chopped onion
1/4 c. drained crushed pineapple
2 tsp. seasoned salt
2 c. chopped pecans

Soften cream cheese. Add green pepper, onion, pineapple, seasoned salt and 1 cup pecans; mix well. Shape into ball and roll in remaining pecans. Chill for several hours; serve with crackers or fresh vegetables.

Mrs Donnabelle Pech
Lincoln Comm HS, Lincoln, Illinois

SALMON YULE LOG

1 1-lb. can salmon
1 8-oz. package cream cheese,
    softened
1 tbsp. lemon juice
2 tsp. grated onion
1 tsp. horseradish
1 tsp. liquid smoke
1/4 tsp. salt
1/2 c. chopped pecans

Drain and flake salmon. Add cheese, lemon juice, onion, horseradish, liquid smoke and salt; combine well. Chill for several hours or overnight. Shape into log; chill for 2 to 3 hours. Sprinkle pecans on waxed paper; roll log in pecans. Chill until ready to serve; serve with crackers. Yield: 2 cups.

Mrs Patsy Stephens
Stamford HS, Stamford, Texas

PORK SAUSAGE-CRANBERRY HORS D'OEUVRES

1 lb. pork sausage
2 eggs
1 c. fresh bread crumbs
1 tsp. salt
1/2 tsp. poultry seasoning
1 16-oz. can jellied cranberry
    sauce
1 tbsp. mustard

Place sausage, eggs, crumbs, salt and poultry seasoning in large bowl; mix well. Shape into 24 meatballs. Place large skillet over medium heat; cook until brown on all sides. Drain on paper towels. Pour all fat from skillet; wipe skillet clean with paper towels. Melt cranberry sauce in same skillet over low heat, stirring occasionally; stir in mustard, meatballs and 1/2 cup water. Cover; simmer for 20 minutes or until meatballs are tender. Yield: 4 servings.

Mrs Judy Bowers
Richland Center HS
Richland Center, Wisconsin

CHRISTMAS BEEF-CHEESE PIE

1 8-oz. package cream cheese,
    softened
2 tbsp. milk
1 2 1/2-oz. jar sliced dried beef
2 tbsp. instant minced onion
2 tbsp. chopped green pepper
1/2 c. sour cream
1/4 c. chopped walnuts

Mix cream cheese and milk well. Chop dried beef; add to cream cheese mixture. Add onion, green pepper and sour cream; mix well. Spread in 8-inch pie plate; sprinkle with walnuts. Bake in preheated 350-degree oven for 15 minutes; serve with crackers.

Mrs Bette L. Sandrock
Shalet Area Jr HS, Pittsburgh, Pennsylvania

SNACK MEATBALLS

1 6-oz. can evaporated milk
5 tsp. Worcestershire sauce
1 env. onion soup mix
1 lb. ground beef
2 c. catsup
3/4 c. (packed) brown sugar

Combine milk, 2 teaspoons Worcestershire sauce and soup mix; blend well. Let stand for about 5 minutes. Add beef; mix well. Mixture will be moist. Shape into balls, using 1 tablespoon for each. Place on rack in broiler pan. Broil 5 to 6 inches from heat for 10 to 12 minutes; do not turn. Combine remaining Worcestershire sauce and remaining ingredients in saucepan; cook, stirring, until heated through. Add meatballs; serve. May be frozen and reheated.

Mrs Joalene Sepke
Mt Clemens HS, Mt Clemens, Michigan

SANTA'S HELPERS SNACKS

Lo Ann's Holiday Meatballs
Ham-Cheese Ball
White Fudge
Elf's Pecan Crunch
Santa's Whiskers
Golden Wassail

LO ANN'S HOLIDAY MEATBALLS

2 lb. lean ground beef
2 eggs
2 pkg. instant oatmeal

3 tbsp. dried minced onion
3/4 c. grated cheese
1/4 c. catsup
1 tsp. salt
1/2 tsp. pepper
1 tsp. sage
1/2 tsp. garlic salt
1 bottle barbecue sauce

Mix ground beef, eggs, oatmeal, onion, cheese, catsup and seasonings; form into tiny meatballs. Melt 2 tablespoons fat in skillet; cook meatballs in fat until brown. Drain well. Pour barbecue sauce over meatballs; add enough water to cover meatballs, if needed. Let stand overnight in refrigerator. Reheat about 20 minutes before serving. Place in chafing dish; serve. Yield: About 5 dozen.

Carolyn S. Heimbuch
Howard D. Crull Intermediate Sch
Port Huron, Michigan

HAM-CHEESE BALL

2 8-oz. packages cream cheese
1/2 lb. sharp cheese, shredded
2 tsp. grated onion
2 tsp. Worcestershire sauce
1 tsp. lemon juice
1 tsp. mustard
1/2 tsp. paprika
1/2 tsp. salt
1 2 1/4-oz. can deviled ham
2 tbsp. chopped parsley flakes
2 tbsp. chopped pimento
2/3 c. chopped pecans

Soften cream cheese in large bowl. Add sharp cheese, onion, Worcestershire sauce, lemon juice, mustard, paprika, salt, deviled ham, parsley flakes and pimento; mix well. Chill until nearly firm. Shape into ball; roll in pecans. Wrap in foil; refrigerate overnight. Sprinkle with additional paprika; slice to serve.

Mrs Margaret Byram
Belmont HS, Belmont, Mississippi

WHITE FUDGE

2 c. sugar
1/2 c. sour cream
1/3 c. light corn syrup
2 tbsp. butter
1/4 tsp. salt
2 tsp. vanilla extract
1/4 c. quartered candied cherries
1 c. coarsely chopped walnuts

Combine sugar, sour cream, corn syrup, butter and salt in heavy 2-quart saucepan; bring to a boil over low heat, stirring until sugar dissolves. Boil, without stirring, over medium heat to 236 degrees on candy thermometer or to soft-ball stage. Remove from heat; let stand for 15 minutes. Do not stir. Add vanilla; beat for 8 to 10 minutes or until mixture starts to lose gloss. Stir in cherries and walnuts; pour into 8-inch square greased pan quickly. Cool; cut into squares. Rum or brandy flavoring may be substituted for vanilla. Yield: 1 1/2 pounds.

Mrs John L. Puffenbarger
Buckhannon-Upshur HS
Buckhannon, West Virginia

ELF'S PECAN CRUNCH

3 sq. semisweet chocolate
1 c. butter
1 c. sugar
1 tbsp. light corn syrup
1/4 tsp. salt
3 tbsp. water
2 c. chopped pecans

Melt chocolate over hot, not boiling, water until soft enough to spread with pastry brush. Melt butter in another saucepan. Add sugar; stir until dissolved. Add corn syrup, salt and water; cook to 290 degrees on candy thermometer, stirring constantly. Remove from heat; add 1 cup pecans. Return to heat; cook for 3 minutes longer, stirring constantly. Pour onto marble slab or cold cookie sheet. Spread half the chocolate over candy with pastry brush; sprinkle with half the remaining pecans. Turn candy over. Brush with remaining chocolate; sprinkle with remaining pecans. Let stand until completely cooled. Break into pieces; store in covered container.

Mrs Joyce D. Phillips
Doyle HS, Knoxville, Tennessee

SANTA'S WHISKERS

1 c. butter or margarine
1 c. sugar
2 tbsp. milk
1 tsp. vanilla or rum extract
2 1/2 c. sifted flour
3/4 c. finely chopped red and green
    candied cherries
1/2 c. finely chopped pecans
3/4 c. flaked coconut

Cream butter and sugar in mixer bowl; blend in milk and vanilla. Stir in flour, candied cherries and pecans; form into 2 rolls, each 2 inches in diameter and 8 inches long. Roll in coconut. Wrap and chill for several hours or overnight. Slice 1/4 inch thick; place on ungreased baking sheet. Bake in preheated 375-degree oven for 12 minutes or until edges are golden. Yield: About 5 dozen.

Mrs Karen Marr
Southwestern HS, Patriot, Ohio

GOLDEN WASSAIL

4 c. unsweetened pineapple juice
1 12-oz. can apricot nectar
4 c. apple cider
1 c. orange juice
1/4 tsp. whole cardamom seeds,
    crushed
2 3-in. sticks cinnamon
1 tsp. whole cloves
1/4 tsp. salt

Pour juices into 20-cup electric percolator. Place remaining ingredients in basket. Allow to go through perk cycle; serve hot. Yield: Twenty 1/2-cup servings.

Sandra Parish
Kennedale HS, Kennedale, Texas

BEEF AU JUS FOR CHRISTMAS

1 6 to 8-lb. standing rib of beef

Let beef stand at room temperature for 1 hour before roasting; place, fat side up, on rack in shallow pan. Insert meat thermometer so tip will be in center. Roast in 325-degree oven for 2 hours and 15 minutes to 3 hours or to 140 degrees on thermometer for medium rare. Let stand for 20 minutes in warm place before carving; roast will continue to cook after being removed from oven. Cut into thin slices across grain. Allow from 1/2 to 1 pound beef per person.

Photograph for this recipe on this page.

DELICIOUS CHRISTMAS RIBBON SALAD

1 1-lb. 4-oz. can crushed
*   pineapple*
2 3-oz. packages lime gelatin
1 3-oz. package lemon gelatin

1/2 c. miniature marshmallows
1 8-oz. package cream cheese
1 c. heavy cream, whipped
1 c. mayonnaise
2 3-oz. packages cherry gelatin

Drain pineapple; reserve 1 cup juice. Dissolve lime gelatin in 2 cups boiling water; stir in 2 cups cold water. Pour into 14 x 7 x 2-inch pan; chill until partially set. Dissolve lemon gelatin in 1 cup boiling water in top of double boiler; place over boiling water. Add marshmallows; stir until melted. Remove from water. Add reserved pineapple juice and cream cheese; beat until well blended. Stir in pineapple; cool slightly. Fold in whipped cream and mayonnaise; chill until thickened. Pour over lime gelatin; chill until almost set. Dissolve cherry gelatin in 2 cups boiling water; stir in 2 cups cold water. Chill until syrupy. Pour over pineapple layer; chill until firm. Yield: 24 servings.

Mrs Donna Hofmann
South Delta Sr Secondary Sch
Delta, British Columbia, Canada

145

DONNIE'S CHRISTMAS EVE FRUIT SALAD

2 1/2 c. diced mixed fruits
1 tsp. unflavored gelatin
2 tbsp. lemon juice
1 3-oz. package cream cheese, softened
1/4 c. mayonnaise
Dash of salt
2/3 c. whipping cream
1/2 c. chopped nuts
1/2 c. sugar

Drain fruits. Soak gelatin in lemon juice; dissolve over hot water. Blend cream cheese with mayonnaise and salt; stir in gelatin. Whip cream until stiff, adding sugar gradually during last stages of beating; fold in cheese mixture, nuts and fruits. Pour into refrigerator tray lined with waxed paper; freeze until firm. Turn out on platter. Remove paper; cut in slices. Serve on crisp lettuce with additional mayonnaise; garnish with red cherries.

Effie Lois Greene
Potts Camp HS, Potts Camp, Mississippi

SANTA'S MIDNIGHT CASSEROLE

1 lb. link sausages
2 1/2 c. medium white sauce
Worcestershire sauce to taste
1/2 lb. Cheddar cheese, cubed
1 can button mushrooms, drained
8 hard-boiled eggs

Brown sausages in skillet; drain on paper towel. Cut sausages in half. Heat white sauce; season with Worcestershire sauce. Fold in sausages, cheese and mushrooms carefully; pour into 1 1/2-quart casserole. Press eggs in sausage mixture. Refrigerate overnight. Bake in preheated 375-degree oven for 45 minutes to 1 hour. Serve with fruit and hot biscuits. Yield: 8 servings.

Sheila Hall
Goodwyn Jr HS, Montgomery, Alabama

AFTER THE PACKAGES BREAKFAST

Breakfast Hot Dish
Butterscotch Coffee Cake
Christmas Brioches
Holiday Hot Chocolate Mix

BREAKFAST HOT DISH

2 1/2 c. herbed croutons
2 c. shredded med. sharp cheese
2 lb. sausage
4 eggs
3/4 tsp. dry mustard
2 1/2 c. milk
1 c. mushroom soup
1 sm. can mushrooms

Place croutons in greased 8 x 8 x 2-inch pan; top with cheese. Cook sausage in skillet until brown; drain on paper toweling. Place sausage over cheese. Beat eggs; mix with mustard, milk, mushroom soup and mushrooms. Pour over sausage. May be refrigerated overnight, if desired. Bake in preheated 300-degree oven for 1 hour and 30 minutes; may be reheated.

Mrs Jean McOmber
Spring Lake HS, Spring Lake, Michigan

HOLIDAY HOT CHOCOLATE MIX

1 25-oz. package instant nonfat dry milk
1 1-lb. box powdered sugar
1 16-oz. package instant chocolate drink powder
1 6-oz. jar non-dairy coffee creamer

Mix all ingredients in large bowl. Place in large container; cover tightly. Place desired amount in cup; fill cup with hot water. Stir well.

Mrs Virginia Ryan McLain
Daingerfield HS, Daingerfield, Texas

BUTTERSCOTCH COFFEE CAKE

1 18 1/2-oz. package yellow cake
   mix
1 3 3/4-oz. package butterscotch
   pudding mix
4 eggs
2/3 c. corn oil
3/4 c. water
1/2 c. sugar
1 tbsp. cocoa
1 tsp. cinnamon

Blend cake mix with pudding mix in large bowl. Add unbeaten eggs, oil and water; beat with electric mixer for 10 minutes. Pour into 10-inch greased and floured tube pan. Combine sugar, cocoa and cinnamon; sprinkle over batter. Cut through batter with knife to marbleize. Bake in preheated 350-degree oven for 1 hour; cool upright for 15 minutes. Loosen edge; turn cake upside down to remove. Sprinkle with powdered sugar, if desired. Yield: 16 servings.

Mrs Esther Colville
Pampa HS, Pampa, Texas

CHRISTMAS BRIOCHES

3/4 c. milk
1 pkg. yeast
1/4 c. lukewarm water
Sugar
1/2 c. butter
3 eggs, well beaten
4 1/2 c. sifted flour
1 tsp. lemon flavoring
1 tsp. grated lemon rind
1 1/4 c. powdered sugar
2 tbsp. warm water

Scald milk; cool to lukewarm. Sprinkle yeast over lukewarm water; add 1 teaspoon sugar. Let stand for 5 minutes. Beat butter with electric mixer at medium speed until soft and creamy. Add 1/2 cup sugar gradually, beating constantly. Add milk, yeast, eggs, 2 cups flour, 3/4 teaspoon flavoring and rind. Beat at low speed for about 2 minutes or until well blended; stir in remaining flour by hand. Turn out on floured cloth-covered board; knead for about 1 minute or until dough is smooth and satiny. Place in greased bowl; cover. Refrigerate for at least 8 hours or overnight. Divide dough in half; roll each half into 6 x 14-inch rectangle. Cut crosswise with floured knife into 16 to 18 strips; tie each strip into simple knot. Place on greased baking sheets; let rise in warm place until doubled in bulk. Bake in preheated 375-degree oven for 10 to 12 minutes. Remove to cooling rack. Mix powdered sugar, warm water and remaining flavoring; drizzle over warm brioches. Serve warm.

Mrs Eunice Gordon
Shattuck HS, Shattuck, Oklahoma

CHRISTMAS DAY CORN STUFFING BALLS

3/4 c. butter
1 1/2 c. water
1 12-oz. package corn bread
   stuffing mix
1 can corn, drained
3/4 c. chopped parsley
2 eggs, slightly beaten

Heat butter with water in large saucepan until butter melts; stir in stuffing mix. Add corn and parsley; stir in eggs. Add more water, if needed. Shape into balls; arrange in buttered, shallow baking dish. Cover; refrigerate for about 1 hour. Remove from refrigerator. Bake, uncovered, in preheated 400-degree oven for 15 minutes. Yield: 20 balls.

Karen L. LeClair
Olivet Comm Schools, Olivet, Michigan

PIMENTO PEAS AND CORN

1   10-oz. package Green Giant peas
    frozen in butter sauce
1   10-oz. package Green Giant
    shoe peg white corn frozen in
    butter sauce
1/3 c. diced onion
1/3 c. chopped celery
1 tbsp. chopped parsley
1   2-oz. jar sliced pimento,
    drained
1/2 tsp. basil
1/2 tsp. salt
Dash of pepper
1 tsp. lemon juice
1/2 c. sour cream

Cook peas and corn according to package directions. Open pouches partially; drain butter sauce into medium saucepan. Saute onion, celery and parsley in butter sauce until tender. Add peas, corn, pimento, basil, salt and pepper; mix well. Add lemon juice and sour cream just before serving; heat through. Yield: 6-8 servings.

Photograph for this recipe on this page.

GREEN BEANS IN MUSHROOM SAUCE

1 No. 10 can green beans
1   3-lb. 2-oz. can cream of
    mushroom soup
1/2 c. minced onion
1/4 c. sherry (opt.)
Slivered almonds

Drain green beans. Heat cream of mushroom soup in large saucepan. Add beans and onion; simmer until well heated. Add sherry; serve topped with slivered almonds. Five 10-ounce cans mushroom soup may be used instead of 1 large can soup. Yield: 24 servings.

Sister M. Josepha Book
Forest Park HS, Ferdinand, Indiana

CLAM-STUFFED MUSHROOMS

24 fresh mushrooms
1 onion
Oil
1 8-oz. can minced clams
1 c. Italian bread crumbs
1/2 tsp. oregano
1/2 tsp. thyme
1/2 tsp. parsley flakes

Cut stems from mushrooms; chop fine. Chop onion. Coat saucepan with oil. Add chopped mushrooms and onion; saute for about 5 minutes, stirring constantly. Add clams, bread crumbs, oregano, thyme and parsley flakes; cook until thoroughly mixed, adding oil, if needed. Stuff mushroom caps with clam mixture; place in baking pan. Bake in preheated 350-degree oven for 30 minutes.

Joan Laura
Cresskill Ind Sch No 166
Cresskill, New Jersey

SURPRISE SWEET POTATO BALLS

2 to 3 lb. sweet potatoes
2 eggs
Large marshmallows
Finely crushed corn flakes
1 c. (packed) brown sugar
1 c. light cream
1 tsp. flour
1/2 tsp. vanilla

Cook sweet potatoes in boiling water until done. Peel; mash fine. Add eggs; mix well. Form into balls around marshmallows; roll in corn flakes. Place in baking dish, being careful not to crowd. Bake in preheated 350-degree oven for about 10 to 15 minutes or until potato balls pop open. Mix brown sugar, cream, flour and vanilla in saucepan; bring to a boil. Pour over potato balls; keep warm in oven until served.

Connie Schlimgen
Edison Jr HS, Sioux Falls, South Dakota

AFTER THE SLEIGH RIDE DINNER

Warm-Up Eggnog
Red-White and Green Salad
Alaska King Crab Soufflé
Holiday Artichoke Casserole
Asparagus-Chestnut Casserole
Tipsy Pudding

HOLIDAY ARTICHOKE CASSEROLE

1 2-oz. can mushrooms, drained
2 9-oz. packages frozen artichoke
   hearts
1 tbsp. lemon juice
4 c. chopped cooked turkey
1/4 c. butter
1/4 c. all-purpose flour
1/2 tsp. salt
1/2 tsp. leaf thyme
1/4 tsp. nutmeg
2 c. milk
1 chicken bouillon cube
1 1/2 c. shredded Cheddar cheese
1/3 c. crumbled bleu cheese

Chop mushrooms. Cook artichokes according to package directions; drain. Place in buttered shallow baking dish; sprinkle with lemon juice. Add turkey and mushrooms. Melt butter in 2-quart saucepan; stir in flour, salt, thyme and nutmeg. Remove from heat; stir in milk gradually. Add bouillon cube; cook over medium heat, stirring until thickened. Cook for 2 minutes longer. Add cheeses; stir until melted. Pour over artichoke mixture. Bake in preheated 350-degree oven for 30 to 35 minutes. Yield: 6-8 servings.

Charwynne Schultz
Rio Vista HS, Rio Vista, Texas

149

VANILLA LIGHT FRUITCAKE

1 lb. candied cherries, diced
1 lb. candied orange peel, diced
1 lb. candied pineapple, diced
*1 15-oz. box golden seedless
    raisins*
*1 lb. walnuts or pecans, coarsely
    chopped*
1 c. shortening
1 c. sugar
1/4 c. pure vanilla extract
2 tbsp. orange juice
1 tbsp. grated orange peel
5 eggs
3 c. all-purpose flour
1 tbsp. baking powder
1 tsp. salt
Butter

Place fruits and walnuts in very large mixing bowl; toss until blended. Set aside. Cream shortening with sugar in large mixing bowl until light and fluffy; blend in vanilla extract, orange juice and peel. Add eggs, one at a time, blending well after each addition. Sift flour, baking powder and salt together; blend half the flour mixture into creamed mixture. Mix remaining flour mixture with fruit mixture in large bowl. Pour batter over fruit mixture; mix with spatula or hands until fruits and nuts are distributed throughout batter. Grease 10-inch tube pan generously with butter; line bottom with buttered heavy brown paper. Place batter in prepared pan; place pan of hot water on bottom rack of oven. Bake cake in preheated 300-degree oven for 2 hours and 30 minutes to 3 hours or until cake tester inserted in center comes out clean. Cool cake on rack in pan for 30 minutes. Turn out on rack; remove paper. Cool completely. Wrap in foil; store in cool, dry place. May be baked in six 5 x 3 x 2-inch loaf pans for 1 hour and 45 minutes, if desired.

Photograph for this recipe on page 151.

DECORATIVE VANILLA BUTTER COOKIES

1 c. butter or margarine, softened
2/3 c. sugar
1 tbsp. pure vanilla extract
1 egg, lightly beaten
2 1/2 c. all-purpose flour
Vanilla Confectioners' Sugar Frosting

Beat butter and sugar in large bowl with electric mixer until light and fluffy; blend in vanilla extract. Add egg; beat for 1 minute. Stir in flour gradually. Cover; refrigerate for 2 hours or until dough is firm and easy to handle. Roll out on lightly floured board to 1/4-inch thickness; cut out into desired shapes with cookie cutter. Place on ungreased cookie sheets. Bake in preheated 325-degree oven for 12 to 15 minutes or until edges just begin to brown; cool on wire racks. Decorate with Vanilla Confectioners' Sugar Frosting. Yield: About 4 dozen.

Vanilla Confectioners' Sugar Frosting

2 c. confectioners' sugar
1 tsp. pure vanilla extract
2 1/2 tbsp. water
Food coloring

Combine sugar, vanilla extract and water thoroughly. Divide into 3 parts; color as desired.

Photograph for this recipe on page 151.

RAINBOW CREME

1 env. unflavored gelatin
1/2 c. cold water
1/2 c. hot water
1 c. sugar
1/4 tsp. salt
4 egg whites, stiffly beaten
1 tsp. vanilla extract
2 sq. chocolate, melted
1 tsp. lemon extract
1/4 c. maraschino cherries,
    quartered and drained
Red food coloring
1/4 c. chopped pecans

Soften gelatin in cold water. Add hot water, sugar and salt; stir until dissolved. Cool to consistency of unbeaten egg whites; do not chill. Add gelatin mixture to egg whites, several spoonfuls at a time, beating constantly; divide quickly into 3 parts. Rinse 1 1/2-quart clear souffle dish with cold water. Add 1/2 teaspoon vanilla extract and melted chocolate to first part, folding until well blended. Pour into prepared souffle dish, making even layer; refrigerate while preparing next layer. Add lemon extract and maraschino cherries to second part, folding carefully until well blended. Pour on top of first layer, making even layer; refrigerate while preparing next layer. Add several drops of red food coloring, remaining vanilla extract and pecans to third part, folding carefully until evenly blended. Pour on top of second layer; smooth top. Refrigerate until firm. Garnish with whipped cream; serve with spoon. May be unmolded before serving. Run wet knife around edge. Cover souffle dish with serving plate; turn over and gently shake out dessert. Cut into pie-shaped slices; serve with whipped cream, if desired. Yield: 8 servings.

Photograph for this recipe on page 152.

WARM-UP EGGNOG

6 eggs, separated
1 c. sugar
1 pt. whipping cream
1 1/2 c. bourbon
1/4 c. dark heavy rum (opt.)
1/2 tbsp. nutmeg

Beat egg whites until stiff, but not dry; fold in 1/2 of the sugar. Beat cream until stiff, adding remaining sugar gradually. Beat egg yolks until thick and lemon colored; fold into cream slowly. Fold in 1/2 of the bourbon; fold in egg whites, folding in remaining bourbon with egg whites. Fold in rum, if desired. Sprinkle with nutmeg; serve in chilled punch cups. Yield: 16 cups.

Mrs Avis F. Scaife
Albany HS, Albany, Georgia

ALASKA KING CRAB SOUFFLE

1 c. chopped green onions
2/3 c. butter
1/2 c. flour
2 tsp. salt
1 tsp. pepper
1 1/4 c. light cream
1/3 c. tomato paste
8 eggs, separated
12 oz. crab meat, flaked

Cook onions in butter until tender. Stir in flour, salt and pepper; cook over low heat until smooth, stirring constantly. Stir in cream and tomato paste; bring to boiling point. Stir in beaten egg yolks; remove from heat. Stir in crab meat; cool to room temperature. Beat egg whites until stiff; fold 1/4 of the egg whites into crab meat mixture. Fold in remaining egg whites gently; place in 2 buttered casseroles. Bake in preheated 375-degree oven for 30 minutes or until knife inserted in center comes out clean. Garnish with parsley and lemon wedges; serve immediately.

Helen Giles
Susan B. English Sch, Seldovia, Alaska

RED-WHITE AND GREEN SALAD

1 3-oz. package lime gelatin
1/3 c. pineapple juice
1 c. crushed pineapple
1 1/2 tsp. unflavored gelatin
1 8-oz. package cream cheese, softened
1/4 c. milk
1 3-oz. package strawberry gelatin
1 10-oz. package frozen strawberries

Dissolve lime gelatin in 1 cup boiling water; stir in pineapple juice and pineapple. Pour into mold; chill until firm. Sprinkle unflavored gelatin over 2 tablespoons cold water to soften; dissolve over hot water. Mix cream cheese with milk; stir in unflavored gelatin. Spread over lime layer; chill. Dissolve strawberry gelatin in 1 cup boiling water. Add frozen strawberries; stir until strawberries are thawed. Cool. Pour over cream cheese layer; chill until firm.

Mrs Vaudene Pruitt
Falls City HS, Falls City, Texas

ASPARAGUS-WATER CHESTNUT CASSEROLE

1 can water chestnuts
1 8-oz. cans mushrooms, sliced
1 sm. jar pimentos
2 cans asparagus spears
4 hard-cooked eggs, chopped
1 can cream of mushroom soup
1 can French-fried onion rings

Drain water chestnuts; slice. Drain and slice mushrooms. Drain and chop pimentos. Drain asparagus; arrange spears in greased casserole. Mix water chestnuts, mushrooms, pimentos and egg with mushroom soup; pour over asparagus. Bake in preheated 350-degree oven for 20 minutes. Top with onion rings; bake for 10 minutes longer. Yield: 6-8 servings.

Mrs Mary Ada Parks
Anna-Jonesboro HS, Anna, Illinois

TIPSY PUDDING

6 eggs
1 1/2 c. sugar
6 c. milk
2 tsp. vanilla
1 lg. sponge cake
1 c. sherry
Slivered toasted almonds
Chopped maraschino cherries
Whipped cream

Beat eggs in saucepan until light; add sugar and milk. Cook over low heat until mixture coats spoon, stirring constantly; add vanilla. Cool; refrigerate until chilled. Break cake into small pieces; place half the cake in large casserole. Sprinkle with half the sherry; add half the custard. Add layer of almonds, then cherries. Repeat layers; cover with whipped cream. Refrigerate for at least 2 hours or overnight.

Violet H. Horne
Forest Hills Sch, Marshville, North Carolina

YULETIME DATE BALLS

1 egg, well beaten
1 c. sugar
1/2 c. margarine or butter
1/4 tsp. salt
1 8-oz. package chopped dates
2 c. Rice Krispies
1/4 c. finely chopped nuts
1 pkg. flaked coconut

Mix egg, sugar, margarine, salt and dates in saucepan; cook, stirring frequently, until dates are soft and mixture is thick. Place saucepan in ice water until mixture is cool enough to handle. Add Rice Krispies and nuts; mix quickly. Shape into small balls with buttered hands; roll each ball in coconut.

Thelma Dilday
East Duplin HS, Beulaville, North Carolina

NUTTY MILLION DOLLAR FUDGE

1/2 lb. marshmallows
3 6-oz. packages chocolate chips
2 c. chopped nuts
1 c. margarine or butter
1 tsp. vanilla
4 1/2 c. sugar
1 lg. can evaporated milk

Mix marshmallows, chocolate chips, nuts, margarine and vanilla in large bowl; set aside. Mix sugar and evaporated milk in large saucepan. Bring to a boil; boil for exactly 12 minutes, stirring constantly. Pour over marshmallow mixture; stir until well mixed. Place in 13 x 9 x 2-inch pan; may be decorated with frosting in pressurized cans. Chill for at least 24 hours. Candy may be placed in tree-shaped, bell-shaped or other pans for different seasons of year. Yield: 5 pounds.

Mrs Irene Knudsen
Del Norte HS, Crescent City, California

EASY CHRISTMAS DIVINITY

3 c. sugar
3/4 c. light corn syrup
3/4 c. water
2 egg whites
1 3-oz. package strawberry or lime gelatin
1 c. chopped nuts
1/2 c. shredded coconut (opt.)

Combine sugar, corn syrup and water in saucepan; bring to boiling point. Reduce heat; cook to hard-ball stage. Beat egg whites until fluffy. Add dry gelatin gradually, beating until stiff peaks form. Pour syrup slowly into egg white mixture, beating constantly until candy holds shape and loses gloss. Stir in nuts and coconut; pour quickly into 9-inch buttered pan. Let stand until firm. Dip knife blade into hot water; cut candy as desired.

Mrs Marjorie H. Kirby
Ole Main HS, North Little Rock, Arkansas

ORANGE JUICE FRUITCAKE

4 c. sugar
1 c. butter
4 eggs
1/3 c. buttermilk
4 c. flour
1 tsp. salt
1 tsp. soda
1 c. chopped dates
1 c. chopped nuts
1 c. maraschino cherries, drained
   and chopped
2 tbsp. grated orange peel
4 lg. oranges

Cream 2 cups sugar and butter; stir in eggs and buttermilk. Mix flour, salt and soda; add dates, nuts, cherries and orange peel; mix well. Add to creamed mixture gradually, mixing well after each addition. Place in greased tube pan. Bake in preheated 300 to 325-degree oven for 1 hour and 30 minutes. Remove from oven; leave in pan. Squeeze oranges; measure 1 cup juice. Add drained cherry juice if orange juice does not make 1 cup. Mix orange juice and remaining sugar in saucepan; cook, stirring, until sugar is dissolved. Pour over cake; cool before removing from pan.

Mrs Charlene Canter
Oakdale HS, Oakdale, Louisiana

CHRISTMAS EVE WHITE CHOCOLATE CAKE

1/4 lb. white chocolate
1/2 c. boiling water
1 c. butter
1 c. sugar
4 eggs, separated
1 tsp. vanilla extract
2 1/2 c. flour
1 tsp. soda
1 tsp. salt
1 c. buttermilk
1 c. chopped pecans
1 c. flaked coconut

Melt chocolate in water; cool. Cream butter and sugar; add egg yolks, one at a time, beating well after each addition. Add chocolate mixture and vanilla. Sift flour, soda and salt together; add to creamed mixture alternately with buttermilk. Fold in stiffly beaten egg whites; stir in pecans and coconut gently. Place in greased 13 x 9-inch pan. Bake in preheated 350-degree oven for 25 to 30 minutes or until cake tests done; cool. Remove from pan.

Frosting

1 c. evaporated milk
1 c. sugar
1/4 c. butter
3 egg yolks, beaten
1 tsp. vanilla extract
1 c. chopped pecans
1 c. flaked coconut

Mix milk, sugar and butter in saucepan; bring to a boil. Stir in egg yolks and vanilla; cook for 15 minutes, stirring frequently. Remove from heat. Add pecans and coconut; beat until thickened. Spread on cake.

Esther Engelhardt
Mt Pleasant Comm Schools, Mt Pleasant, Iowa

POUND CAKE WITH FRUIT

1 8-oz. package cream cheese,
   softened
1 c. margarine
1 1/2 c. sugar
1 1/2 tsp. vanilla extract
4 eggs
2 1/4 c. sifted cake flour
1 1/2 tsp. baking powder
1 c. chopped candied fruits
1/2 c. chopped pecans
1/2 c. ground pecans
Candied cherries
Candied pineapple slices

Blend cream cheese, margarine, sugar and vanilla thoroughly. Add eggs, one at a time, mixing well after each addition. Sift 2 cups flour with baking powder; combine remaining flour with candied fruits and chopped pecans. Fold both flour mixtures into batter. Grease 10-inch bundt pan; sprinkle with ground pecans. Pour batter into pan. Bake in preheated 325-degree oven for 1 hour and 20 minutes. Cool for 5 minutes; remove from pan. Garnish with cherries and pineapple slices.

Mrs Mary Vermillion Watson
Sullivan West Sch, Kingsport, Tennessee

CANDY CANE COOKIES

1/2 c. butter
1/2 c. shortening
1 c. sifted confectioners' sugar
1 egg
1 1/2 tsp. almond extract
1 tsp. vanilla extract
2 1/2 c. flour
1 tsp. salt
1/2 tsp. red food coloring
1/2 c. crushed peppermint candy
1/2 c. sugar

Mix butter, shortening, confectioners' sugar, egg and extracts thoroughly; stir in flour and salt. Divide into halves; blend food coloring into 1 half. Roll 1 teaspoon each color dough into strip about 4 inches long; place strips side by side. Press together lightly; twist as for rope. Place on ungreased cookie sheet; curve top down to form handle of cane. Repeat with remaining dough. Bake in preheated 375-degree oven for about 9 minutes; remove from cookie sheet while warm. Mix peppermint candy and sugar; sprinkle over cookies. Yield: About 4 dozen.

Mrs Frances Huntington
Brady HS, Brady, Texas

CHRISTMAS COOKIE HORNS

Milk
1 pkg. dry yeast

Sugar
1/2 tsp. salt
4 c. flour
1 c. butter
1/4 tsp. cinnamon
1/2 lb. walnuts, ground
1 egg, beaten
Confectioners' sugar

Heat 1 cup milk in saucepan until lukewarm. Add yeast and 1 teaspoon sugar; set aside in warm place to rise until bubbly. Place salt and flour in bowl; cut in butter as for pastry. Add yeast mixture; mix lightly. Shape into ball. Place on lightly floured board; shape into walnut-sized balls. Roll each ball out flat. Combine cinnamon, walnuts, 1 cup sugar and enough milk to moisten; spread 1/4 teaspoon walnut mixture on each cookie. Roll and shape into horn. Place on ungreased cookie sheet; brush with egg. Bake in preheated 400-degree oven for 15 minutes or until brown; roll in confectioners' sugar.

Madeline Franchiso
Rome Free Acad, Rome, New York

CHRISTMAS PECAN TASSIES

1 3-oz. package cream cheese,
*   softened*
Softened margarine
1 c. sifted all-purpose flour
1 egg, lightly beaten
3/4 c. (packed) brown sugar
1 tsp. vanilla extract
Dash of salt
2/3 c. chopped pecans

Blend cream cheese with 1/2 cup margarine until smooth. Add flour; blend well. Chill for about 2 hours or overnight. Shape dough into twenty-four 1-inch balls; press into 1 3/4-inch muffin cups. Blend egg, brown sugar, vanilla, 1 tablespoon margarine, salt and pecans in small bowl; fill pastry cups with egg mixture. Bake in preheated 375-degree oven for 20 minutes or until lightly browned.

Mrs Paula Calhoun
Fisher HS, Fisher, Illinois

157

FESTIVE LOUISIANA YAM PIE

2 c. mashed cooked Louisiana yams
1 c. (firmly packed) brown sugar
1 c. light cream
1/2 c. milk
3 eggs
1/2 tsp. salt
1 tsp. cinnamon
1 tsp. ground nutmeg
1/2 tsp. ground ginger
1   11-in. unbaked pastry shell
2 c. sour cream
1/4 c. sifted confectioners' sugar
1/2 tsp. vanilla extract

Combine yams, brown sugar, cream, milk, eggs, salt, cinnamon, nutmeg and ginger in large mixing bowl; pour into pastry shell. Bake in preheated 350-degree oven for 1 hour or until knife inserted in center comes out clean; cool. Mix sour cream, confection-ers' sugar and vanilla; spoon around edge of pie and in center. Two 8-inch pastry shells may be used instead of 11-inch shell; bake for about 50 minutes.

Photograph for this recipe on this page.

ORANGE AND CRANBERRY STEAMED PUDDING

1/4 c. butter or margarine
1 c. (packed) light brown sugar
2 eggs
2 c. sifted all-purpose flour
2 tsp. baking powder
1/2 tsp. salt
1/2 tsp. soda
1/4 c. milk
1/2 c. Florida orange juice
1 tbsp. grated orange rind
1/2 c. raisins

2 c. fresh cranberries, halved
Foamy Orange Sauce

Cream butter and sugar; add eggs, one at a time, beating until light after each addition. Sift flour, baking powder, salt and soda together; add to sugar mixture alternately with milk and orange juice, beginning and ending with flour mixture. Stir in orange rind, raisins and cranberries; turn into well-greased 2-quart pudding mold. Cover mold tightly; place on rack in heavy, deep kettle. Add about 2 inches boiling water; cover kettle. Steam for about 2 hours, keeping water simmering and adding boiling water, if necessary. Unmold; serve warm with Foamy Orange Sauce. Garnish with orange sections, if desired. May be made ahead, wrapped and refrigerated. Resteam for about 30 minutes. Yield: 8 servings.

Foamy Orange Sauce

1/3 c. butter
2 c. sifted confectioners' sugar
1 egg, separated
1/8 tsp. salt
1 tsp. grated orange rind
1/4 c. Florida orange juice

Cream butter. Add about 1/2 of the sugar gradually; continue creaming until fluffy. Add egg yolk, salt and orange rind; beat well. Add remaining sugar alternately with orange juice; place in top of double boiler over hot water. Cook for 8 to 10 minutes or until slightly thickened. Remove from heat; cool. Beat egg white until stiff; fold lightly into sauce. Serve cold or warm. Yield: 2 cups.

Photograph for this recipe on page 136.

EGGNOG CHARLOTTE

12 to 14 ladyfingers
2 env. unflavored gelatin
3/4 c. sugar
1/4 tsp. salt

4 eggs, separated
2 1/4 c. milk
1/4 c. rum or brandy
2 c. heavy cream, whipped

Split ladyfingers; stand upright around inside of 9-inch springform pan. Mix gelatin, 1/4 cup sugar and salt in saucepan. Beat egg yolks with 1 cup milk; stir into gelatin mixture. Place over low heat; cook, stirring constantly, for 5 to 6 minutes or until gelatin dissolves and mixture thickens slightly. Remove from heat; stir in remaining milk and rum. Chill, stirring occasionally, until mixture mounds slightly when dropped from spoon. Beat egg whites until stiff, but not dry. Add remaining sugar gradually; beat until very stiff. Fold in gelatin mixture; fold in whipped cream. Turn into prepared pan; chill for several hours or until firm; may be chilled overnight. Release spring; remove side of pan. Garnish with additional whipped cream, pieces of maraschino cherry and chopped pistachio nuts, if desired. One tablespoon rum or brandy flavoring may be substituted for rum or brandy. Yield: 12 servings.

Mrs Norman Sands
Ware Co HS, Waycross, Georgia

SANTA'S TANGY PUNCH

2/3 c. Tang
1/2 c. sugar
3 c. water
2 c. pineapple or cranberry juice
1/4 tsp. almond extract
1 qt. ginger ale

Mix Tang, sugar, water, pineapple juice and almond extract; place in ice tray. Freeze until mushy. Add ginger ale just before serving. Tang mixture may be frozen ahead of serving, then thawed to a mush. Yield: 20 punch cups.

Mrs Francys Putnam
Grey Culbreth Jr HS
Chapel Hill, North Carolina

Congratulations!

special occasions

Those special personal occasions in everyone's life—Weddings, Anniversaries and Birthdays . . . your day for individual memories and expectations.

These are times when you like to combine those family recipes with bright new ideas. To assist you in making these celebrations a delicious success, we have selected menus and recipes that make lovely dishes you'll be proud to serve. Each has been tried and proven in the kitchen of a home economics teacher who wants to share with you her many years of experience in planning parties for these special affairs . . . a delicious bridal shower, an elaborate anniversary party or a fun birthday party for your child.

Plus, there are menus for all those festive events that call for a distinctive celebration with a personal touch . . . Graduation Day, a tea for the teenager in your family; Father's Day, a feast for the king of the castle; or maybe you'd like to entertain a special group of friends—the bridge group with a cool salad plate or the before-the-game crowd with a hearty brunch.

These and many other festive events are covered in the following menus and recipes. Try them all . . . then, mix and match them in your own style for your next party.

◁ Recipe on page 175.

MENU

Bridal Shower

Midsummer Night's Dream
Miniature Cream Puffs
Frosted Ribbon Loaf
Delightful Ham Rolls
Tea Party Orange-Pecan Balls
Teatime Tassies
Cream Mints
Hazel's Mention-The-Groom Cake
Champagne Punch

MIDSUMMER NIGHT'S DREAM

1 fresh pineapple, pared and cubed
2 c. green grapes
2 lg. grapefruit, peeled and
   sectioned
3 lg. oranges, peeled and
   sectioned
3 lg. bananas, peeled and cut
   in 1/2-in. slices
1 pt. fresh strawberries, washed
   and hulled
1/3 to 1/2 c. Cointreau
1 8-oz. bottle Seven-Up or
   ginger ale
2 tbsp. powdered sugar

Drain fruits; arrange in layers in bowl. Combine Cointreau, Seven-Up and powdered sugar; pour over fruit. Top with 1 perfect, unhulled strawberry, if desired. Chill for at least 6 hours before serving.

Linda Armstrong
Union City Comm Schools, Union City, Michigan

MINIATURE CREAM PUFFS

6 tbsp. butter
3/4 c. water
3/4 c. sifted all-purpose flour
3 eggs
1 12-oz. can chicken, chopped
1 c. chopped celery
1 c. mayonnaise
1 tbsp. Good Seasons onion salad
   dressing mix
1/4 c. lemon juice

Bring butter and water to a boil in saucepan. Reduce heat; add flour all at one time, stirring rapidly. Cook and stir until mixture thickens and leaves side of pan. Remove from heat. Add eggs, one at a time, beating well after each addition. Beat until mixture looks satiny and breaks off when spoon is raised. Drop from teaspoon onto ungreased baking sheets. Bake in preheated 425-degree oven for 20 to 30 minutes or until brown.

Let cool. Place chicken in mixing bowl. Add remaining ingredients; mix well. Fill cream puffs with chicken sandwich filling. Yield: 4 1/2 dozen.

Mrs Taylor Cowan, III
Fulton HS, Knoxville, Tennessee

DELIGHTFUL HAM ROLLS

12 thin slices boiled ham
1 8-oz. package cream cheese
1 c. finely chopped nuts
1 clove of garlic, chopped and
   mashed
Mayonnaise

Have butcher slice boiled ham paper thin. Combine cream cheese, nuts and garlic; add a small amount of mayonnaise. Do not get mixture too thin. Spread each slice of ham with mixture; roll as for jelly roll. Chill thoroughly; cut into slices. Serve each slice on round cracker, if desired.

Mrs Robin A. Moore
Breckenridge HS, Breckenridge, Texas

TEATIME TASSIES

1 3-oz. package cream cheese,
   softened
1/2 c. butter, softened
1 c. flour
1 c. (packed) brown sugar
1 egg
1/2 tsp. vanilla
1/2 c. chopped nuts

Cream cheese and butter together. Add flour; blend to make a smooth dough. Roll dough into 24 balls the size of walnuts; press each in a muffin cup. Place in refrigerator; chill for 1 hour. Beat brown sugar, egg and vanilla together until frothy; stir in nuts. Fill muffin cups. Bake in preheated 300-degree oven for 25 to 30 minutes. Yield: 24 tassies.

Mavis M. Holley
Palatka Central Sch, Palatka, Florida

FROSTED RIBBON LOAF

1 unsliced sandwich loaf
Softened butter
Ham Filling
Egg Filling
Crab Filling
4 3-oz. packages cream cheese,
    softened
1/3 c. milk
Minced parsley

Remove crust from bread; cut lengthwise into 4 equal slices. Butter the top of 3 slices; spread 1 buttered slice with Ham Filling, 1 with Egg Filling and 1 with Crab Filling. Stack slices; place unbuttered slice on top. Wrap in foil; chill thoroughly. Combine cream cheese and milk in mixer bowl; beat until fluffy. Place loaf on serving plate; frost sides and top with cheese mixture. Sprinkle generously with parsley. Cut into slices to serve. Yield: 10 servings.

Ham Filling

1 c. ground cooked ham
1/3 c. finely chopped celery
2 tbsp. drained pickle relish
1/2 tsp. prepared horseradish
1/4 c. mayonnaise

Combine all ingredients; mix well.

Egg Filling

4 hard-cooked eggs, chopped
1/3 c. chopped stuffed green olives
2 tbsp. chopped green onion
2 tsp. prepared mustard
1/4 c. mayonnaise

Combine all ingredients; mix well.

Crab Filling

1 can crab
1 tbsp. lemon juice
1/4 c. mayonnaise

Remove any cartilage from crab. Combine all ingredients; mix well.

Beverly Romney
Montera Jr HS, Oakland, California

TEA PARTY ORANGE-PECAN BALLS

1/2 c. butter or margarine,
    softened
1 box confectioners' sugar
1 box vanilla wafers, crushed
1 sm. can frozen orange juice
    concentrate
1 c. chopped pecans

Combine butter, sugar, wafer crumbs and orange juice concentrate; mix well. Roll into 3/4-inch balls; roll balls in chopped pecans. Refrigerate until ready to serve.

Mrs Mildred Sanders
Clint HS, Clint, Texas

HAZEL'S MENTION-THE-GROOM CAKE

5 lb. candied fruit and nuts
4 c. flour
12 eggs, separated
2 c. butter, softened
2 1/4 c. sugar
1 tsp. cloves
1 tsp. nutmeg
1 tsp. cinnamon
1 tsp. baking powder
1 tsp. salt
1 c. sherry
1 c. brandy

Dredge candied fruit and nuts with 1/2 of the flour. Beat egg whites until stiff peaks form; beat egg yolks until thick. Beat butter until soft and creamy. Add sugar to butter gradually; blend in egg yolks. Fold in egg whites. Sift remaining flour, spices, baking powder and salt together; stir into batter. Add sherry and brandy, blending well. Stir in dredged fruit and nuts; place batter in large greased and lined baking pan. Bake in preheated 290-degree oven for about 3 hours or until cake tests done. May bake in three 3-pound cake pans or nine 1-pound pans, if desired.

Hazel R. Johnson
Central Jr HS, Sheridan, Wyoming

CREAM MINTS

1 3-oz. package cream cheese,
     softened
2 1/2 c. sifted confectioners' sugar
2 drops of red food coloring
2 drops of strawberry flavoring or
     oil of cinnamon

Cream cheese; add 1 cup sugar, food coloring and flavoring. Continue to add sugar until mixture is stiff enough to knead. Knead until smooth and creamy. Roll out into balls about the size of a dime; let stand for 5 minutes. Press into rose-shaped molds for teas and showers or bells for weddings. Turn out of mold onto waxed paper by grasping edge of mold and pressing back of mold with thumb. Green food coloring and oil of peppermint flavoring or yellow food coloring and lemon flavoring may be substituted for the red food coloring and strawberry flavoring.

Mrs Shirley Shandley
Leakey HS, Leakey, Texas

CHAMPAGNE PUNCH

1 1/2 c. sugar
2 c. lemon juice
2 qt. sauterne, chilled
1 qt. champagne, chilled

Dissolve sugar in lemon juice; pour mixture into punch bowl. Add sauterne, then pour in champagne. May garnish with lemon slices, if desired.

Fern Alexander
Big Spring Sr HS, Big Spring, Texas

ANNIVERSARY CELEBRATION

Anniversary Fruit Cup
Savory-Sauced Bean Salad
Wild Rice and Chicken Casserole
Avocado Sherbet

ANNIVERSARY FRUIT CUP

2 c. watermelon balls
2 c. honeydew melon balls
2 c. cantaloupe balls
2 c. fresh pineapple cubes
2 c. seedless grapes or peaches
Lemon juice
Pink champagne or ginger ale

Mix fruits together gently; arrange in parfait glasses. Sprinkle with several drops of lemon juice. Fill glasses with champagne. Garnish each glass with a mint sprig. Yield: 8-10 servings.

Patricia Shradel Mundy
Perry Jr HS, Perry, Iowa

SAVORY-SAUCED BEAN SALAD

1 16-oz. can cut green beans,
     drained
2 tomatoes, cut in eighths
2 tbsp. chopped onion
1/3 c. spicy French dressing
1/2 c. sour cream
1 tsp. prepared horseradish
1/2 tsp. seasoned salt
1/2 tsp. dry mustard
Lettuce cups (opt.)

Combine beans, tomatoes and onion; add French dressing, stirring gently to coat well. Chill for several hours, stirring occasionally. Combine sour cream, horseradish, salt and mustard; toss with bean mixture. Chill; serve in lettuce cups.

Jean Searcy
Silver Lake HS, Silver Lake, Kansas

WILD RICE AND CHICKEN CASSEROLE

1 6-oz. can sliced mushrooms
1 c. Uncle Ben's long grain and
wild rice
1/2 c. chopped onion
1/2 c. butter
1/2 c. flour
1 1/2 c. chicken broth
1 1/2 c. cream
3 c. diced cooked chicken
1/2 c. diced pimento
2 tbsp. minced parsley
1/4 tsp. pepper
1/2 c. slivered blanched almonds

Drain mushrooms; reserve liquid. Prepare rice according to package directions. Saute onion in butter until transparent. Stir in flour; add chicken broth and reserved mushroom liquid. Add cream; cook until thick, stirring constantly. Combine all ingredients except almonds; mix well. Place in baking dish. Sprinkle almonds over top. Bake in preheated 350-degree oven for 25 minutes. Additional seasonings may be used, if desired.

Mrs Virginia O. Savedge
Northampton Sr HS, Eastville, Virginia

AVOCADO SHERBET

1 c. sugar
3/4 c. mashed avocado
1/2 c. lemon juice
1/2 c. orange juice concentrate
1 tsp. grated lemon rind
1 c. whipping cream, whipped

Combine first 5 ingredients; stir until sugar is dissolved. Pour into refrigerator tray; freeze for 30 minutes. Transfer to chilled bowl; stir well. Fold in whipped cream. Return to refrigerator tray; freeze until firm without stirring. Yield: 6-8 servings.

Mrs Van Jones
Marlin HS, Marlin, Texas

GROOM'S DARK FRUITCAKE

1 c. Grandma's West Indies molasses
1/2 c. water
1 15-oz. package raisins
2 8-oz. packages dates, finely cut
2 1-lb. jars mixed candied fruits
1 c. butter or margarine
1 1/4 c. sugar
6 eggs
2 1/4 c. sifted all-purpose flour
1/4 tsp. soda
1 1/2 tsp. cinnamon
1 1/4 tsp. nutmeg
3/4 tsp. allspice
1/2 tsp. ground cloves
1/2 c. orange juice or brandy
3 c. coarsely chopped nuts

Blend molasses and water in large, deep saucepan; bring to a boil over low heat, stirring constantly. Add raisins; bring to a boil again. Reduce heat; simmer for 5 minutes. Remove from heat; stir in dates and candied fruits. Set aside. Cream butter and sugar; blend in eggs, one at a time. Sift flour, soda and spices together; add to butter mixture alternately with orange juice. Stir in molasses mixture; stir in nuts. Turn into 2 waxed paper-lined 9 x 5 x 2 3/4-inch loaf pans. Bake in preheated 275-degree oven for 3 hours. May be placed in waxed paper-lined tube pan and baked for 3 hours and 30 minutes. Cut each loaf into 1-inch slices to package cake for distribution at wedding. Cut each slice into thirds; wrap in waxed paper-lined individual gift boxes. Boxes for wedding cake gifts are available at specialty stores. Batter may be placed in baking cups in 1 3/4-inch cupcake pans for bonbons, if desired; bake at 325 degrees for 25 minutes. Yield: 27 gift portions per cake.

Photograph for this recipe on page 166.

GRADUATION TEA

Easy Avocado Dip

Special Sandwich Cake

Frozen Lemon Sherbet Pie

Coconut Chews

Graduation Punch

FROZEN LEMON SHERBET PIE

1 pkg. Nabisco wafers, crushed
3 eggs, separated
Juice of 1 lemon
2 tsp. lemon rind
1/2 c. whipping cream, whipped
3/4 c. sugar

Press layer of wafer crumbs in well-buttered 9-inch pie pan, reserving some for topping. Beat egg yolks until thick; stir in lemon juice, rind and whipped cream. Beat egg whites until soft peaks form. Add sugar gradually, beating constantly; beat until stiff peaks form. Fold into egg yolk mixture; pour over wafer crumbs. Cover with a layer of wafer crumbs. Place in freezer; freeze until firm. Let pie soften slightly before serving. Yield: 6-8 servings.

Judith A. Evans
Desert Jr HS, Wamsutter, Wyoming

SPECIAL SANDWICH CAKE

1 8-in. round loaf bread
Softened margarine
Ham Filling
Egg Filling
2 8-oz. packages cream cheese, softened
1/3 c. light cream

Trim crust from bread; cut loaf crosswise into 3 circles 1 inch thick. Spread bottom slice with margarine; spread Ham Filling over margarine. Spread center slice with margarine; spread Egg Filling over margarine. Spread bottom side of top slice with margarine. Stack slices back together to form loaf; wrap tightly in aluminum foil or plastic wrap. Cover with moist towel; chill for several hours. Beat cream cheese until smooth; add cream gradually, beating until fluffy. Frost loaf with cream cheese mixture. Decorate loaf with pimento, parsley, green pepper or other garnishes cut in designs appropriate for a special occasion. One unsliced sandwich loaf bread may be used, if desired.

Ham Filling

2 4 1/2-oz. cans deviled ham
1/3 c. pickle relish
1/4 c. finely chopped celery

Combine all ingredients; mix well.

Egg Filling

6 hard-cooked eggs, chopped
1/3 c. chopped stuffed olives
1/3 c. mayonnaise
1 1/2 tsp. prepared mustard
1 tsp. grated onion
Salt and pepper to taste

Combine all ingredients; mix well.

Mrs Mary Ada Parks
Anna-Jonesboro HS, Anna, Illinois

EASY AVOCADO DIP

2 lg. ripe avocados
1 lg. package cream cheese,
*   softened*
2 tbsp. lemon juice
Dash of Worcestershire sauce
Dash of garlic powder or salt
Dash of onion powder or salt
1 tomato, chopped

Mash avocados; blend in cream cheese until smooth. Stir in remaining ingredients; mix well. Serve with chips, if desired.

Mrs Elizabeth Muennink
Cedar Bayou Jr HS, Baytown, Texas

GRADUATION PUNCH

4 tbsp. or 4 bags black tea
Rind and juice of 3 lemons
2 c. sugar
1 1/2 tsp. vanilla extract
1 1/2 tsp. almond extract
2   46-oz. cans unsweetened pineapple
*   juice*
2 qt. ginger ale
1 pkg. frozen pineapple chunks, thawed

Pour 2 cups boiling water over tea; cover and let steep for 10 minutes. Strain tea, if needed. Combine lemon rind, sugar and 4 cups cold water in saucepan; heat to boiling point. Remove rinds. Add lemon juice, strained tea and extracts; let cool. Pour mixture over ice blocks in punch bowl. Add pineapple juice and ginger ale; float pineapple chunks in punch. Serve immediately.

Jeanne Scheinoha
Valders HS, Valders, Wisconsin

COCONUT CHEWS

3/4 c. margarine or Crisco
3/4 c. confectioners' sugar
1 1/2 c. all-purpose flour
2 eggs

1 c. (packed) brown sugar
1/2 tbsp. baking powder
1/2 tbsp. salt
1 tsp. vanilla
1/2 c. chopped walnuts
1/2 c. coconut

Cream margarine and confectioners' sugar until light and fluffy. Blend in flour; press evenly in 13 x 9 x 2-inch pan. Bake in preheated 350-degree oven for 12 to 15 minutes. Combine remaining ingredients; spread over hot baked layer. Bake for 20 minutes longer.

Orange-Lemon Icing

1 1/2 c. confectioners' sugar
2 tbsp. melted margarine or butter
3 tbsp. orange juice
1 tbsp. lemon juice

Combine all ingredients; mix until smooth. Spread over warm layer. Let cool; cut into bars to serve. Yield: 32 servings.

Emily J. Rickman
Asst State Supvr of Home Ec, State Dept of Ed
Danville, Virginia

CHILD'S BIRTHDAY PARTY

Cake In Cups
Birthday Lemon Velvet Ice Cream
All-Occasion Punch

CAKE IN CUPS

1   9-oz. package cake mix
12 chocolate ice cream cups
1 can white frosting or 1 pkg.
*   frosting mix*
Colored cake decorations

Preheat oven to 350 degrees. Prepare cake batter according to package directions. Pour batter into ice cream cups, filling about 1/2 full. Place on baking sheet or in muffin tins. Bake for 25 to 30 minutes or until cakes test done. Let cool; mound fluffy white icing over top of each cake, rounding to resemble a scoop of ice cream. Sprinkle decorations over frosting. Yield: 12 servings.

Mrs Eleanor Weatherhead
Northridge Middle Sch, Dayton, Ohio

BIRTHDAY LEMON VELVET ICE CREAM

4 oranges
4 lemons
2 c. sugar
1 can evaporated milk
9 c. milk

Squeeze juice and pulp from oranges and lemons; stir in sugar. Add milk; pour into freezer container. Stir in milk; freeze according to manufacturer's directions.

Susan N. Benjamin
Austin Area Sch, Austin, Pennsylvania

ALL-OCCASION PUNCH

1 box lime or strawberry gelatin
2 c. sugar
1 can pineapple juice
1 1-oz. bottle almond extract
Green or red food coloring (opt.)
1 qt. ginger ale

Dissolve gelatin in 2 cups hot water. Add sugar; stir until dissolved. Add pineapple juice and almond extract; stir in food coloring. Pour half the pineapple mixture into a freezer container; freeze until firm. Place frozen pineapple mixture in punch bowl; pour remaining mixture over the top. Pour in ginger ale; serve immediately.

Mrs Rachel Nicholson
Union HS, Union, Mississippi

BRIDGE LUNCHEON

Bridge Club Surprise Snack
Fake Tomato Aspic
Hot Chicken Salad Deluxe
Girdle-Buster Pie
Wine Party Punch

BRIDGE CLUB SURPRISE SNACK

1 5-oz. jar cheese-bacon spread, softened
4 tsp. butter, softened
Dash of Worcestershire sauce
Dash of Tabasco sauce
3/4 c. flour
1 jar med. stuffed olives
Paprika

Beat cheese spread and butter together until fluffy. Add sauces; mix well. Stir in flour to make a dough-like consistency. Shape about 1 teaspoon dough around each olive. Place on ungreased cookie sheet. Bake in preheated 400-degree oven for 12 to 15 minutes. Sprinkle with paprika.

Mrs Frances VanLandingham
Greene Central HS, Snow Hill, North Carolina

FAKE TOMATO ASPIC

1 can stewed tomatoes
1 pkg. lemon-lime gelatin
1 c. hot water
1 tbsp. Worcestershire sauce
3 drops of Tabasco sauce

Process tomatoes in blender or mash to break up. Dissolve gelatin in hot water; stir in Worcestershire sauce, tomatoes, and Tabasco sauce. Pour into mold; chill until firm.

Mrs Kathryn Frazior
Nederland HS, Nederland, Texas

HOT CHICKEN SALAD DELUXE

2 c. cubed cooked chicken
2 c. sliced celery
1/2 c. chopped almonds
1 c. mayonnaise
2 tsp. grated onion
2 tbsp. lemon juice
1/2 tsp. salt
1/2 c. grated American cheese
1 c. crushed potato chips
3 hard-boiled eggs, sliced
Parsley sprigs

Combine chicken, celery and almonds in mixing bowl. Add mayonnaise, onion, lemon juice and salt; mix well. Place in baking dish; top with cheese and potato chips. Bake in preheated 400-degree oven for 10 minutes. Garnish with egg slices and parsley sprigs.

Mrs Ruth L. DeFriese
Young HS, Knoxville, Tennessee

WINE PARTY PUNCH

2 6-oz. cans frozen Hawaiian punch
2 6-oz. cans frozen orange juice
    concentrate
2 bottles sauterne, chilled
2 qt. club soda, chilled
1 pt. whole strawberries
1 c. sliced peaches

Mix frozen juices and sauterne together until juices are thawed. Pour into punch bowl. Add ice ring or block of ice; pour in club soda just before serving. Garnish with strawberries and peaches. Other fruit may be used as garnish, if desired. Yield: Fifty 3-ounce servings.

Mrs Karin Bargar
Pattengill Jr HS, Lansing, Michigan

GIRDLE-BUSTER PIE

20 Oreo cookies, crushed
1/4 c. melted butter
1 qt. vanilla ice cream, softened
1 sm. can evaporated milk
2 tbsp. butter
1/2 c. sugar
2 sq. bitter chocolate
1/2 tsp. vanilla
Whipped cream
Toasted slivered almonds

Combine cookie crumbs and melted butter; pack into pie pan to make a crust, then freeze. Spoon in vanilla ice cream; store in freezer. Combine milk, butter, sugar, chocolate and vanilla in saucepan; cook over low heat until sauce is smooth, stirring frequently. Let cool. Serve pie topped with sauce, whipped cream and slivered almonds.

Mrs Sara Martin Conkle
Chelsea HS, Chelsea, Alabama

LUCKY SEVEN SANDWICH

4 slices rye bread
4 slices Swiss cheese
8 slices tomato
8 crisp lettuce leaves
8 slices crisp bacon
4 to 8 slices cooked breast of turkey
Favorite Thousand Island Dressing

Place 1 slice rye bread on luncheon plate for each sandwich; top with 1 slice Swiss cheese, 2 tomato slices, 2 lettuce leaves, 2 strips bacon and 1 or 2 turkey slices. Top each sandwich with generous portion of Favorite Thousand Island Dressing; serve with additional Thousand Island dressing. Yield: 4 sandwiches.

Favorite Thousand Island Dressing

2 eggs
1/2 tsp. mustard
1/4 tsp. salt
3 tbsp. sugar
2 tbsp. vinegar
Dash of paprika
Dash of red pepper
2 c. salad oil
1 1/2 c. catsup

1 sm. can pimentos, drained and
    finely chopped
1 sm. onion, finely grated
1/2 c. drained sweet pickle relish

Beat eggs until thick; stir in mustard, salt, sugar, vinegar, paprika and red pepper. Add salad oil gradually, almost drop by drop at first, beating constantly until oil is used and dressing is thick. Add catsup gradually; stir in pimentos, onion and pickle relish. Store in covered jar in refrigerator for several hours before using. Yield: 1 quart.

Photograph for this recipe on this page.

FATHER'S DAY SUPPER

Congealed Waldorf Salad
He-Man Jiffy Turkey and Stuffing
Father's Day Caramel Cake

FATHER'S DAY CARAMEL CAKE

1   16-oz. package butterscotch bits
2 1/4 c. sifted all-purpose flour
1/2 tsp. soda
1 tsp. baking powder
3/4 tsp. salt
1 3/4 c. sugar
3/4 c. margarine, softened
1 tsp. vanilla
3 eggs

Combine butterscotch bits and 1/4 cup water in saucepan; stir over low heat until bits are melted and mixture is smooth. Remove from heat. Sift flour, soda, baking powder and salt together; set aside. Combine sugar, margarine and vanilla in bowl; beat until blended. Add eggs, one at a time, beating well after each addition. Blend in butterscotch mixture. Stir in flour mixture alternately with 1 cup water; pour into 2 greased and floured 9-inch layer cake pans. Bake in preheated 375-degree oven for 30 to 35 minutes. Cool; frost with favorite caramel or butterscotch frosting.

Mrs D. J. Dear
Stringer HS, Stringer, Mississippi

HE-MAN JIFFY TURKEY AND STUFFING

8 to 10 lg. slices cooked turkey
1 10-oz. package frozen broccoli
spears, cooked and drained
1 can cream of chicken soup
1/3 c. chopped celery
1/3 c. chopped onion
1/2 tsp. salt
1/8 tsp. pepper
1 egg
1 10-count can refrigerator
biscuits

Cover bottom of ungreased 8 x 8-inch or 11 x 7-inch baking pan with turkey slices; arrange broccoli over turkey. Combine half the soup, celery, onion, seasonings and egg in medium bowl; mix well. Separate biscuits; cut each biscuit into 10 pieces. Stir into soup mixture; spoon mixture down center of broccoli. Bake in preheated 350-degree oven for 35 to 45 minutes or until golden brown and the biscuit pieces are done. Combine remaining soup and 1/4 cup water in small saucepan; heat thoroughly. Cut turkey and stuffing into squares; serve sauce over squares.

Mrs Pauline R. Bluhm
Flatonia HS, Flatonia, Texas

CONGEALED WALDORF SALAD

2 c. ground fresh cranberries
2 c. sugar
2 pkg. red gelatin
2 c. hot water
2 c. pineapple syrup
1 orange, chopped
2 c. crushed pineapple,
well drained
1 c. chopped walnuts
2 c. chopped celery

Combine cranberries and sugar; set aside. Dissolve gelatin in hot water; stir in pineapple syrup. Chill until partially congealed.

Add cranberry mixture, orange, pineapple, walnuts and celery. Pour into 1 1/2-quart ring mold. Chill until firm. Unmold on lettuce to serve. Yield: 18-20 servings.

Ruth K. Ockman
Maplewood Jr HS, Maplewood, New Jersey

MARDI GRAS PARADE REFRESHMENTS

Fun Punch
Harlequin Bonbons
Mardi Gras Pound Cake

MARDI GRAS POUND CAKE

1 8-oz. package cream cheese,
softened
4 eggs
1 pkg. white cake mix
3/4 c. milk
3/4 c. instant strawberry powder
for milk
1 tsp. vanilla extract
3/4 c. instant chocolate powder
for milk
Confectioners' sugar

Combine cream cheese and eggs in large bowl; beat until smooth. Add dry cake mix and milk; blend until moistened, then beat according to package directions. Divide batter into thirds. Add strawberry powder to 1/3 of the batter; pour into greased and floured 10-inch bundt pan. Add vanilla extract to 1/3 of the batter; pour over strawberry layer. Add chocolate powder to remaining 1/3 of the batter; pour over vanilla layer. Bake in preheated 350-degree oven for 45 to 55 minutes or until cake tests done. Let cool for 10 minutes; turn out of pan. Sprinkle with confectioners' sugar.

Karen Ann Mathisen
Little Falls HS, Little Falls, New York

HARLEQUIN BONBONS

1 c. peanut butter
1 c. confectioners' sugar
2 tbsp. butter
1 c. chopped dates
1 c. chopped nuts
1 c. chocolate bits, melted
1/4 1/4-lb. bar paraffin, melted

Combine peanut butter, confectioners' sugar, butter, dates and nuts; form into balls. Mix chocolate and paraffin together; dip balls into chocolate mixture. Place on waxed paper to harden.

Mary E. Seifert
Brookside Jr HS, Albert Lea, Minnesota

FUN PUNCH

1/2 fifth Triple Sec
1 fifth sauterne
2 fifths champagne
1 lg. bottle club soda

Chill all ingredients; pour into punch bowl in order listed. Garnish with orange slices and cherries; serve immediately.

Diane Manono May
Gove Jr HS, Denver, Colorado

BEFORE THE GAME BRUNCH

Fruit Kabobs

Oven-Scrambled Eggs

Eggs with Peppers and Onions

Garlic-Cheese Grits

Golden Biscuits

Breakfast Apple Muffins

Basic Sweet Dough Orange Rolls

Homecoming Party Punch

FRUIT KABOBS

1 pt. firm large strawberries
4 firm bananas
1 fresh pineapple
3 Winesap apples
1 cantaloupe
1 honeydew melon
1/4 c. Fruit Fresh
1 can frozen orange juice concentrate
1 pkg. large marshmallows (opt.)
Sugar

Remove stems from strawberries; cut bananas, pineapple, apples, cantaloupe and melon into cubes. Place fruits in bowl; add Fruit Fresh and orange juice concentrate, stirring gently. Let stand for at least 1 hour. Arrange fruits and marshmallows on kabobs; sprinkle each kabob with a small amount of sugar.

Mrs Brett W. Slusser
Agra HS, Agra, Oklahoma

OVEN-SCRAMBLED EGGS

4 tbsp. butter or margarine
13 eggs, well beaten
1 c. warm milk
1/4 tsp. salt
1/4 tsp. seasoning salt
1 tbsp. cheese
1/2 can mushrooms, drained (opt.)

Place butter in 13 x 9-inch baking dish; place in warm oven to melt. Combine eggs, milk, seasonings and cheese; stir well. Add mushrooms; pour into baking dish. Bake in preheated 350-degree oven for 10 minutes. Remove from oven; stir well. Return to oven for 20 to 25 minutes or until mixture is set. Cut into squares to serve.

Lorene L. Arent
Wausa Public Schools, Wausa, Nebraska

173

BREAKFAST APPLE MUFFINS

1 1/2 c. sifted flour
1 3/4 tsp. baking powder
1/2 tsp. salt
1/2 tsp. nutmeg
Sugar
1/3 c. shortening
1 egg, beaten
1/4 c. milk
1/2 c. grated apple
1 tsp. cinnamon
1/2 c. melted butter

Sift flour, baking powder, salt, nutmeg and 1/2 cup sugar together; cut in shortening until mixture resembles fine crumbs. Mix egg, milk and apple together. Add to dry ingredients all at one time; mix quickly but thoroughly. Fill greased muffin pans 2/3 full. Bake in preheated 350-degree oven for 20 to 25 minutes or until golden brown. Remove from pans. Mix 1/3 cup sugar and cinnamon together. Roll muffins in melted butter, then in cinnamon mixture. Yield: 12 muffins.

Mrs Lester Clarke
Central HS, Aberdeen, South Dakota

EGGS WITH PEPPERS AND ONIONS

6 green peppers, sliced thin
2 lg. onions, sliced thin
4 tbsp. olive oil
5 tomatoes, peeled
1 garlic clove, crushed
Salt and pepper to taste
10 eggs
1/2 c. whipping cream
4 tbsp. butter

Saute green peppers and onions in olive oil until soft. Add tomatoes, garlic and seasonings; simmer until vegetables are very soft, crushing occasionally with fork. Beat eggs lightly with cream. Heat butter in a large skillet. Add eggs; cook over low heat, stirring constantly, until just set. Arrange eggs on a heated platter; spoon vegetable mixture around eggs. Garnish with diamonds of sauteed or toasted white bread.

Mrs Dorothy M. Scanlon
West Mifflin North HS
West Mifflin, Pennsylvania

GOLDEN BISCUITS

2 pkg. refrigerator butter flake rolls
1/2 c. melted butter or margarine
1/4 tsp. garlic salt
1/4 tsp. parsley flakes
1/2 tsp. onion flakes

Remove rolls from packages; place in 2 rows in loaf pan. Separate tops of rolls slightly. Combine remaining ingredients; pour over rolls. Bake in preheated 375-degree oven for 15 to 20 minutes or until golden. Bacon bits, shredded cheese, sesame seed or poppy seed may be added to the butter, if desired. Yield: 6-8 servings.

Cathy DiOrio
Reavis HS, Burbank, Illinois

BASIC SWEET DOUGH ORANGE ROLLS

2 c. milk, scalded
Sugar
2 tsp. salt
1/3 c. fat
2 eggs, well beaten
1 pkg. or cake yeast
1/4 c. lukewarm water
6 c. (about) flour
1/4 c. raisins
1/4 c. grated orange rind
1/4 c. melted margarine

Combine milk, 1/3 cup sugar, salt and fat; let cool to lukewarm. Stir eggs into milk mixture. Dissolve yeast in lukewarm water; stir in yeast mixture and enough flour to make a soft dough. Place dough in well-greased bowl; cover with cloth. Let stand in a warm place until doubled in bulk. Combine raisins, 1 cup sugar and orange rind. Roll out dough on a floured surface into a rectangle; brush with melted margarine. Sprinkle with orange mixture; roll up, starting at long side. Cut into slices; place in greased pan. Cover; let rise until doubled in bulk. Bake in preheated 375-degree oven for 25 minutes.

Margenia F. Keeton
Cumberland County HS, Burkesville, Kentucky

GARLIC-CHEESE GRITS

3 1/2 c. water
1 tsp. salt
1 c. grits
1 roll garlic cheese
2 eggs, beaten
Milk
1/2 c. melted margarine or butter

Bring water and salt to a boil in a heavy saucepan. Stir in grits; cook until thick. Stir in cheese until melted. Pour eggs into a 1-cup measure; add enough milk to make 1 cup liquid. Stir margarine and milk mixture into grits; pour into greased 9 x 12-inch baking pan. Bake in preheated 400-degree oven for 1 hour.

Louise J. Teague
Jr HS, Iola, Kansas

HOMECOMING PARTY PUNCH

6 c. sugar
4 3-oz. packages lemon gelatin
1 6-oz. can frozen orange juice concentrate
1 6-oz. can lemon juice
2 lg. cans pineapple juice
1 1/2 oz. almond extract
4 qt. ginger ale

Combine sugar and 4 cups water in kettle; cook until sugar is dissolved and mixture is syrupy. Add gelatin; stir until dissolved. Add fruit juices, 1 gallon water and almond extract; let stand until ready to use. Pour 1/8 of the juice mixture over ice in punch bowl; add 1/2 quart ginger ale. Continue adding ingredients in the same proportions to punch bowl as needed. Yield: 100 servings.

Mrs Wynn Bragg
Ware County HS, Waycross, Georgia

ELEGANT VEAL WITH AN AVOCADO FLAIR

1 lb. veal cutlets
2 tsp. parsley flakes
1/4 tsp. salt
1/8 tsp. pepper
2 eggs, beaten
1 c. bread crumbs
4 tbsp. corn oil
2 tbsp. butter
1 California avocado, sliced
2 med. tomatoes, sliced
1/2 c. hollandaise sauce

Trim fat from veal cutlets; pound cutlets until 1/4 inch thick. Mix parsley, salt, pepper and eggs in shallow bowl. Immerse veal in egg mixture; coat with bread crumbs. Heat 2 tablespoons oil and 1 tablespoon butter in large frying pan over medium heat until bubbly. Saute breaded cutlets in oil mixture on both sides until brown and crisp, adding remaining oil and butter as needed. Place cutlets on cookie sheet; do not crowd. Place avocado slices in center of each cutlet; top avocado with tomato slices. Spoon hollandaise sauce over top. Broil under medium-hot heat for several minutes or until sauce is lightly browned and all ingredients are heated through. Yield: 4 servings.

Photograph for this recipe on page 160.

175

GOURMET Gifts

Everyone loves a homemade gift straight from the good cook's kitchen . . . breads, jellies, candies, desserts, pickles or your own speciality. There's just no gift appreciated quite as much as delicious food.

Of course, you'll want to package your extra special gift in an attractive container which can be used again after the food has disappeared. We suggest wicker or reed baskets for large gifts of bread or desserts and cute little apothecary or fancy glass jars for the jellies and candies. You can also make your own containers by painting the tin cans of the products that came with plastic tops. These will make lovely presents when decorated with your own imaginative ideas.

◊ Recipe on page 185.

BANANA-ORANGE BREAD

2 c. unsifted flour
1 tsp. soda
1/4 tsp. salt
1/2 c. butter
1 1/3 c. sugar
2 eggs
3 lg. or 4 med. bananas, finely
    mashed
1/4 tsp. grated orange rind
1 1/2 tbsp. orange juice
1/2 c. chopped pecans

Grease bottom and sides of 9 x 5 x 3-inch loaf pan. Stir flour, soda and salt thoroughly on waxed paper. Cream butter and sugar in large mixing bowl; beat in eggs. Mix bananas, orange rind and orange juice; stir into creamed mixture alternately with flour mixture in 4 additions. Stir in pecans; turn into prepared pan. Bake in preheated 350-degree oven for 1 hour and 10 minutes or until bread tests done. Cool on wire rack for 10 minutes; remove from pan. Cool on rack.

Vergie Hill
Owensboro HS, Owensboro, Kentucky

CRANBERRY-NUT BREAD

2 c. flour
1 c. sugar
1 1/2 tsp. baking powder
1/2 tsp. soda
1 tsp. salt
1/4 c. shortening
3/4 c. orange juice
1 tbsp. grated orange rind
1 egg, beaten
1/2 c. chopped nuts
1 c. chopped fresh cranberries

Sift flour with sugar, baking powder, soda and salt into bowl; cut in shortening until mixture resembles cornmeal. Combine orange juice and rind with egg. Pour into flour mixture; mix just until flour is dampened. Fold in nuts and cranberries. Pour into floured and greased loaf pan. Bake in preheated 350-degree oven for 1 hour.

Susan Carothers
Franklin Reg Sr HS, Murrysville, Pennsylvania

DELICIOUS CRANBERRY MUFFINS

3/4 c. halved cranberries
1/2 c. powdered sugar
2 c. flour
1 tbsp. baking powder
1/2 tsp. salt
1/4 c. sugar
1 egg, well beaten
1 c. milk
1/4 c. melted shortening

Mix cranberries with powdered sugar; let stand until muffin mixture is prepared. Sift dry ingredients together into bowl. Mix egg, milk and shortening. Add to dry ingredients all at once; mix until dry ingredients are just dampened. Do not beat. Fold in cranberry mixture; fill greased muffin cups 2/3 full. Bake in preheated 350-degree oven for 20 minutes.

Mrs Jean Lang
Bonita HS, La Verne, California

DATE-PUMPKIN BREAD

2/3 c. shortening
2 2/3 c. sugar
4 eggs
1 1-lb. can pumpkin
2/3 c. water
3 1/3 c. flour
2 tsp. soda
1 1/2 tsp. salt
1/2 tsp. baking powder
1 tsp. cinnamon
1 tsp. cloves
2/3 c. chopped nuts
2/3 c. chopped dates

Cream shortening and sugar in bowl until fluffy. Stir in eggs, pumpkin and water; set aside. Sift flour, soda, salt, baking powder, cinnamon and cloves together; stir into pumpkin mixture. Stir in nuts and dates; pour into 3 greased and floured 1-pound coffee cans. Bake in preheated 350-degree oven for about 1 hour or until wooden pick inserted in center comes out clean. Slice off any bread that is above top of can; cover with plastic lid that comes with coffee can. Box, wrap and mail.

Barbara Ann Ware
Metropolitan HS West, Dallas, Texas

MARASCHINO CHERRY-NUT BREAD

1 c. sugar
1 tsp. salt
2 eggs, beaten
1 1/2 c. flour
1 1/2 tsp. baking powder
1 8-oz. bottle maraschino cherries

Mix sugar, salt and eggs in bowl. Add flour, baking powder and cherries and liquid; mix well. Place in greased loaf pan. Bake in preheated 350-degree oven for 1 hour or until bread tests done. May be placed in greased soup cans and baked for 35 to 45 minutes or until done.

Mrs Betty Anderson
Laurel Public Schools, Laurel, Nebraska

ORANGE-NUT BREAD

1 lg. orange
1 c. chopped dates
1 tsp. vanilla extract
2 c. flour
1/4 tsp. salt
1 tsp. soda
1 c. sugar
2 tbsp. shortening
1 egg
1 tsp. baking powder
1 c. chopped nuts

Grate orange; reserve grated rind. Squeeze juice from orange; add enough water to make 1 cup liquid. Place all ingredients in large bowl; beat well. Place in greased 9 x 5-inch loaf pan. Bake in preheated 350-degree oven for 1 hour or until bread tests done; cool. Remove from pan; spread with Orange Butter.

Orange Butter

1/2 lb. margarine
Grated rind of 1 orange
Juice of 2 oranges

Soften margarine. Add remaining ingredients; mix well.

Betty Ambrose
Robert E. Lee HS, Midland, Texas

STRAWBERRY-NUT BREAD

2 c. margarine
3 c. sugar
2 tsp. vanilla extract
1/2 tsp. lemon extract
8 eggs
6 c. flour
2 tsp. salt
2 tsp. cream of tartar
1 tsp. soda
2 c. strawberry preserves
1 c. sour cream
2 c. broken nuts

Cream margarine, sugar, vanilla and lemon extracts thoroughly; add eggs, one at a time, beating well after each addition. Sift dry ingredients together. Combine preserves and sour cream; add to creamed mixture alternately with flour mixture. Stir in nuts; place in greased and floured loaf pan or aluminum juice cans. Bake in preheated 350-degree oven for 50 to 55 minutes or until bread tests done. Cool for 10 minutes. Remove from pan; cool completely on wire racks. Wrap in foil or gift paper; may be frozen.

Mrs Joe Wayne Carter
Hamlin HS, Hamlin, Texas

RHUBARB-NUT BREAD

1 1/2 c. (packed) brown sugar
2/3 c. oil
1 egg
1 c. buttermilk
1 tsp. salt
1 tsp. soda
2 1/2 c. flour
1 tsp. vanilla extract
2 c. diced rhubarb
1 c. chopped nuts
1/2 c. sugar
1/2 tsp. cinnamon
1 tbsp. butter

Beat brown sugar, oil, egg and buttermilk in bowl. Blend salt and soda into flour. Add to sugar mixture; blend in vanilla. Fold in rhubarb and nuts; pour into 2 greased and floured loaf pans. Mix sugar, cinnamon and butter; sprinkle over batter in pans. Bake in preheated 325-degree oven for 50 to 60 minutes or until toothpick inserted in center comes out clean.

Susan Knopfle
Edison Jr HS, Sioux Falls, South Dakota

THREE-C BREAD

3 eggs, beaten
1/2 c. cooking oil
1/2 c. milk
2 1/2 c. sifted flour
1 c. sugar
1 tsp. soda
1 tsp. cinnamon
1/2 tsp. salt
2 c. shredded carrots
1/2 c. chopped maraschino cherries
1/2 c. raisins
1/2 c. chopped pecans

Combine eggs, oil and milk in large bowl. Sift flour, sugar, soda, cinnamon and salt together. Add egg mixture; mix just until ingredients are combined. Stir in carrots, cherries, raisins and pecans; place in 4 small or 2 large greased loaf pans. Bake in preheated 350-degree oven for 45 to 50 minutes or until bread tests done.

Jane A. Bower
Del Norte HS, Crescent City, California

HARD BUTTERSCOTCH SQUARES

1 c. light corn syrup
2 c. sugar
2/3 c. water
1/4 tsp. salt
3/4 c. butter
1 tsp. vanilla extract

Combine syrup, sugar, water and salt in 2-quart saucepan; cook over medium heat to 310 degrees on candy thermometer. Do not stir. Remove thermometer; cook over low heat for 4 to 5 minutes, adding butter small amount at a time and stirring vigorously until thoroughly blended with syrup. Add vanilla. Pour into buttered 14 x 10-inch baking pan; spread, if necessary. Let stand for several minutes; mark into 3/4-inch squares with knife. Do not cut all way through candy. May be necessary to retrace markings as candy cools. Remove from pan when nearly cool; place on waxed paper to cool completely. Break into squares; store in airtight container. Yield: 1 3/4 pounds.

Photograph for this recipe on page 180.

HOLIDAY CREAMY CARAMELS

1/2 c. butter
2 c. sugar
3/4 c. light corn syrup
Dash of salt
2 c. cream
1 tsp. vanilla extract
1 1/2 c. chopped nuts

Mix butter, sugar, corn syrup, salt and 1 cup cream; bring to boiling point. Add remaining cream slowly; cook to hard-ball stage. Add vanilla and nuts; pour into buttered pan. Cool; turn out onto flat surface. Cut and wrap. Do not substitute margarine for butter.

Cynthia Atkins
Altoona-Midway Jr-Sr HS, Buffalo, Kansas

CHRISTMAS WREATHS

30 marshmallows
1/4 c. butter or margarine
5 c. crisp rice cereal
1/2 pkg. shredded coconut

Melt marshmallows and butter in top of double boiler over hot water; blend well. Place cereal in large, greased bowl. Pour marshmallow mixture over cereal; mix well. Pack tightly into greased individual ring molds; sprinkle coconut on top. Chill for about 30 minutes. Remove from molds; place on waxed paper. Place in refrigerator to harden. Add small bow of red cellophane to each ring; wrap in colorful cellophane paper.

Lorene L. Arent
Wausa Public Schools, Wausa, Nebraska

MINTED WALNUTS

1/4 c. light corn syrup
1 c. sugar
1/2 c. water
10 marshmallows
1 tsp. essence of peppermint
3 c. walnut halves

Mix syrup, sugar and water in saucepan; bring to a boil over medium heat, stirring constantly. Cook to soft-ball stage or 238 degrees on candy thermometer; remove from heat. Add marshmallows and peppermint; stir until marshmallows are dissolved. Add walnuts; stir until coated. Pour onto waxed paper; separate walnuts with forks while still warm. May be tinted pink or green before pouring onto paper.

Gaynelle C. James
Gardner HS, Gardner, Illinois

ALMOND CARAMEL CLUSTERS

2 c. unblanched almonds
1 c. sugar
1/3 c. (firmly packed) light brown
    sugar
3/4 c. milk
1/2 c. light corn syrup
1/2 c. butter
1/4 tsp. salt
1 tsp. vanilla extract

Spread almonds in shallow pan. Bake in pre-heated 350-degree oven for 20 minutes; cool. Combine sugar, brown sugar, milk, corn syrup, butter and salt in 2-quart sauce-pan; bring to a boil over medium heat, stir-ring constantly until sugar dissolves and but-ter melts. Continue cooking, stirring occasionally, until mixture reaches 248 de-grees on candy thermometer; remove from heat. Add vanilla and almonds; stir lightly until mixture just starts to hold shape. Drop by tablespoonfuls onto buttered baking sheets; cool at room temperature. Wrap indi-vidually; store in tightly covered container. Yield: About 48 clusters.

Photograph for this recipe on page 180.

CREAMY MARSHMALLOW FUDGE

1 lg. jar marshmallow creme
1 8-oz. Hershey bar, broken into
    pieces
1 12-oz. package chocolate chips
1 lg. can evaporated milk
1 c. butter
4 1/2 c. sugar
Chopped pecans to taste (opt.)

Mix marshmallow creme, Hershey bar and chocolate chips in large bowl; set aside. Mix milk, butter and sugar in saucepan; place over medium heat. Bring to a boil, then boil for 5 minutes, stirring constantly. Pour over ingredients in bowl; beat until chocolate is dissolved. Add pecans; mix well. Pour into well-greased 9 x 12-inch pan; place in refrig-erator overnight before cutting.

Ardith Wakefield
Eisenhower Jr HS, Darien, Illinois

CHRISTMASTIME HARD CANDY

1 c. sugar
1/3 c. light corn syrup
1 c. water
1/4 tsp. peppermint flavoring
1/4 tsp. green food coloring

Mix sugar, corn syrup and water; bring to a boil. Cook to 300 degrees on candy ther-mometer. Add flavoring and coloring; mix quickly. Pour on ice cold buttered marble slab; cut into small pieces with scissors. Fill apothecary jars or jelly jars with candy; add ribbon. Other flavoring and food coloring combinations are anise with blue, winter-green with red, cinnamon with brown, clove with orange, lemon with yellow and spear-mint clear.

Ruth Mounts
Rahway Jr HS, Rahway, New Jersey

EASY-TO-MAKE PEANUT BRITTLE

2 c. sugar
1 c. light corn syrup
1 c. water
1/4 tsp. salt
1 1/2 c. unroasted Spanish or
    Virginia peanuts
1 tsp. butter
1/4 tsp. soda

Combine sugar, corn syrup and water; cook over low heat, stirring, until sugar dissolves. Cook to soft-ball stage or 236 degrees on candy thermometer, stirring constantly. Add salt and peanuts; cook to hard-crack stage or 295 degrees on thermometer, stirring con-stantly. Remove from heat. Add butter and soda; stir lightly. Pour evenly onto well-greased waxed paper; cool partially, lifting around edges with knife. Cool until firm; turn. Cool completely; break into pieces. Yield: 2-3 dozen pieces.

Margaret A. Bruce
Redwood HS, Larkspur, California

MISSISSIPPI PECAN PRALINES

1 1/2 c. (packed) brown sugar
1 1/2 c. sugar
3 tbsp. dark corn syrup
1 c. milk
1 tbsp. vanilla extract
1 1/2 c. pecan halves

Butter side of heavy 3-quart saucepan. Combine sugars, corn syrup and milk in buttered saucepan; cook over medium heat, stirring, until sugar dissolves and mixture comes to a boil. Cook to soft-ball stage or 234 degrees on candy thermometer, stirring occasionally; cool for 10 minutes. Add vanilla; beat with spoon for about 2 minutes. Add pecans; beat until mixture loses gloss. Drop by heaping tablespoonfuls onto buttered foil or waxed paper-lined cookie sheet.

Mrs Jesse Clausel
Kossuth HS, Kossuth, Mississippi

CANDIED FRUIT SLICES

1 c. butter
1 c. confectioners' sugar, sifted
1 egg
1 tsp. vanilla extract
2 1/4 c. sifted cake flour
1 c. candied red cherries
1 c. candied green cherries
1 c. pecan halves

Cream butter. Add powdered sugar gradually; cream well. Add unbeaten egg and vanilla; stir in flour. Stir in cherries and pecan halves; chill for 1 hour. Divide into thirds; shape into rolls. Wrap in waxed paper; chill for 3 hours. Slice 1/8 inch thick; place on ungreased cookie sheet. Bake in preheated 325-degree oven for 13 to 15 minutes. Do

not substitute margarine for butter. Yield: About 7 dozen.

Martha Harless
Bayside Jr HS, Virginia Beach, Virginia

HARD ROCK CANDY

2 c. sugar
3/4 c. water
3/4 c. light corn syrup
1/4 tsp. desired food coloring
1/4 tsp. desired flavoring
Confectioners' sugar

Mix sugar, water and corn syrup in large saucepan; cook over medium heat until mixture reaches 300 degrees on candy thermometer or hard-crack stage. Remove from heat. Add food coloring and flavoring; mix well. Pour into well-greased cookie pans; cool enough to touch. Cut or break into bite-sized pieces; dust with confectioners' sugar. Pack in junior baby food jars for gift giving; pack in small plastic containers with lids for mailing.

Mrs Sharon Schultz
Owosso Jr HS, Owosso, Michigan

PARTY CANDY STRAWBERRIES

2 c. finely chopped almonds or
    pecans
3 c. finely shredded coconut
3/4 c. strawberry gelatin
1 can sweetened condensed milk
1 tsp. vanilla extract
Red food coloring
Green butter frosting

Mix almonds, coconut and gelatin in bowl; stir in milk, vanilla and enough food coloring for strawberry color. Chill overnight. Shape into strawberries, using about 1 teaspoon gelatin mixture for each strawberry; roll each in additional strawberry gelatin. Let stand until dry. Shape butter frosting into leaves; place on top of each strawberry. Yield: 80 to 100 strawberries.

Mrs Geraldine Mayo Beveridge
East Carteret HS, Beaufort, North Carolina

FRUITCAKE BONBON GOODY TREE

1/2 c. Grandma's West Indies
  molasses
1 6-oz. can frozen Florida orange
  juice concentrate, thawed
1 15-oz. package seedless raisins
1 1-lb. jar mixed candied fruits
1/2 c. butter or margarine
2/3 c. sugar
3 eggs
1 1/4 c. sifted all-purpose flour
1/8 tsp. soda
3/4 tsp. cinnamon
3/4 tsp. nutmeg
1/4 tsp. allspice
1/4 tsp. ground cloves
1/2 c. chopped nuts

Blend molasses and half the orange juice concentrate in saucepan; bring to a boil over low heat, stirring constantly. Add raisins; bring to a boil again. Reduce heat; simmer for 5 minutes. Remove from heat. Reserve about 1/4 of the candied fruits for garnish; stir remaining fruits into molasses mixture. Set aside. Cream butter and sugar; blend in eggs, one at a time. Sift flour, soda and spices together; add to creamed mixture alternately with remaining orange juice concentrate. Add molasses mixture and nuts; blend. Line 1 3/4-inch cupcake pans with miniature paper cups; fill 3/4 full with fruit-cake mixture. Sprinkle with reserved candied fruits. Bake in preheated 350-degree oven for 25 to 30 minutes. Cool; remove paper cups. Place each bonbon in center of 6-inch square of clear plastic wrap; pull edges together at top. Tie with 10-inch piece of 3/8-inch wide red ribbon; tie to small tree and make bow. Decorations require 17 yards ribbon. Yield: 60 bonbons.

Photograph for this recipe on this page.

WILLIAMSBURG WHITE FRUITCAKE

1/2 c. butter
1 c. sugar
2 c. flour, sifted
1/2 tsp. soda
1 tsp. cream of tartar
1/4 tsp. salt
6 egg whites, stiffly beaten
1 lb. citron, cut in slivers
3/4 lb. blanched almonds, sliced
2 pkg. frozen coconut, thawed

Cream butter and sugar. Sift flour with soda, cream of tartar and salt; stir into creamed mixture gradually. May have to add small amount of egg whites in order to stir in entire amount of flour mixture. Fold in egg whites. Add about 1/3 of the citron to batter; mix well. Pour 1/3 of the batter into 2 buttered and waxed paper-lined loaf or tube pans. Mix remaining citron, almonds and coconut; sprinkle half the mixture over batter in pan. Add half the remaining batter; cover with remaining coconut mixture. Add remaining batter. Bake in preheated 325-degree oven for 1 hour. Cake keeps well.

Mary Alice Bird
Southwestern HS, Detroit, Michigan

LITTLE WHITE FRUITCAKES

2 c. white raisins
1/2 c. candied cherries

1/2 c. chopped candied pineapple
1/4 c. ground citron
3/4 c. butter
1 c. sugar
3 eggs
2 c. sifted flour
3/4 tsp. baking powder
1/2 c. chopped nuts
1/2 c. heavy cream, whipped

Wash raisins; place in saucepan. Cover with boiling water; simmer for 30 minutes. Drain; dry. Add remaining fruits. Cream butter; add sugar gradually, beating until light. Add eggs, one at a time, beating well after each addition. Sift flour with baking powder; add fruits and nuts. Add to sugar mixture alternately with whipped cream. Place cupcake containers in muffin cups; fill 2/3 full with batter. Bake in preheated 325-degree oven for about 20 minutes; let stand until cool. Yield: Sixteen 2 1/2-inch cupcakes.

Phyllis T. Krumrine
Susquehannock HS, Glen Rock, Pennsylvania

LIGHT OLD-FASHIONED FRUITCAKES

4 c. sifted all-purpose flour
1/2 tsp. baking powder
1 1/2 tsp. salt
1 1/2 tsp. cinnamon
1 tsp. nutmeg
7 c. walnut halves
1 3/4 c. candied red cherries
1 3/4 c. chopped candied pineapple
3 1/4 c. golden raisins
1 c. butter
2 1/4 c. sugar
6 eggs
3 tbsp. lemon extract

Line two 9 x 5 x 3-inch pans with aluminum foil. Sift flour with baking powder, salt, cinnamon and nutmeg into 4-quart bowl. Add walnuts and fruits; mix until well coated. Set aside. Cream butter; add sugar gradually, creaming until light and fluffy. Add eggs, one at a time, beating well after each addi-

tion; stir in lemon extract. Add fruit mixture; mix well. Pour into prepared pans. Bake in preheated 275-degree oven for 2 hours. Cool cakes completely; remove from pans. Wrap tightly in foil, then in plastic bag for shipping.

Mrs Tomoe Nimori
Reedley HS, Reedley, California

APPLE-CINNAMON JELLY

4 c. apple juice
1 pkg. powdered fruit pectin
4 1/2 c. sugar
1/4 c. red cinnamon candies

Combine juice and pectin in large saucepan; bring to a full, rolling boil. Add sugar and candies, stirring constantly; bring to a boil. Boil for 2 minutes; remove from heat. Let boiling subside; skim foam from top. Pour into sterilized jars; seal. Yield: Seven 1/2 pints.

Dee Broughton
Agra HS, Agra, Oklahoma

FRESH STRAWBERRY-ORANGE JAM

2 California oranges
4 c. crushed strawberries
7 c. sugar
1/2 bottle liquid pectin
Melted paraffin

Cut unpeeled oranges into very thin wedges; remove ends and seeds as necessary. Place in saucepan; cover with water. Bring to a boil; boil for 15 minutes. Drain. Repeat, boiling with fresh water; drain thoroughly. Chop or dice fine. Combine oranges and strawberries in large saucepan. Add sugar; mix well. Place over high heat; bring to a full, rolling boil. Boil hard for 1 minute, stirring constantly. Remove from heat; stir in pectin immediately. Stir and skim for 5 minutes to cool slightly and prevent floating fruit. Ladle into hot, sterilized jars; seal immediately with paraffin. Yield: 10 medium glasses.

Photograph for this recipe on page 176.

BURGUNDY JELLY

2 c. Burgundy
1 tbsp. lemon juice
3 c. sugar
1/2 bottle liquid fruit pectin
Melted paraffin

Combine Burgundy, lemon juice and sugar in 3-quart saucepan. Place over high heat; stir until sugar is dissolved. Bring to full boil; boil for 1 minute. Remove from heat; stir in pectin immediately. Pour quickly into hot sterilized jars, cups or glasses; cover with 1/4 inch paraffin. Yield: About 2 pints.

Mrs Betty Rassette
Central HS, Salina, Kansas

CRANBERRY WINE JELLY

1 1/4 c. cranberry juice
3 c. sugar
1/2 bottle liquid fruit pectin
3/4 c. wine
Melted paraffin

Place cranberry juice and sugar in large kettle; bring to full, rolling boil. Boil for 1 minute. Add pectin; boil for 1 minute longer. Add wine; bring to a boil. Boil for 1 to 2 minutes longer. Let stand for 5 minutes; skim. Pour into jars; cover with paraffin.

Margaret A. Campbell
Sierra Middle Sch, Roswell, New Mexico

GREEN PEPPER JELLY

6 lg. green peppers
1 hot pepper
1 1/2 c. vinegar
1/2 tsp. salt
6 c. sugar
1 bottle liquid pectin
Green food coloring

Cut all peppers into pieces; place in blender container. Add vinegar; process until lique-

fied. Pour into saucepan; add salt and sugar. Bring to a full boil; boil for 1 minute. Remove from heat; stir in pectin. Let stand for 5 minutes; stir in several drops of green food coloring. Pour into sterilized jars; seal. Yield: Four 1/2 pints.

Mrs Helen M. Godwin
Northwest Sr HS, Greensboro, North Carolina

HOT PEPPER JELLY

1/4 c. chopped red or green
  hot peppers
1 1/2 c. chopped green sweet peppers
6 1/2 c. sugar
1 1/2 c. white vinegar
1 bottle liquid pectin

Grind hot and green peppers, using fine blade of food chopper. Mix peppers, sugar and vinegar in saucepan; bring to a brisk boil. Boil for 3 minutes. Add pectin; boil for 1 minute longer. Remove from heat; strain. Let stand for 5 minutes. Pour into hot, sterilized jars; seal.

Mrs Mary Vermillion Watson
Sullivan West Sch, Kingsport, Tennessee

LUSCIOUS LIME JELLY

1 c. bottled lime juice
2 1/2 c. water
1 pkg. powdered fruit pectin
5 c. sugar
1/4 tsp. green food coloring
Melted paraffin

Combine lime juice and water in large saucepan. Add pectin; mix well. Bring to a hard boil over high heat, stirring constantly; stir in sugar. Bring to a full rolling boil; boil for 1 minute, stirring constantly. Remove from heat; stir in food coloring. Skim off foam. Pour into sterilized jars; cover immediately with 1/8 inch paraffin. Yield: 5 cups.

Mrs Virginia Claypool
Marshall HS, Marshall, Illinois

CALIFORNIA FIG CONSERVE

1 orange
2 lemons
1 lb. California dried figs
2 c. water
1   1 3/4-oz. package powdered
*   fruit pectin*
5 c. sugar
1   3 1/2-oz. can flaked coconut

Slice orange and lemons paper thin; cut each slice into quarters. Slice figs. Combine orange, lemons, figs and water in large kettle; bring to a boil. Reduce heat; cover. Simmer for 30 minutes. Add pectin; mix well. Stir over high heat until mixture comes to a hard boil; stir in sugar at once. Bring to full, rolling boil; boil hard for 1 minute, stirring constantly. Remove from heat; stir in coconut. Ladle into scalded jelly glasses. Yield: About ten 6-ounce glasses.

Photograph for this recipe on this page.

SPICY WATERMELON PICKLES

2 c. diced watermelon rind
1 tbsp. salt

3 c. sugar
3/4 c. vinegar
1 tbsp. pickling spice
2 drops of green food coloring

Peel watermelon rind, removing red and green portions and leaving white section only; place in bowl. Mix salt and 2 cups cold water; pour over rind. Let stand overnight. Drain. Cook rind in boiling water until tender; drain. Mix sugar, vinegar, pickling spice and food coloring; pour over rind. Bring to a boil. Place in sterilized jars; seal.

Mrs Sherri Day
Bartlett-Begich Sec Sch, Anchorage, Alaska

FAVORITE WATERMELON RIND PICKLES

Rind of 1 watermelon
3 tbsp. slaked lime
3 sticks cinnamon
2 tbsp. whole cloves
2 pieces of gingerroot
1 lemon, thinly sliced
1 qt. white vinegar
8 c. sugar
2 tbsp. green or red food coloring

Trim dark skin and pink watermelon from rind; cut rind into 1-inch squares. Dissolve lime in 2 quarts cold water; pour over rind to cover. Let stand for 2 hours; drain. Rinse. Cover rind with water; cook until tender. Drain. Tie spices in cheesecloth bag. Combine spices with remaining ingredients and 1 quart water; simmer for 10 minutes. Add watermelon rind; simmer until rind is clear, adding boiling water as needed if syrup becomes too thick. Remove spice bag. Pack rind and liquid in hot, sterilized jars, leaving 1/4 inch space at top; seal jars. Process in boiling water bath for 10 minutes. One cup pickling salt may be used instead of slaked lime; soak rind for 6 hours instead of 2 hours. Yield: 7 pints.

Mrs Oleta M. Smith
O'Donnell HS, O'Donnell, Texas

SQUASH PICKLES

8 c. thinly sliced yellow squash
2 c. thinly sliced onions
Salt
2 c. vinegar
3 c. sugar
4 green peppers, sliced
1 tsp. celery seed
1 tsp. mustard seed

Mix squash and onions; sprinkle with desired amount of salt. Set aside. Combine vinegar and sugar; add green peppers, celery seed and mustard seed. Bring to boiling point. Drain squash mixture. Rinse with cold water; drain well. Add squash mixture to vinegar mixture; bring to boiling point. Pack in jars; add lids. Process in water bath for 5 minutes or until water in cooker comes to a boil; remove from water bath. Cool. Yield: About 4 pints.

Mrs Chris Weems
Hazen HS, Hazen, Arkansas

JEZEBEL SAUCE

1/3 to 1/2 sm. box dry mustard
1 lg. glass apple jelly
1 lg. glass pineapple preserves
1/2 sm. jar horseradish
2 tsp. coarsely ground pepper

Mix mustard and apple jelly well. Add remaining ingredients; mix thoroughly. Place in decorative jars; tie ribbons on jars. Tie on recipe card and serving suggestion for ham, pork roast or sausage. Store in refrigerator; will keep indefinitely.

Mrs Emely Sundbeck
Manor HS, Manor, Texas

ALL-SUMMER BARBECUE SAUCE

1 qt. tomato juice
1/2 c. Worcestershire sauce
1 sm. jar mustard

1   1-lb. box brown sugar
1/2 sm. can pepper
2 bottles catsup
2 bottles hickory barbecue sauce
2 tbsp. garlic salt
1/2 c. salt
1   6-oz. can tomato paste
1 pt. white vinegar
1 1/2 pt. salad oil
1 lg. onion, chopped
1 can beer

Mix all ingredients in large saucepan; bring to a boil. Reduce heat; simmer for 1 hour. Place in sterilized jars; seal. May be placed in jars, covered and refrigerated. One Number 2 can pineapple juice may be used instead of beer. Yield: 5 quarts.

Janet Wommack
Hood Jr HS, Odessa, Texas

BARBECUE SAUCE FOR FAVORITE MEAT

1 lg. onion, chopped
1 clove of garlic, chopped
2 tbsp. bacon fat
2 tbsp. brown sugar
1 tbsp. paprika
1 tsp. salt
1 tsp. dry mustard
1/4 tsp. chili powder
1/8 tsp. cayenne pepper
1/4 c. vinegar
1/4 c. catsup
2 tbsp. Worcestershire sauce
1 sm. can tomato paste
1 tomato paste can water

Cook onion and garlic in bacon fat until tender. Combine remaining ingredients in saucepan; stir in onion mixture. Simmer for 1 hour. Place in jars; cover. Store in refrigerator.

Mrs Evelyn F. Grabowski
Plant City Sr HS, Plant City, Florida

CARL'S HOT MUSTARD

1 c. dry mustard
1 c. cider vinegar
1/2 c. sugar
2 egg yolks

Mix mustard and vinegar in top of double boiler; let stand for 2 hours. Beat in sugar and egg yolks; cook over simmering water, stirring occasionally, for 1 hour. Cool. Place in small jars; cover. Store in refrigerator.

Mrs Emely Sundbeck
Manor HS, Manor, Texas

POPPY SEED SALAD DRESSING

1 egg
1/4 c. sugar
1/4 c. lemon juice
1 tbsp. poppy seed
1 tsp. dry mustard
1 tsp. grated onion
1/2 tsp. paprika
1/2 tsp. salt
1 1/2 c. salad oil
1/4 c. honey

Place egg, sugar, lemon juice, poppy seed, mustard, onion, paprika and salt in blender container. Blend at high speed, adding oil gradually. Add honey; blend at medium speed until well mixed. Yield: 2 cups.

Mrs Agnes Foster
Home Economics Supervisor
State Department of Education
Frankfort, Kentucky

ZIPPY FAT-FREE SALAD DRESSING

1 tbsp. finely chopped onion
1/2 tsp. finely chopped green pepper
1/4 c. finely chopped carrot
1 tsp. minced parsley
1/3 tsp. sucaryl solution
1 c. tomato juice
1/4 c. vinegar
Salt and pepper to taste

Combine all ingredients in jar with tight fitting top. Cover; shake until blended. Store, covered, in refrigerator. Shake well before using.

Mrs Elwanda McCall
Brantley Co HS, Nahunta, Georgia

ROSETTES

1 c. flour
1 c. milk
1/2 tsp. salt
1 to 3 tsp. sugar
2 eggs
Food coloring (opt.)
1 1/2 lb. shortening
Powdered sugar

Combine first 6 ingredients, adding enough food coloring for desired tint. Heat shortening in deep fat fryer to 365 degrees. Dip rosette iron in shortening for 15 seconds; dip iron into batter, holding level and letting batter come not quite to top of iron so that shell can slide off. Place mold in shortening; fry for about 45 seconds or until lightly browned. Remove shell from iron. Drain on paper towels; dust with powdered sugar. Repeat with remaining batter.

Mrs Clara Clark
Trailridge Jr HS, Shawnee Mission, Kansas

INSTANT SPICED TEA

1   1-lb. jar Tang
1 pkg. lemonade mix
3/4 c. instant tea
2 c. sugar
1 tsp. ground cloves
2 tsp. ground cinnamon

Mix all ingredients well. Place in jar; cover tightly. Place 2 teaspoons in cup of boiling water to serve. Yield: 30 servings.

Laurena C. Ward
Ashford HS, Ashford, Alabama

index

PHOTOGRAPHY CREDITS: Green Giant Company (Cover Photo); American Lamb Council; Standard Brand Products: Planter's Peanut Oil, Planter's Peanuts, Fleischmann's Yeast, Fleischmann's Margarine; American Concordgrape Association; Florida Citrus Commission; General Foods Kitchens: Birds Eye Cool Whip, Swans Down Cake Flour, Baker's Unsweetened Chocolate; Vanilla Information Bureau; Corning Glass Works; The McIlhenny Company; American Molasses Company: Grandma's West Indies Molasses; Idaho Potato and Onion Commission; Campbell Soup Company; Gerber Products Company; National Kraut Packers Association; California Strawberry Advisory Board; National Macaroni Institute; California Apricot Advisory Board; Spanish Green Olive Commission; Charcoal Briquet Institute; Louisiana Yam Commission; American Home Foods; California Avocado Advisory Board; Best Foods, a Division of CPC International, Inc.; National Dairy Council; The Borden Company; California Beef Council; National Biscuit Company; Quaker Oats Company; National Turkey Federation: Turkey Information Service; The Popcorn Institute; Sunkist Growers; American Dairy Association; California Dried Fig Advisory Board.

FAVORITE RECIPES®
of HOME ECONOMICS TEACHERS —
offer endless variety and ideas a'plenty

Blue Ribbon Poultry Cookbook — Hundreds of new and easy award-winning poultry recipes. A cookbook featuring creative recipes from home economics teachers across the country. A must for all homemakers who enjoy good food!

"Life-Saver" Cookbook — Introducing a new way of thinking for our changing life style! A beautiful and unique cookbook featuring Craft Projects and tested recipes for creative home-makers.

Canning, Preserving and Freezing — Here is a most timely edition in the Home Economics Teachers' Cookbook series. This book is filled with recipes for delicious canned, preserved and frozen fruits and vegetables to laden a pantry!

Meats Cookbook — The way to a man's heart? Nothing beats beef, veal, lamb, pork . . . or any other meat dish. Plain or fancy, mouth-watering main dishes for every occasion and taste are included in this valuable recipe book.

Americana Cookery — Exciting regional history and time-proven recipes such as Yankee Pot Roast, Southern Pecan Pie, New England Clam Chowder . . . here are these and other favorite American dishes that best reflect our great heritage.

Quick and Easy Cookbook — The perfect answer to all those last minute meals — for families on the go! Hundreds of recipes to make delicious desserts, dinners, suppers and snacks in a snap. Sure to be a real family favorite!

Money-Saving Cookbook — Prepare delicious and appealing meals — for dollars less with these thrifty, budget-pleasing recipes. Here is the perfect answer to today's rising prices.

Desserts Cookbook — Flaming crepes to frosted cakes . . . desserts are the crowning complement to every meal. Here are hundreds of tempting desserts — sure to bring smiles of delight to everyone at your table.

AMERICA'S HOME ECONOMICS TEACHERS bring you the best of holiday fare!

This is a book about holidays, and more specifically, about delightful holiday foods. About the foods served on those very special occasions when the ordinary, day-to-day world stops and holiday magic takes over.

Here to make your holidays unforgettable are hundreds of holiday recipes which are favorites of Home Economics Teachers throughout the country. Find countless inspiration for parties, dinners and treats that do justice to your special way of entertaining. Recipes for soups, meats, vegetables, salads, breads, relishes, desserts, beverages and snacks are found in this one cookbook. And each one is a Home Economics teacher's favorite, tested and tried out by her in her own kitchen.

Every homemaker knows the pleasure of working with a recipe until each ingredient is right . . . until the proper combination of seasonings blends for an unforgettable taste treat. The recipes in this book have been developed with this same loving care, and have won acclaim for the women who now share them with you.

But New Holiday is much more than a recipe collection. Menus for each of the major holidays are plentiful in each section and throughout the categories — to eliminate that ever-present question of "What could I serve *with* it?" This comprehensive Holiday collection has a Special Occasions section with a sampling . . .

*A Before The Game Brunch   *Graduation Tea

*Father's Day Supper   *Maypole Madness Party

Good Neighbors Coffee . . . just to name a few. And many of these "special occasion menus" include decorations and entertainment ideas. Another exciting "first" is the "Gourmet Gifts" section, with that "just right" idea for something different and especially thoughtful!

Be sure to order New Holiday, as well as the other idea-packed editions of the *Favorite Recipes of Home Economics Teachers* cookbook series. Don't miss this opportunity to really show off your cooking — and gift-giving — talents!

Favorite Recipes® of Home Economic Teachers Cookbooks

Add To Your Cookbook Collection

Select From These ALL-TIME Favorites

Book Title	Item Number
Desserts — Original Edition Revised (1962) 304 pages	01422
Our Favorite Meats (1966) 384 pages	70114
Our Favorite Desserts (1967) 384 pages	70106
Our Favorite Salads (1968) 384 pages	01791
Quick & Easy (1968) 384 pages	70297
Money-Saving Cookbook (1971) 256 pages	70092
Americana Cooking (1972) 192 pages	70351
Poultry Cookbook (1973) 192 pages	70319
New Holiday (1974) 200 pages	70343
Canning, Preserving & Freezing (1975) 200 pages	70084
Life-Saver Cookbook (1976) 200 pages	70335
Foods from Foreign Nations (1977) 200 pages	01279

For ordering information write to:

FAVORITE RECIPES PRESS
P.O. Box 77
Nashville, Tennessee 37202

Books Offered During 1978 Subject To Availability